SLEEPING WITH A SUNFLOWER

A
Treasury of Old-Time Gardening Lore

By Louise Riotte

with illustrations by the Author

Sleeping with a sunflower (Helianthus annuus) *under your pillow will permit you to know the truth of any matter.*

A Garden Way Publishing Book

STOREY

Storey Communications, Inc.
Schoolhouse Road
Pownal, VT 05261

Cover art by Sue Storey

Designed by Cindy McFarland

Typeset at Hemmings Motor News, Bennington, Vermont

Printed in the United States by The Alpine Press

Second Printing, McK. edition, December 1988

Library of Congress Cataloging-in-Publication Data

Riotte, Louise.
    Sleeping with a sunflower.

    Bibliography: p. 214
    Includes index.
    1. Gardening — Folklore. 2. Plants — Folklore. 3. Folklore — United States.
4. Gardening — United States. I. Title.
GR895.R56   1987   398'.368   87-45008
ISBN 0-88266-502-2 (pbk.)
ISBN 0-88266-503-0

CONTENTS

A.E. McKENZIE CO. LTD.

McKenzie is proud to be able to support new, innovative and unique methods of bringing gardening information to the marketplace. *Sleeping with a Sunflower* is one in a series of new books McKenzie will be introducing to gardeners in the coming years. We at McKenzie are dedicated to the belief that gardening is for everyone and that gardening can be "Fun" and "Rewarding."

We have been practicing this belief since the Company was founded in 1896 at Brandon by Dr. A.E. McKenzie. The seed company quickly flourished under his gardening spirit plus a high demand for quality seeds: in fact, customer requests increased to the point that in the late eighteen hundreds, McKenzie released its first seed catalogue.

The Company has grown since then and has acquired other companies to the point where it has become the largest consumer-oriented Flower and Vegetable Seed Company in Canada. The Company serves Canada from Coast to Coast and trades under the name "McKenzie-Steele-Briggs." However, recently the company has moved to reestablish its roots and is now known as McKENZIE.

We hope you enjoy *Sleeping with a Sunflower* and we look forward to bringing you other informative products for gardening in the future.

McKENZIE
SERVING THE HOME GARDENER
SINCE 1896

McKENZIE

TWELVE MONTHS

of Old-Time Gardening Folk Wisdom

Includes weather signs, astrological lunar lore, wild foods, vegetables, flowers, mysterious and medicinal powers of herbs, non-poisonous pest controls, companion planting and folklore of early America, month by month with sensible and easy-to-follow directions

WOULDN'T IT BE FUN to go back in time to an earlier, simpler day when you could enjoy the fruits and vegetables your garden produced without being afraid of getting poisoned on something? Last fall there was even a scare concerning apples — growers had used a chemical to prevent a certain problem and then, after they were harvested and coming on to the market, it was found that the chemical used was one that supposedly caused cancer.

Reading old garden books, it's intriguing to discover how American home gardeners were coping with their problems, enjoying their gardens, and living better because of them, in the last couple of hundred years. We may even go back a little further than that, for much of early American gardening was imported from still earlier times in the Old World.

Our country has a rich and varied heritage of gardening practices and traditions and, as we go through the twelve months of the year, we are not only going to review those of the early New England settlers but remember there were others as well. First, there were the Indians, who were here first of all. And then there were the French and Spanish, whose cuisine and customs have also enriched our lives. And, having come from a family of Western pioneers, I'm going to tell you about my folks, too, particularly my mother, whose knowledge of herbs and medicinal plants I was to learn and make my own.

Even so the early settlers found it necessary to experiment or starve. They had to adapt their gardening knowledge to a new climate, and different soil conditions in order to survive. It is a tribute to their ability to adapt that survive they did. During the winter of 1609–1610, two-thirds of the settlers in Jamestown, Virginia, the first permanent English settlement in America, died. That winter was remembered as the "starving time." The survivors, who experimented with Indian corn and Indian farming, produced food and lived.

In 1621, Edward Winslow of Plymouth Colony wrote: "Our corn did prove well; and, God be praised, we had a good increase of Indian corn, and our barley indifferent good, but our pease not worth the gathering.... Our harvest being gotten in, our governors sent four men on fowling, that so we might, after a special manner, rejoice together, after we had gathered the fruits of our labors."

The Pilgrim settlers in Massachusetts had, under the guidance of a friendly Indian, experimented with Indian corn. In the spring of 1621 they planted five acres of English grain and twenty acres of corn, fertilizing the corn by burying fish with the seed (decaying fish provide nitrogen). The corn succeeded; the English grain failed. While today it might be both dif-

ficult and expensive to get enough fish to plant with your corn, much the same result can be obtained with companion planting of beans, soybeans or black-eyed peas. Just let the corn get a head start and plant the nitrogen-providing legumes a bit later so their vigorous growth will not smother the corn.

The new crop and new methods brought the first Thanksgiving. However, continued experimentation with English wheat, barley and other crops eventually led to their successful cultivation under the soil and climatic conditions of America. This was done mainly by saving and replanting seeds from the few early plants which produced grain. And so, by trial and error, British crops were acclimated to the New World.

Corn, which insured survival in Jamestown, Plymouth, and many later settlements in America, had been developed by the American Indians, through a series of experiments that have been impossible to duplicate since. Today corn is America's most valuable single crop.

Those early settlers weren't behind the door when the brains were given out. Being sharp and quick to learn, they adapted their diet to other fruits and vegetables they noticed the Indians growing. In what is now the United States they also raised avocados, kidney and lima beans, squashes, pumpkins, and probably an early type of tomato, while those in Central and South America also grew sweet potatoes, white potatoes, peanuts, and other crops. They also grew types of cotton.

Famous Early Gardeners

So far we've just been considering early gardeners in general, but there were some among them whose names we are all familiar with. Have you been thinking of George Washington as a crotchety old man, unwilling to smile because his wooden teeth made him very uncomfortable? Or, as a slave owner and someone insensitive to his soldiers' suffering at Valley Forge? No, George was human, just like the rest of us, and basically he was a farmer who, pressed into military life, excelled in that realm as well. He loved his farm and he loved to walk or ride through his fields and woods. But probably, says Wheeler McMillen (an expert on the life and times of Washington), he most loved plants and trees. He grafted English mulberries on wild ones and new improved cherries onto old trees, and he imported Siberian wheat. He wanted Mount Vernon to have every kind of native tree or shrub noted for its form, leaf or flower.

In his travels as a young man in America and Europe he learned landscaping. While riding around his farm, he laid down plans for a serpentine road flanked with contrasting shade trees. He was intensely aware of the beauty of the flower of the sassafras — "an admixture of this and Redbud I conceive would look very pretty."

Benjamin Franklin, the old "apple-a-day man" was another who was interested in plants. He even promoted American apples in England and helped start an export business. He is said to have brought the first rhubarb to the Colonies. John Quincy Adams ordered his consuls to send home any promising plants, and he tended his own garden at Quincy very carefully.

Just as hooked on gardening as Washington was Thomas Jefferson. In 1953 the American Philosophical Society published his sixty-year diary of gardening and it is a marvel of minute observation as well as precise, vivid writing. There is a story that he grew tomatoes, then thought to be poisonous, in his garden and that at one time he publicly ate one to prove that they could be eaten without harm. Tomatoes were regarded as decorative but dangerous, and in truth they are a relative of poisonous and narcotic plants of the Solanaceae family, one of which is deadly nightshade. The tomato's bright red color did nothing to allay the suspicions of early-day people.

Indeed, though we all know tomatoes are delicious and harmless, the leaves have been used against certain garden pests. A late-19th-century gardener in West Virginia observed, "It is said that the water in which tomato leaves and stems have been boiled will, if sprinkled over plants which are infected with aphis and other pests, effectually destroy the pests."

And in 1886, a California gardener said, "I have got rid of several insect pests by simply placing tomato leaves among the plants infested. The black fleas or bugs did not stay on the plants ten minutes after placing leaves among them."

Native American Full Moons

The native Americans were a very poetic people, intelligent and creative, and they gave the Moon many names. To them, each Full Moon of the year had a particular name and a story to go with it. The Indians named the various Moons long before the settlers came to the New World.

★ ★ ★

January, they believed, brought the *Wolf Moon*, describing the hungry wolf packs that roamed about in the dead of winter. They were greatly feared.

★ ★ ★

February's Full Moon was called the *Snow Moon*, because of the blizzards that often struck during this month.

★ ★ ★

March's Full Moon was given a strange name — the *Worm Moon*, because with the spring thaw the earthworms would come to the soil surface.

★ ★ ★

April's Full Moon had several interesting names — *Pink Moon* for the flowers (mostly pink) that covered the land at this time, *Fish Moon*, *Sprouting Grass Moon*, *Egg Moon*, and *Shad Moon*.

★ ★ ★

An important Full Moon, the *Corn Planting Moon*, came in May — but another name, *Flower Moon* described the burst of flowers now apparent.

★ ★ ★

June's Full Moon was called the *Strawberry Moon*, describing the time when the strawberries were fruiting over most of the land and might be gathered and enjoyed.

★ ★ ★

The *Thunder Moon* describes July's fierce storms which often come up suddenly, apparently out of nowhere.

★ ★ ★

August's Full Moon has three descriptive names: the *Green Corn Moon*, the *Sturgeon Moon* (named for the fish), and the *Red Moon* (named for the heat and haze of the month).

★ ★ ★

September brings the *Harvest Moon*.

★ ★ ★

October's Full Moon is also very descriptive — the *Hunter's Moon*. Then, as now, elk, deer and bear were hunted.

★ ★ ★

November brought the *Beaver Moon*, named for the trapping that was done before winter hit in earnest and the rivers were frozen over.

★ ★ ★

December's Full Moon was aptly named — the *Cold Moon*.

★ ★ ★

Wolf Moon
JANUARY

*Seed and nursery catalogs arrive ★ A time for
dreaming by the fire ★ Planning your garden ★
Seedsmen of long ago ★ Buying seed from suppliers ★
Almanacs ★ An astrological guide to planting ★
Old-fashioned vegetables ★ Pecan pie in January ★
Forcing flowers to brighten dull days ★*

CELEBRATE NEW YEAR'S DAY and do it right! Eat the traditional southern hog jowls and black-eyed peas for good luck in the coming year. I hope that you grew your own peas last summer and put up an ample supply in your freezer. They are filling, warming and just great to eat "when the wind blows cold," and you are lucky if you have them.

January is a time for dreaming by the fire and planning your spring garden. Soon a feast of seed and nursery catalogs will arrive with a bewildering array of new and old flower, fruit, and vegetable varieties for you to choose from — but won't it be a pleasure! (Look in the back of this book to find a list of companies you may write to and request their catalogs. Lucky you!)

SEEDSMEN OF LONG AGO

Back in 1784, there wasn't all that much in the way of acclimated seeds. At that time nearly all seeds came from Holland and England and, as one customer, George Washington, could have told you, you just couldn't depend on foreign seeds. That, how-

ever, was going to change. A young Englishman named David Landreth left for the New World, stopping in Quebec, where the cold was not to his liking, and in New York, which he described as a "mere hamlet." His itching foot finally brought him to the glamorous capital of Philadelphia, where he set up a seed store in 1784.

Almost at once, Landreth began growing his own seeds, and in the true American way began advertising and casting discreet aspersions on his competitors. His ad in an early newspaper ran:

> Just imported in the ship *Fame*, from London, and for sale by David and Cuthbert Landreth at their seed shop in Market and Twelfth Street, being the next house to the French minister's, and at their stall ... a general collection of kitchen garden and flower seeds. They have likewise a considerable quantity of their own saving, which are very good. They have tried the imported seeds and will sell none but such as are found to grow.

In 1790 the wily Landreth, in the true tradition of nurserymen and seedsmen, had something new for his buyers — a freestone peach, as well as strawberries in two colors, both red and yellow. His Virginia Green Grass soon became the talk of all visitors to the capital. Ever enterprising, he next unveiled a new flower, the zinnia, found growing wild in Mexico. No wonder the Landreth emporium was popular with Washington, John Quincy Adams, and Jefferson, gentlemen who undoubtedly made gardening a highly social avocation. Landreth's was a gathering place for people to come and discuss their favorite vegetables, exchange ideas and brag a little.

And, as to vegetables, except for sweet corn our founding fathers had them all, plus a few others:

corn salad, a green; orach, used somewhat like spinach; rocambole, a garliclike plant; skirret, a root used like salsify; plus several dozen herbs.

Legend has it, and it may well be true, that it was in Landreth's seed house that Jefferson, with his fascination for new plants, planned a trip of exploration over the vast land known as Louisiana, which he had just bought from the French. One of the explorers he sent, Meriwether Lewis, was a trained botanist. Along the Osage River, he found the seed of the Osage orange, and sent it to Landreth's for propagation. It was first advertised as a hedge plant in the catalog they later produced.

In the best American way business cooperated with government — and so through five generations of Landreths, the American way continued to take shape.

Down the competition: "Cheap seed is always nasty seed," wrote Landreth. "Don't be shanghaied into buying seed because it is cheap." Incredibly, to us, Landreth's seed cost five cents a package, including postage.

But competition moved in anyway and, one by one, other seed and nursery firms started up — Dreers' in 1838, Vaughan's in 1877, and Star Roses in 1897. According to George Seddon, author of *Your Kitchen Garden*, the first nationally known seedsmen were the eighteenth-century Shakers. They distributed seeds imported from Europe, but also grew their own strains on American soil.

Gradually, purely American seed

houses developed. Some of the nineteenth-century firms are still doing business today, but offer greatly improved varieties bred especially for disease resistance, flavor and adaptability. Sweet corn, the first home vegetable to be widely available as an improved hybrid, appeared in the W. Atlee Burpee Seed Company catalog in 1945, soon followed by tomatoes and cucumbers.

Enter Luther Burbank

Naturally every seed house proclaimed their seeds as "the best." But it was not until Luther Burbank that seedsmen achieved the ultimate in American hyperbole. Burbank, a plant breeder and horticulturist, moved to California in 1875 and settled in Santa Rosa, where he purchased a small piece of land and started a nursery. In his catalog he wrote:

> World travelers find my seed under cultivation by the temples of Hindustan, near the pyramids of Egypt, the Botanical gardens of Java, Western China and on Pacific Islands. Burbank fruits and flowers are household words everywhere. My 65,000 customers live in Iceland, Brazil and Australia, Patagonia, Alaska, China, Tasmania and far-off Cathay. Is it necessary to say more?

No, it wasn't necessary, but he did. The old plant wizard knew the value of advertising his wares and, unblushingly, did so. He offered Burbank flax, Burbank peppers, and the earliest tomato in the world, naturally enough, the Burbank. "Luther Burbank," we read in his own catalog, "is unquestionably the greatest student of life and living things in America if not in the world." A truly worthy successor to the tradition established by David Landreth.

But, thank God for seed catalogs! And again, in the true American way, for the competition, without which we might still be planting the same seeds as the colonists did — or depending on friends and neighbors for new ones.

Buying Seed From Suppliers

I know seed, like everything else, has increased in price, but seeds are still one of the biggest bargains going. All the work has been done for you. And I can't say enough nice things about the seedsmen and nurserymen I have dealt with during the last forty years or so. They are absolutely dependable. Their seeds are true to name, and if they say they will replace their nursery stock if it doesn't grow, *they will.* Seedsmen like Parks and Burpee have been at it a long time.

The old seed catalogs were perhaps even more full of advice than they are now. In addition to giving advice, however, the old seedsmen sometimes sought it, so that years ago the customers helped with the testing of some novelties and occasionally named them as well.

In 1883 the W. Atlee Burpee company sent free packets of a

likely-looking new lettuce to a few hundred customers to try out under various local growing conditions. It was designated Sample No. 33, and a gardener in Connecticut waxed lyrical in his report — "Large, handsome, firm..." He was so carried away by the lettuce's appealing center that he suggested it be called Golden Heart, which it promptly was.

★ ★ ★

ALMANACS

Speaking of advice, early day gardeners were devoted to an informative little book called an "almanac." Many scholars believe that the earliest almanacs contained predictions made by ancient Persian astrologers. Later, almanacs appeared in Rome. The oldest still-existing copies of almanacs were written in the 1300's and 1400's.

Almanacs appeared in Colonial America in the 1600's. *Poor Richard's Almanack*, the best known of these, was first published in 1733 and its author, Benjamin Franklin (who published it under the name Richard Saunders), kept it going for 25 years. People loved it for its astrological predictions, jokes and verses. It was also famous for its sayings, many of which are applicable today, such as: "God helps those who help themselves" and "A penny saved is a penny earned."

The *Old Farmers Almanac*, launched in 1792, still appears today and continues to predict the weather and times to plant, as does *Baer's Agricultural Almanac*, now in its 161st year. The *Llewellyn Moon Sign Book*, first published in 1906, gives detailed information on fishing dates, weather, horoscopes, stock market, planting dates, moon tables, "What to do When" Guide, moon lore, Lunar Almanac, lucky dates, politics, earthquakes, etc.

Early gardeners and farmers relied heavily on their almanacs to tell them when to plant and to harvest, and many still do. And right here seems to be a good place to stop and explain what is meant by "planting by the Moon."

❫ ❫ ❫

Early day settlers in America believed in witches and magic spells. Mostly these were practiced secretly — that they were forbidden made them all the more alluring. In some form or other many of these are still with us today and, oddly enough, many times they "work." Most are simple, practical, and the ingredients easy to find.

★

Keep alfalfa (Medicago sativa) in the home to protect from poverty and hunger.

ASTROLOGICAL GUIDE TO PLANTING

Planting by astrological signs is centuries old, but the information is just as valid today as it was hundreds, even thousands of years ago.

The ancient agriculturists in the valleys of the Euphrates and the Nile did their planting with special regard to the Moon's phase and its zodiacal signs. Their remarkable farming success has been heralded through the ages.

Early Calendars

Egyptians were probably the first people to adopt a predominantly solar calendar. Every year the Nile flooded and left behind rich black soil. They depended upon these annual deposits for growing many of their crops.

They observed that the Dog Star, Sirius, reappeared in the eastern sky just before sunrise after several months of invisibility, and that the annual flood of the Nile River occurred soon after this. Using this event to fix their calendar, they came to recognize a year 365 days long, with an extra dividend of five days added at the end. But they did not allow for the necessary extra fourth of a day, and their calendar slowly drifted into error.

The Romans borrowed their first calendar from the Greeks, who got it from the Egyptians. In 46 B.C., Julius Caesar asked the astronomer Sosigenes to review the calendar and improve it. He solved the problem by adding a day to February every fourth year. The Julian calendar was widely used for more than 1,500 years but it, too, was not completely correct — after a while the equinox was not occurring on the correct date.

In 1582, on the advice of astronomers, Pope Gregory XIII corrected the discrepancy between the Sun and the calendar by ordering ten days dropped from October that year only. This procedure restored the equinox to its proper date. To correct the Julian calendar's error regularly, the Pope decreed that February would have an extra day in century years that could be divided by 400, such as 1600 and 2000, but not in other century years, such as 1700, 1800, and 1900. We still use this Gregorian calendar today.

I've gone into this rather lengthy explanation to assure you of the accuracy of the Gregorian calendar, which is very important to all of us who use calendars for calculating the Moon's phases and the best planting signs. Many believe that the signs of the zodiac govern not only planting but human and animal life as well.

★ ★ ★

To see your future love, wear a piece of goldenrod (Solidago odora) and he or she will appear on the morrow.

The Twelve Signs of the Zodiac

Aries, the Ram — March 21 to April 19. A dry, barren sign but good for cultivating, spraying and weeding. A fine sign for harvesting fruit and root crops. Harvest during decrease of Moon for lasting results.

Taurus, the Bull — April 20 to May 20. A fairly productive sign, good for planting root crops such as potatoes and bulbous plants. This sign is good for sturdy growth and hardiness.

Gemini, the Twins — May 21 to June 21. Dry and barren. Do not plant or transplant. Good for cultivation or for killing unwanted growths. Good sign for harvesting fruit or root crops — 3rd and 4th quarters best for these operations. Mow lawns to retard growth.

Cancer, the Crab — June 22 to July 22. Moist and very fruitful. A good time to bud, graft and irrigate. Plant root crops. Good for cover crops, rye, oats, wheat.

Leo, the Lion — July 23 to August 22. Most dry and barren of all signs. Time to kill weeds and trees, destroy roots. Good for harvesting fruit and root crops. Mow lawns to retard growth.

Virgo, the Virgin — August 23 to September 22. Moist but barren. Do not plant or transplant vegetables. Good for cultivation or destroying weeds. Especially good for planting flowering vines.

Libra, the Scales — September 23 to October 23. Good for crops that bear above ground, flowers, and vegetables whose flower part is eaten. Good for tubers for seed.

Scorpio, the Scorpion — October 24 to November 21. Next to Cancer in productiveness. Do not harvest root crops such as potatoes. Good sign for irrigation. Plant flowers for abundance. Plant vegetables, berries and cereals.

Sagittarius, the Archer — November 22 to December 21. Fairly good for onions and cucumbers. Do not use for transplanting. Good sign for making pickles and jelly. Plant endive, leeks, chicory, maple, oak, garlic, peppers, potatoes and radishes. Good harvest sign.

Capricorn, the Goat — December 22 to January 19. Fairly productive, earthy sign, much like Taurus, but drier. Good sign for root crops, potatoes, peanuts, onions, beets, turnips, etc. Good for all flowers. Good sign for applying organic fertilizer.

Aquarius, the Waterman — January 20 to February 18. Rather barren but good for cultivation, and for destroying pests. Good for harvesting fruit and root crops.

Pisces, the Fish — February 19 to March 20. Use for same purpose as Cancer. Good for planting or transplanting all crops bearing above ground, and all flowers. Good sign for root crops, except potatoes.

The word zodiac comes from the Greek zodiakos, meaning a circle or zone of animals. It was originally a time-measuring device and was of immense benefit to early humans. All ancient civilizations were based on agriculture, and a knowledge of natural rhythms, planting times, and animal husbandry was essential.

Moon-Planting in Your Own Garden

Planting success in your garden is largely dependent upon moisture, presupposing that you have done everything possible to assure a fertile soil, plentifully supplied with organic matter, which will hold the moisture for the use of the plant for a reasonable period of time once rain appears. As I have mentioned in my book *Planetary Planting*, "organic gardening teaches us *how* to plant in harmony with nature; astrology teaches us *when*."

Practical-minded early gardeners did not consider lunar gardening a miracle cure for inescapable problems. They knew that even Moon-planted crops could not completely withstand drought or get along without a program of weeding, watering, mulching, composting, and fertilizing. However, given the same odds and care, they felt that growth advanced at a more rapid and satisfactory rate if gardening tasks were performed when the signs were right.

To follow in their firm and careful footsteps you will need a good astrological calendar. There are many on the market — *Llewellyn's Astrological Calendar* (Llewellyn Publications, St. Paul, MN 55164-0383), *Planting by the Moon* (published by Astro Computing Services, San Diego, CA 92116), and *Raphael's Ephemeris* (Starlog Press, New York, NY 10016), to name but a few — and they are published yearly. Usually they carry conversion tables for time changes in all parts of the United States, including Hawaii and Alaska.

As you slip easily into consulting your calendar for gardening practices you will come to note that it is useful for much more

---

Moon Signs

Just as each month of the year is dominated by one of the Zodiac signs, so is each day of the month, as the moon moves through the different Zodiac signs. Each sign will appear at least once a month for two or three days, and each is useful for some specific gardening practice. (You will need to refer to an annual almanac, as previously explained.)

Aries — Harvest, weed or cultivate.

Taurus — A feminine sign, moist and earthy; good for sturdy growth.

Gemini — A good sign to harvest, chop and weed.

Cancer — A watery and fruitful sign. Good for planting or transplanting.

Leo — Fiery, barren and dry, but good for harvesting.

Virgo — A rather dry but earthy sign, good for planting vines. Produces many blossoms but little fruit.

Libra — A lovely sign for flowers; airy and moist.

Scorpio — Good planting sign for seed or nursery stock.

Sagittarius — Good sign for weeding and cultivating.

Capricorn — Earthy, moist and feminine. A good "second best" sign.

Aquarius — Masculine, airy, barren and dry. Good for cultivation.

Pisces — Good for both planting and irrigation, a very fruitful sign.

than just planting dates. For instance, the zodiac period of Capricorn (December 22 to January 20) is said to hold earthy, moist, productive, and feminine qualities. Accordingly, grafts should be cut under Capricorn and held to be grafted under Pisces. Remember also that moon sign and quarter are even more important than month.

From a book on early day gardening I found this bit of advice which was passed along to readers of *Park's Floral Magazine* in the fall of 1886 by a gardener in Maryland.

"I used to laugh at persons sowing seeds in the different signs but experience has taught me better. One of my neighbors planted her garden peas this spring in the days sign of the Virgin (Virgo). Consequently they have done nothing but blossom, and now I am very sorry I did not plant my sweet 'flowering peas' in the same sign. But I always try to make it suit to sow my flower seeds in that sign and just before the full moon. You will be amply repaid, especially with single varieties that you must save seeds from, such as petunias, ten-week stock, daisies, and so forth." Many believe that fruiting vines such as English peas should not be planted in Virgo. It is thought that they will bloom and bloom but bear very little fruit.

Virgo is generally considered fine for planting blooming vines such as honeysuckle, moon vine and morning glory. It is also a good planting sign for asters, chrysanthemums, crocus, daffodils, dahlias, endive, gladiolus, iris, peonies, petunias, poppies, portulaca, and tulips.

In general, when planting flowers for abundance, plant under the signs of Cancer, Pisces and Virgo, first quarter.

For beauty use first quarter and Libra.

For sturdiness use first quarter and Scorpio.

For hardiness use first quarter and Taurus.

Moon Quarters

The Moon is considered to be on the increase from New Moon to Half Moon to Full Moon, and on the decrease from Full Moon to dark of moon to New Moon. Simplifying further, the first quarter and the second quarter are considered as increasing, the third and fourth quarter as decreasing.

Combine these divisions with the correct sign and you will increase your accuracy when you time planting and other gardening practices to coincide with natural rhythms. Remember that moon "day" sign and quarter are the important considerations — rather than month.

Many gardeners simply plant crops that produce above ground during moon increase and crops that produce below ground at moon decrease. However, following this practice without *consulting the signs* may lead to possible selection of planting days governed by barren signs.

Phases of the Moon

NEW MOON
BEGINNING
OF THE FIRST
QUARTER

SECOND
QUARTER
BEGINS

FULL MOON
BEGINNING
OF THE THIRD
QUARTER

FOURTH
QUARTER
BEGINS

Moon Quarters

Here are some suggestions for using the correct quarters for gardening operations, being sure also to check the appropriate sign for what you are planning to do.

First Quarter. Plant asparagus, broccoli, Brussels sprouts, barley, cabbage, cauliflower, celery, cucumbers, corn, cress, endive, kohlrabi, lettuce, leek, oats, parsley, onions, spinach and seeds of herbs and flowering plants. Avoid the first day of the New Moon for planting, also the days on which it changes quarters.

Second Quarter. Plant beans, eggplant, muskmelons, peas, peppers, pumpkins, squash, tomatoes, watermelon. In both the first and second quarters it is best to plant seed while the Moon is in the fruitful signs of Cancer, Scorpio or Pisces. The next best signs are Taurus and Capricorn. For flowers use Libra. For flowering vines use Virgo. Onion and garlic seeds may be planted in Sagittarius.

Third Quarter. Plant artichoke, beets, carrots, chicory, parsnips, potatoes, radish, rutabaga, turnip and all bulbous flowering plants. Good also for planting apple trees, beech trees, biennials, deciduous trees, maple trees, oak trees, onion sets, peach trees, peanuts, pear trees, perennials, plum trees, rhubarb (under Aries), sage, strawberries, tubers for seed, and sunflowers.

Fourth Quarter. During the Fourth or last quarter of the moon turn sod, pull weeds and destroy unwanted growths, especially when the Moon is in the barren signs of Gemini, Leo or Virgo. Not considered a good planting time, but possible for planting onion sets and sunflower seeds with some hope of success.

(Later, in proper sequence, I will give the proper times and phases of the Moon for other gardening operations such as weeding, watering, fertilizing, harvesting, and so on, so that you may correctly use your calendars or almanacs.)

OLD-FASHIONED VEGETABLES

Jerusalem Artichokes

In many areas January is a very cold month and there is little opportunity to search for and gather wild foods of any sort. But in many regions of the South and Southwest, with their milder climate, it is often possible to dig Jerusalem artichokes (Helianthus tuberosus), that strange relative of the sunflower, which has a delectable base similar to that of the artichoke.

This cousin of the sunflower is not an artichoke, however; nor does it come from Jerusalem. Jerusalem is actually a corruption of the Italian girasole, meaning "turning to the sun." Several Indian tribes knew and raised this Native American vegetable, calling it "sunroot," or sought it out as an edible wild plant. The plant was known and domesticated in Massachusetts as early as 1605.

The Jerusalem artichoke has something quite unique going for it. The artichoke is 100 percent starchless. It stores its carbohydrates as inulin rather than as starch and its sugar as levulose, the way most healthful fruits and honey do. It has practically no caloric value (all you dieters take note!). Because of these facts, medical authorities strongly recommend it as a substitute for other carbohydrates on the diabetic's menu, and in the diet of all who should or must restrict their starch and calorie intake.

The Jerusalem artichoke also offers a good source of some minerals and vitamins (particularly potassium and thiamine) — a result of its being a plant-world union of tuber roots and sunflower growth.

Planting and Preparing

Planting artichoke tubers is very much like planting potatoes, and is done with cut pieces each having a seed or "eye." The tubers may be set out in fall as well as in early spring. As they grow so tall gardeners often find them useful for their screening effect to hide or block off some undesirable area.

Even though they do resemble potatoes a little and both grow in the earth, they are entirely different in taste. French cooks wash and peel Jerusalem artichokes, cube them, and simmer them gently in butter for ten minutes, or until almost done. They season with pepper and salt, cover them with a thin cream sauce made with a roux of two tablespoons of butter (or margarine), one tablespoon of flour, one cup of milk and one cup of cream (or just use two cups of "half and half"), a sprig of thyme, a little grated nutmeg, and more pepper and salt if needed. Cook the artichokes very slowly in the cream sauce and serve them in a deep dish.

Or you may prefer to serve them very simply, blanched in boiling water for three minutes, peeled, then boiled until soft, drained and served with butter, salt and pepper.

Kale

Kale, another old-fashioned plant, was mentioned as growing in Virginia in 1669, although its willingness to grow along through winter cold suggests it was grown even earlier in American gardens. For years its name was spelled "cale"; another name for it is "borecole," meaning, in the original Dutch, "peasant cabbage." Although it has never approached the popularity of cabbage, kale has continued to be familiar through the centuries in our home gardens, now grown as an annual.

Stokes carries an elite strain — Green Curled Scotch — imported from Denmark. The pretty, ribbed leaves are yellowish green, curled and bushy, and the plant is best harvested after frost.

Dandelions

It is fairly certain that the dandelion leaves and roots the early colonists ate in America were from the wild plant, and not a domesticated one. The dandelion (*Taraxacum officinale*), a perennial, did not move into the household garden until after the Civil War. In 1821 Cobbett called it "a most wicked garden weed," but he did not hesitate to recommend it to those of the poor who had no gardens. It began to be listed in seed catalogs in the 1870's. Given a choice, Dandelions will grow best in rich soil and sun, but the bright, courageous little weed will grow just about anywhere. I love dandelions, even in my lawn, and I don't think they are the least bit wicked.

The leaves are a happy accompaniment to spinach, but must be partly cooked before the spinach is added.

Dandelion Coffee

Dandelion coffee is made from the roots of the plants and is so beneficial to human organs that it is sold in superior stores and health-food shops and served as an after-dinner beverage in vegetarian restaurants. To make it, clean the roots and dry them thoroughly. Now roast them to coffee color in a warm oven. They may be stored for a short time in airtight cans or jars to be freshly ground just before brewing.

Burpee offers an improved strain of dandelion seed with large, thick, dark green leaves that may be used as greens for boiling. If the hearts are blanched, they may be eaten raw if the leaves are tied together.

Chickweed

Chickweed (*Stellaria media*) is an annual that lasts through winter and seldom lacks flowers and seeds. It is even established in the Arctic Circle. This friendly herb is among the few plants possessing a rich copper content. This, along with its other valuable constituents, makes it a highly beneficial cress in the diet of man, beast, and bird.

For sandwiches, chickweed can be given a fillip by a squeeze of lemon juice, a seasoning of salt and pepper, and a few drops of Worcestershire sauce on the bread and butter. Like any cress, this one goes well with tomato or any other sandwich filling, and can be put into salads.

The early settlers knew chickweed as a medicinal plant, using it as a tea or tisane. To make this, gather a good handful of the plants, wash them, and pour ten ounces of boiling water over them. The thin yellow peel of a lemon or orange may be added for flavoring. Cover the vessel to prevent the steam from escaping.

Drink this amount daily in several doses to relieve constipation, to soothe an upset stomach, or to act as a helpful slimming potion of ancient reputation. The same infusion makes an excellent lotion to relieve tired or inflamed eyes.

A delicious vegetable, chickweed is very like the tenderest early spring spinach, and it is equally wholesome. Gather quite a lot as it shrinks when boiled. Wash them and put them in a pan without shaking off the water, just as you would spinach. Add a dab of butter and a light seasoning of salt and pepper. Now put in some chopped chives, shallots or spring onions, and a sprinkling of nutmeg. Cook carefully to avoid burning.

Drain and serve hot. A squeeze of lemon juice before serving gives the vegetable a piquancy that is good with rich meats.

Leeks

Leeks, distinguished members of the onion group, were also grown in early American gardens. They have fine eating qualities and endeared themselves to the early settlers because of their willingness to remain in the ground until wanted, needing no more than a light covering of straw even in the coldest climates.

If you blanch them you will get a larger area of usable stem. As the leeks grow, earth them up by degrees as you would celery; and at last you will have leeks 18 inches long underground, as thick as your wrist and as tender as a mother's heart.

I love leeks and cook them with a cream sauce as I do the Jerusalem artichokes. I may add fresh picked early dandelion buds, a sprinkling of my winter-grown parsley, and even early asparagus. Don't be afraid of dandelion buds; like the leaves they are just chock full of Vitamin A.

Gout and Sciatica Pains

These problems seem to have been more prevalent in an earlier day. Grandmother made grandfather a poultice of crushed roasted onions boiled with neatsfoot oil to give him ease.

FORCING BLOOMS

Forcing branches to bloom in winter is one of the most rewarding off-season pleasures for gardeners and nature lovers everywhere. Flower buds of spring-blooming shrubs and trees are fully formed in the fall. After a long winter's nap, the buds are all ready to grow when warmth and moisture are supplied.

Ordinarily, at least six weeks of cold temperature are required before flower buds awake. Thus, branches may be brought indoors for forcing at any time after the first of the new year.

Most shrubs have an abundance of buds along the younger shoots. Check for the large, plump ones — these are usually the flower buds, while the smaller ones are the leaves. Try to select branches that contain as many flower buds as possible. Look for "spurs" when selecting from quinces or ornamental crabs — it is on these short branches that they bear their flowers.

Don't do a lot of random cutting. Keep in mind where you will use these branches and what container you will put them in. This will avoid waste (and believe me, the colonial housewife abhorred waste), and help you select types and lengths that will be most useful. Try to select interesting curves and angles.

Make a clean cut. Prune the branches you decide upon flush with the trunk or main branch so no stubs are left. Try to shape the remaining plant as well.

The cut stem will seal over, defeating your purpose, if you don't make it possible for the branches to absorb water by shredding or mashing the end of the stem. If you live in a cold area, you must also moisten the bud scales. Soak the branches overnight in room-temperature water. Try using the bathtub.

The next morning, place the crushed ends in a deep container or pail. Add a piece of charcoal to keep the water sweet, and change the water once or twice a week. Place the containers in a cool room to let the buds develop. They do best in a temperature at around 60 to 65 degrees. Higher temperatures speed things up, but you will have smaller flowers and less color.

At this stage they do not need light — just keep them in a convenient cool place. As soon as the buds begin to "fatten," however, they will need light to develop the colors. Never place them directly in the sun.

When the buds are nicely plump and color is becoming evident, remove them from their pails. Creating arrangements gives you a chance to display your artistic talents, so gather some other decorative material as well — moss, bark, pine cones, pebbles, and vases and other containers.

Remember, taller branches look best in tall containers, and low bowls are excellent for vertical arrangements. Red Japanese quince gives a lovely Oriental effect; in a black or other dark colored bowl it is simply exquisite. Used alone, rhododendron makes a very dramatic floral arrangement.

To keep your arrangement looking well as long as possible, move it to a cool room at night — or even during the daytime if you will not be at home.

What can you force? Just about anything you want to. Any shrub that leafs out in early spring can be forced indoors. If you vary your species and times of cutting you can have almost continuous bloom indoors until spring arrives. Pussy willows, both white and the lovely pink, are enchanting, and so is the pink-flowering almond. My beloved old book, *Watkins Household Hints*, by Elaine Allen (1941), recommends bittersweet, sumac, milkweed, autumn leaves, huckleberry, laurel, pine, spruce and hemlock as cutting material, which may be used at various seasons throughout the year. You may even find a friendly farmer who will let you cut a few branches of wild plum or some other wild tree or shrub on his land. In January, when your spirit is hungry for something green, even leaves, nicely arranged, are satisfying to the soul. I say this with reverence — it is almost a religious experience.

★ ★ ★

Oklahoma Pecan Pie

Here where I live in Southern Oklahoma, the high winds of January often provide us with a light harvest of pecans, shaking down the very last nuts on the trees. I compete with the squirrels for these, for they are the necessary ingredient for that delicious southern dessert known as "pecan pie." I'm a devout contester and I once won a prize for the following recipe:

Unbaked 9" deep dish pie shell
3 eggs, slightly beaten
½ cup sugar
1 cup corn syrup (½ light, ½ dark)
1 teaspoon vanilla
⅛ teaspoon salt

2 tablespoons melted butter or margarine
1 cup pecans, chopped (makes cutting pie easier)
Whipped cream or vanilla ice cream for topping (optional)

Preheat oven to 375° F. Perforate pie shell. Mix ingredients in order given, making sure pecans are well coated, as this gives them an attractive glossy appearance. Place pie on a cookie sheet in oven. Bake 40 minutes. Cool and cover with topping if desired just before serving. *Makes one 9-inch pie.*

★ ★ ★

Aquarius the Water Bearer   (January 21 - February 19)

Snow Moon
FEBRUARY

A time of beginning — a time of warming and awakening in the natural cycle of food-getting ★ Signs in the sky ★ Starting seeds right ★ Growing plants in eggshells ★ Freebies — "Use it up, wear it out, make it do, or do without!" ★ Using the earth's magnetic field ★ Native North American plants ★ Early exploration for new plant varieties ★ Controlling orchard pests safely ★ A spray you can trust ★ Harmless herbal pesticides ★ Wild foods for February ★ Grow narcissus in February ★

OLD-TIME GARDEN-ERS — just like garden-ers today — just couldn't wait to get started. But they hurried *slowly*, firmly believing that what was done at this time could make or break their gardening program and activities for the rest of the year.

Even as now they were greatly concerned with the weather. They looked for certain signs in the sky to give them a clue as to what they might expect for the gardening season, which would get into full swing a bit later on.

Many believed along with the Indians, who were great observers of such things, that the position of the Moon during the first two weeks of February indicated whether the growing season would be wet or dry. Horns pointing down at that time were believed to mean that the Moon was "empty-ing its water," and that the follow-ing spring and summer would be wet. With this in mind they would select the type of seed and the location of the crops in their gar-den. A dry February moon — one with the horns pointing up — told them to plant their gardens as early as possible and to use drought-resistant seeds.

Seeding-frame soil was prepared early in February under the sign of Aquarius — this being considered a dry or barren sign and the best for turning sod. The last quarter of the moon was also favored for preparing the soil for cultivation.

STARTING SEEDS RIGHT

A seed is a little bundle of determination to grow. To grow effectively, it needs moisture, oxygen, and warmth. Certain seeds such as lettuce, spinach and peas, however, will sprout in soil as cool as 40° F. Lettuce will not sprout in soil whose temperature is over 70° F, and I always hope for a cool, rainy day in the autumn so I can get my fall lettuce started. Once started, it will often continue to grow well if I keep it watered.

In the spring, when warmth is needed, here is a good old-fashioned way to hold the sun's heat in the soil for sprouting seeds. If the earth was cultivated the previous fall, hoe and rake just the surface before seeding, since the upper six inches of soil is much warmer than that below it.

A 19th-century gardener advised the following way of sprouting extremely small seeds. Fill a clay pot with a very fine soil mixture and sprinkle seeds on the soil surface, without covering them. Place a sheet of glass over the pot and put the pot in a pan of water. "The water will draw up to the surface of the soil," the gardener claimed.

Here's another hint from an early day gardener for germinating hard-coated seeds: "Procure a box 6 inches deep, put in 2 inches of broken crock pieces, then three inches of fine, porous soil. Plant the seeds in the soil and cover with an inch of finely chopped moss. Sink the box in the garden in a shady spot to keep it moist until seeds germinate. Sow only one kind of plant per box, as germination times differ."

Some seeds that did well treated this way were cyclamen, Christmas roses, cannas, gentians, nasturtiums, smilax and violets. The practice of nicking or scoring hardcoated seeds is also often followed to speed up germination.

As time marched on, thrifty early day gardeners also made good use of milk cartons cut the long way with holes poked in the bottom and sides of one of the halves. The planter half with the holes is placed inside the other half, which catches the drip, and may have an inch or so of gravel or sand in the bottom. The planter part is filled, using alternately, one handful of compost plus two of sand. Sand, while containing little in the way of nutrients makes removal easy, and the compost supplies the needed nutrients.

February is still a cold month in much of the country, often with little sunshine so, unless you live farther south, it is best not to plant seeds in windowsill boxes until the latter part of the month.

Most seedlings should be ready to plant permanently in approximately ten weeks, so if you would like to follow the moon-sign lore, start your indoor seedlings under the sign of Pisces — which covers the period from February 19th to March 21st. This is considered a highly fruitful zodiac sign. Under Pisces the moon emerges above the plane of the earth's orbit and is "good for planting." Pisces has watery, feminine and productive characteristics, and astrologers believe that it is the best sign under which to make seeding-frame plantings.

Of course, our gardening forefathers didn't have peat pots, but these crafty and ingenious fellows did have eggshells. Here is advice from an experienced 1880 gardener. "Take eggshells cut in half, make two or three small holes in bottom of each, fill with sifted soil, sink in a box of sand, sow seeds and cover with glass, of course keeping them in the right light. Water only the sand, for they will absorb enough through the holes. In transplanting, all you have to do is break off the shells, leaving the lump of earth intact without the roots being jarred or disturbed."

Windowsill Gardening

What will you plant in your eggshells or milk cartons for your windowsill gardening? Traditionally, cabbage seeds are started indoors first and last. Choose a mild-flavored variety for early slaw and kraut and seed it about the last week of February, moon-willing. Later decide on a winter variety you like and plant it for "keeping" cabbage.

Eggplant and peppers are of rather slow growth and, being set out later in the season, should be seeded after cabbage. You don't like eggplant? Try slicing it thinly, dipping in egg and flour and frying in hot vegetable oil. Season lightly with freshly ground pepper and sea salt and I'll bet you'll be converted.

Sweet peppers, containing vitamins A, C, and B1, are good in just about everything and good for you, so plant plenty. Lush peppers grow readily in windowsill boxes and produce late in the garden season when appetites for regular garden fare have paled. And peppers, like eggplants, are so pretty that you can plant some in your flower beds, along with tomatoes, parsley and borage.

Brussels sprouts and broccoli are very vigorous seedlings. Since I live in the southern part of the United States I do not usually plant Brussels sprouts until fall, but they grow well in spring for gardeners farther north. Now, for me, broccoli is something else again. My family likes it so much that we plant rows and rows in several different varieties, which my friends, the seedsmen, often send me for testing. I've been a broccoli fan for years and years — maybe broccoli knows I admire it and so it grows especially well for me. Now I find that broccoli is one of the very best plants for containing calcium. My broccoli-eating proclivities may be one of the reasons why, at my advanced age, I do not have either osteoporosis or arthritis.

Transplanting Tricks

And I might mention here that gardeners a century or so ago were just as careful to *transplant* on the right day and under the right sign (Cancer, Scorpio or Pisces), as they were to *plant* the seed in the first place. While the Water Signs were preferred, gardeners could also use so-called "secondary signs," such as Gemini, Taurus or Capricorn. Capricorn was considered best for all crops that bear above the ground. Libra was best and Capricorn second best for planting or transplanting flowers.

★ ★ ★

Useful and Free

"Use it up, wear it out, make it do, or do without," — this old New England saying still makes good sense for vegetable gardeners. Early gardeners did not have the plethora of things available to us today but they made good use of what they had. Since I, myself, come from a long line of bottle, string, and papersack savers I can appreciate their leaning toward economy. If they were living now, you can just bet they would have taken note of the many, many useful items for the garden that can be scrounged:

Plastic buckets with sealable lids are often available at donut stores and supermarket delis for a dollar or so. These are great for storing extra quantities of granular fertilizer, manure, lime and other materials purchased in large quantities. They are also handy for hauling water to remote gardens.

The local hockey rink is a great source of **broken hockey sticks.** They make tall, durable tomato stakes.

Year after year I use discarded **shock absorbers** obtain garages to mark my garden They are handy for stretching to mark the rows to keep the straight and later, being round, the watering hose slides smoothly around them rather than whipping across and breaking or bruising the plants.

Chimney flues come in a variety of sizes and are made of red clay, like flower pots. They are often damaged in shipment and can't be sold by building supply companies. For an attractive garden focal point or patio border, sink them into the ground at varying levels, fill them with soil, and plant them with a variety of flowers and vegetables.

Of late years old **railroad ties** have become much desired. They are great for making raised beds which are becoming very popular in some sections of the country. I have also seen them out in random lengths and set upright to border flower beds, and they were very decorative.

Carry-out salad bars often provide **foil containers** with transparent plastic lids. Washed out, these make fine mini-greenhouses for starting plants indoors.

Small, clear plastic glasses are often used in offices for employees use in drinking coffee and other beverages, being discarded just like paper or plastic cups. These are useful for placing over small transplants of broccoli, cabbage, tomatoes, eggplant, peppers, etc. Eggplant, in particular, needs protection when very young, being frequently attacked by tiny flying flea beetles which chew out the

ives, giving
t and weak-
eetles are so
them.

es

But to get back to window-sill gardening, I always have the most pleasure growing my tomato seedlings. It's psychologically uplifting to watch tomatoes grow, bringing closer the gardening days of spring. There is a school of thought that believes praying over seedlings helps — maybe so. Anyway, I always give silent thanks to Thomas Jefferson (see "January") when I start the tomato seed rites. A superstition once held that toma-

---

Cutting the Cutworm

Try crushing eggshells and working them into the soil around plants. Soot sprinkled around the garden is also said to drive cutworms off, and so is a mixture of equal parts of salt, ashes and plaster of Paris, or just salt and ashes. Henry Ward Beecher used weeds to guard plants against cutworms that were cutting up on his tomatoes and cabbages. "Keep the weeds down just about the hill," he wrote, "and permit them to grow for a few weeks between the rows. Never mind the slovenly look — this will save the cabbages by giving ample food to the cutworm." When the weeds grew tough in the stem he lightly spaded them in and leveled the surface with the rake.

---

toes stimulated love — and I certainly love tomatoes.

Cutworms love them, too, so when you later transplant them to your garden be sure to wrap the stem, set a small stick next to the stem (so the cutworm can't wrap itself around it and cut), or make a cardboard collar. These collars are also effective used about other vegetable transplants.

Stagger your tomato-seed plantings, so as to ensure fruit all summer. I like to plant several varieties of tomatoes, including a special type for canning. I have a theory that several varieties cross-pollinate and make for bigger crops. If you love tomatoes, but they don't reciprocate, try a low-acid yellow variety. And let your canner be a late bearer, to span out the work. Can tomatoes after peas, corn, beans, and other early crops are out of the way.

And a word to the wise — a ladybug is a tomato's best friend, so if they come flying around when you set them out, rejoice and let them be!

🌱 🌱 🌱

Hotbeds

The hotbed, to protect tender plants from cold weather and to speed the sprouting of seeds, is centuries old. It was a great favorite with early-day gardeners and still is with many who can obtain the needed ingredients. Manure, the principal ingredient, is used to supply the heat, and a vegetable compost will do this in a shorter time. Today electric cables can serve the purpose, but with electric rates steadily spiraling upward many gardeners are returning to the old ways — just as they are once again using wood to heat their houses. (My son's new home, for example, has a fireplace with ducts all over the house.)

A simple explanation of a hot-bed from an old seed catalog ran: "Simply a boarded-up garden covered with glass." Glass was not always used, though. "Those who are too poor to afford sash of glass," an 1880 gardener observed, "use muslin covers for hotbeds. I am using them and find them just the thing. I am often away from home at the time it is necessary to attend to glass, and yet my plants have not suffered." In this he was referring to the need for ventilation of the hotbed. I like the idea of using clear plastic instead of breakable glass — where I live we have hailstorms.

If you would set up a hotbed similar to the ones the 19th century gardeners used, here is some advice from an old gardening book.

Fresh stable manure in which there is plenty of litter [straw or hay] is most suited for hotbeds. There should be at least one-third litter in the heap. Shape it up well and mix it well together, adding water if at all dry and musty, and throw it into a compact heap to ferment. Let it remain a week and then work it over thoroughly as before, and water if necessary.

[Note: In the early day farming economy, stable manure was easy to come by. Gardeners today might try a dairy farmer, hog farmer, riding stable (or ranches), poultry farmers, or even obtain the cleanings from the animal cages if a circus comes to town!]

On this heap place the frame, which should be smaller than the heap of manure. Get a lot of boxes about five or six inches high. Sow the seeds in these, and place them on the manure inside the frame; this is much better than to fill soil in the frame.

Great care must be taken after the plants appear, to prevent them from becoming scorched or slender. During mild sunny days the heat inside the frame will be intense, and unless given air freely the plants will wither and die. On the other hand, there is often a spell of cold weather after the hotbed is set up, and when this prevails the frames should be sheltered with old carpet or mattresses so that the soil inside may not become cold and thus cause the seeds to rot or the plants to die. As the season advances and the rays of the sun become more genial, give the glass one or two coats of whitewash.

Another coating used was one part of linseed oil to five parts of turpentine, brushed on lightly.

A coldframe is a hotbed without an interior source of warmth, depending solely on the sun for heat. I have a sheltered area where I keep my coldframe, which is made of an old aluminum door on top of a wooden frame. Since the glass was broken I obtained it for a dollar and covered it with clear plastic. My warm climate lets me start plants of cabbage, broccoli, lettuce, and so on in it in early spring and later tomatoes, eggplant and peppers. In the winter months I use it again for growing an ample supply of parsley.

★ ★ ★

Using the Earth's Magnetic Field

We have known for many years that the earth possesses not only a magnetic field, but also a certain amount of electricity within the ground itself. We also know that the earth's magnetic field is always shifting, changing the positions of the poles.

A compass needle points north because the north magnetic pole of the earth is near the North Pole. But the magnetic pole and the geographical pole are not exactly at the same spot. The north magnetic pole is about 1,054 miles from the north geographic pole. It is near Prince of Wales Island in far northern Canada. The south magnetic pole is directly south of Sydney, Australia, about 1,526 miles from the south geographic pole. Because of these differences, magnetic compasses seldom point exactly north.

The angle between the directions of the north magnetic pole and the north geographic pole is called *magnetic declination* or *variation*. Declination varies from place to place on the earth, and also changes in a single place as the years pass as the earth's magnetic field shifts.

Persons who use magnetic compasses must use special declination charts that show differences in declination from place to place on earth. The magnetic equator, or *aclinic line*, is the place on the earth where the attraction of the north and south magnetic poles is equal.

How can we use this knowledge to advantage in gardening? I'm not sure just who first discovered that we could, or how long ago, but there is definitely a way to increase the productivity of your land making use of the earth's magnetic field.

Old timers discovered that by marking out the boundaries of their gardens with poles, and then stretching bare copper wires from pole to pole, they could achieve good effects. To complete the "circuit," another bare copper wire was hooked to the boundary wire and this wire was then placed in the ground.

I have tried this in my own garden and you might like to give this idea some thought in the quiet month of February when you are planning your own garden for later on in the spring.

I found that it gives good results, sometimes enabling me to raise crops two or three times larger than normal and at no extra effort on my part. There is a variation, since weather and fertility of soil play a part in garden operations, and some years are more favorable than others in this respect. In a good season, when the weather conditions cooperate, the results are very noticeable. I do not pay any more attention to the garden than normal, simply planting, weeding and watering as usual and, of course, planting and transplanting by the signs.

I harvest much more than usual and for a longer period of time. Another peculiar thing about this is that the keeping qualities of the vegetables and fruits seem to be definitely improved.

Early Use of Magnetism

We have proof that magnetism was used by early day gardeners in a report written in 1877 by an experienced New York State rose grower. Electricity, which has also been called magnetism, was used to stimulate growth of a tea rose. He writes:

I went to a tinsmith and directed him to cut a strip of sheet copper, three-quarters of an inch wide and 15 inches long — also one of sheet zinc of the same size. One end of the zinc was fastened to the copper with a small rivet. They made a strip 29 inches long, which I bent over the plant in the shape of a horseshoe, and stuck the two ends well down into the earth on each side of the plant, the earth between them completing the circuit. In three weeks the plant had more than half doubled its original size, and is still growing like Jack's bean stalk. I am now experimenting on other plants with good results. I set them in short rows, and bend the electrical strips from one end of the rows to the other. I am also trying it in pots with good results. After the plants get a good start I take the strips away.

🍎 🍎 🍎

TRAVELING PLANTS

Columbus brought wheat to the Western Hemisphere when he returned to the West Indies in 1493. Cortez took wheat from Spain to Mexico in 1519. Missionaries carried it from there into what is now Arizona and California. (Wheat will do best if planted in the 1st or 2nd quarter under the sign of Cancer, Scorpio, Pisces or Libra.)

The colonists brought many of their Old World garden favorites to the New World. These contributions to the culture of our country can be seen today in the restored gardens of Colonial Williamsburg, in Virginia. At that historic center only the garden and herb plants of colonial times are used in landscaping the restored area.

Efforts to introduce ornamental plants in the early 1800's were largely those of wealthy landowners who received plants to grace their estates on every ship arriving from Europe.

H.H. Hunnewell, of Massachusetts, was such a person. He reportedly imported over 2,000 forest trees, fruit and ornamental plants in 1847 alone. Undoubtedly, many of these early importations failed, for this was strictly a trial-and-error approach. Sim-

Sweet bay magnolia (Magnolia virginiana) has deliciously fragrant, creamy white blossoms that are produced in May and June, followed in early autumn by dark red fruits. Evergreen in the South and parts of the Midwest, this magnificent tree may reach a height of 60 feet.

ilarly, plantation owners in the South introduced camellias and other broadleaved evergreens from Europe.

Many of our most popular garden plants are native to the Orient. Most of the European collectors had sent these plants from Japan and China to Europe in earlier centuries. Indirectly, at first from Europe, these broadleaved evergreens, flowering trees and shrubs, and perennials have become our major landscaping resources.

Dr. George R. Hall (an American physician turned foreign trader) was responsible for the first shipment of ornamentals from Japan directly to the United States shortly after the visit to that country by Admiral Perry. In 1861–62, Dr. Hall, on returning to his home in Rhode Island, sent many of the plants he had collected in his Yokohama garden to Francis Parkman, noted historian and horticulturist, and to the famous Parsons Nursery, at Flushing, N.Y.

Some of Hall's first introductions were Japanese maples, Cryptomerias, hydrangea, procumbent juniper, star magnola, Japanese red pine, dwarf Japanese yew, wisteria and zelkova.

Establishment of the Arnold Arboretum in Boston, Mass. in 1872 provided for the first extensively organized effort to collect and introduce ornamentals from foreign countries.

With the United States Department of Agriculture the first organized efforts to conduct plant exploration began in 1898 under the leadership of David Fairchild. While the Department's interests were chiefly economic plants, ornamentals could scarcely be overlooked. During this grand period of plant collecting by Americans, from 1890 to 1930, we find flowering cherries, bamboos, Chinese elms, lawn grasses (zoysia), roses, and lilacs among the plants made especially popular through USDA collections.

There were few import restrictions, if any, during the very earliest days of settlement in the New World. Many colonists, notably those from the wine-producing countries of the Old World, sometimes brought grape cuttings, carefully packed, with them when they emigrated. Some cuttings or small fruit trees sometimes came along as well.

In California and other western states, missionaries were great gardeners, tending grapes, fruit trees, and vegetables as well as following the traditions of their various orders in producing herbs and herbal remedies.

OLDER VARIETIES OF APPLES

Many of the early trees, particularly fruit trees, and flowering shrubs have been improved and hybridized down through the years. By careful research, however, it is still possible to find the older varieties, especially of apples, which are still being produced and sold. Flowering shrubs, once with single blossoms, have in many instances been "taught" to produce double ones. Oddly, many of the double flowers and flowering plants have, on their trip through the beauty parlor, become almost scentless. The older types of single blossoms still retain greater fragrance.

Apples, still America's favorite fruit, came to America during the earliest Colonial days and were already the national fruit when the American colonies became a united nation. The tasty fruit spread westward on the new continent ahead of the settlers, carried by explorers and missionaries, and some Indian tribes planted them around their villages.

John Chapman, the legendary Johnny Appleseed, roamed Ohio and Indiana during the early 19th Century, preaching the gospel and planting apples. Marcus Whitman carried apple seeds across the continent in 1836 and planted them at his mission near Walla Walla, Washington. A sea captain carried an apple seed in his pocket from England to Fort Vancouver, Wash., in 1826. The resulting tree is still producing apples today.

If you plan to enlarge your orchard, or start a new one, the last of February is an excellent time to do so. Early planting of fruit trees gives them a chance to become established before hot weather arrives.

Here is a suggestion I have often given to northern gardeners. Dig the holes for your fruit trees and shrubs in the fall while the soil is still fairly soft. Mix it with compost, peat moss or sand (no fertilizer), return it to the hole, and place a few boards over it. It will not become compacted. When your plants arrive in the spring the soil will be very easy to remove again, so that you can plant even when other areas of your ground may still be frozen. Getting the trees and ornamentals in early will give them a head start for they begin to grow a little and establish themselves underground even though you may not see any signs of this in the top growth until much later on in the spring.

Barking Up the Wrong Tree

In 1898 a gardening magazine advised a reader complaining of a white "scaly bug" on apple tree trunks to make a strong solution of sal-soda, and apply it with a bristle white-wash brush, using it as well on ornamental shrubs.

Stark Bro's, which has been supplying high-quality fruit trees since 1816, tells a fascinating story: "It all began in 1816 with my great-great-great-grandfather Judge James Hart Stark. He was just a young man at the time, when he struck out on his own to make a home for himself — across the Mississippi River from Kentucky to Missouri. He traveled the entire way with a bundle of apple twigs which he protected as if his life depended on it. In a way it did! When he reached Pike County, Missouri, Judge Stark grafted these few twigs to wild seedling roots, thus creating the very first cultivated fruit trees west of the Mississippi River, and founding our nursery.

"By the late 1800's the Judge had passed away and his grandsons, Clarence and Edgar, took the reins and greatly expanded the business here in Pike County."

Clarence and Edgar determined to find the perfect apple and began sponsoring contests to discover new varieties. "In 1892, at one such contest, Clarence bit into an oddly shaped apple entry and exclaimed 'Delicious! That will be its name. Who sent them?' " It was discovered that no one knew because the entry card was missing. This apple was the best Clarence had ever tasted, and he determined to find the grower — which he did at the following year's fruit contest. Everyone told him it couldn't possibly succeed, but Clarence was a stubborn man — and he was right! Today the Red

Delicious is the most popular apple in the entire world.

In an effort to reach more customers than was possible by word-of-mouth, Clarence, an astute businessman, put together his first catalog in 1894. Modest, like all seedsmen and nurserymen, he spoke of the company's early beginnings, stating: "Back then the company's motto was 'Stark Trees Bear Fruit.' It's the same today, because it's true! And now we've got 170 years of experience to back it up." He was right; no one has finer trees than Stark Bro's — and furthermore, there are no finer, more dependable people to deal with. I know from my own experience.

It was about this same time that Clarence was introduced to Luther Burbank, the famous "Plant Wizard." Recognizing Burbank's genius, he offered him $9,000 (a great sum in those days) for three of his new varieties. With Stark Bro's continued support throughout the years, Burbank pioneered the field of plant breeding and went on to worldwide fame. The Burbank July Elberta Peach and the Burbank Red Ace Plum are still in the company's catalog today.

Since many of my readers reside in the northern tier of states I would also like to mention another old and reliable firm which has an equally interesting history — in Canada. Established in 1896 by Dr. A.E. McKenzie, the seed company flourished under his gardening spirit and released its first seed catalog in the late 1890's. The company continued to grow and acquired other companies to the point where it has become the largest consumer-oriented flower and vegetable seed company in Canada, serving the nation from coast to coast. Formerly known as "McKenzie-Steele-Briggs" it has recently moved to reestablish its roots and is now known simply as "McKenzie."

McKenzie sells its seeds and nursery products through the Mc-Fayden Seed Co., Ltd., P.O. Box 1800, Brandon, Manitoba, R7A 6N4. I am also proud to say that McFayden's catalog also offers my two books *Carrots Love Tomatoes*

With all this background where can I go to give you better advice on the "Bear Facts" than to Stark Bro's? They recommend that you ask yourself, just what it is that you personally want in your fruit trees. "Do you want an apple that ripens early? A peach that bears up North, or are you after that special berry that makes the best jam?

They sensibly suggest that you check your zone (their catalog gives you the necessary map), and choose a variety suited to your area. You should also check ripening times, selecting varieties that ripen over a period of time and avoiding choosing fruits that ripen all at once.

The importance of proper pollination is also emphasized — with the description of each variety in their catalog suggesting compatible pollinators.

and *Roses Love Garlic*, which emphasize companion planting.

McFayden's catalog offers many winter-hardy plants and seeds, such as their Early Prolific sweet pepper, which combines high quality with a short growing season. Did you know peanuts would grow in the North? Early Spanish will, and give good crops. Do you have trouble getting your tomatoes to ripen? Consider the fine introduction, Floramerica Hybrid, which bears heavily in hot or cold weather, or Rocket, recommended by the University of Manitoba.

How about prairie-hardy apples? Battleford, Collet and Goodland bear well and store well, and Battleford is especially delicious for eating out of hand. The sub-zero apricot is hardy through zones 1 to 4 and its white spring flowers add to its beauty as well.

Cucumber Beetles

In the mid-19th century a Dr. B.S. Barton of Philadelphia was quoted as recommending sprinkling cucumber vines with a mixture of tobacco and red pepper to rid them of cucumber beetles. Other weapons included teas made of tobacco, elder leaves, walnut leaves, or hops. One tactic of the day that became popular was to stick lighted splinters of pine knots in the ground around the plants at night to attract and incinerate the beetles!

Native Shrubs and Trees

Here are some noteworthy native shrubs for your garden:

Flame azalea (*Rhododendron calendulaceum*)

Flannel bush (*Fremontia mexicana*)

Mescalbean (*Sophora secundiflora*)

Mountain laurel (*Kalmia latifolia*)

Santa Barbara ceanothus (*Ceanothus impressus*)

Fringe-tree (*Chionanthus virginica*)

Mountain stewartia (*Stewartia ovata*, var. grandiflora)

Yaupon (*Ilex vomitoria*)

Cranberrybush (*Viburnum trilobum*)

Oakleaf hydrangea (*Hydrangea quercifolia*)

Oregon-grape (*Mahonia aquifolium*)

Creosotebush (*Larrea tridentata*)

Anacahuita (*Cordia boissieri*)

Sagebrush (*Artemisia tridentata*)

Native American trees include such species as:

White fir (*Abies concolor*)

Huisache (*Acacia farnesiana*)

Red maple (*Acer rubrum*)

Sugar maple (*Acer saccharum*)

Ohio buckeye (*Aesculus glabra*)

Madrona (*Arbutus menziesii*)

Hickory (*Carya spp.*)

Catalpa (*Catalpa spp.*)

Hackberry (*Celtis occidentalis*)

Paloverde (*Cercidium torreyanum*)

Port Oxford cedar (*Chamaecyparis lawsoniana*)

Flowering dogwood (*Cornus florida*)

Pacific dogwood (*Cornus nuttallii*)

Monterey cyprus (*Cupressus macrocarpa*)

American beech (*Fagus grandifolia*)

White ash (*Fraxinus americana*)

Red ash (*Fraxinus pennsylvanica*)

Honey locust (*Gleditsia triacanthos*)

American holly (*Ilex opaca*)

Walnut (*Juglans spp.*)

Juniper (Red cedar) (*Juniperus spp.*)

Larch (*Larix spp.*)

Incense cedar (*Calocedrus decurrens*)

Sweet gum (*Liquidambar styraciflua*)

Tuliptree (*Liriodendron tulipfera*)

Catalina ironwood (*Lyonothamnus floribundus*)

Magnolia (*Magnolia spp.*)

Red mulberry (*Morus rubra*)

Blackgum (*Nyssa sylvatica*)

Sourwood (*Oxydendron arboreum*)

Blue spruce (*Picea pungens*)

Pines (*Pinus spp.*–of these there are about 40 species, nearly all cultivated.)

Sycamore (*Platanus spp.*)

Douglas fir (*Pseudotsuga menziesii*)

Oaks (*Quercus spp.*)

Black locust (*Robinia pseudoacacia*)

Cabbage palmetto (*Sabal palmetto*)

Sassafras (*Sassafras albidum*)

Redwood (*Sequoia sempervirens*)

Sequoia (*Sequoiadendron giganteum*)

Cypress (*Taxodium spp.*)

Western red cedar (*Thuja plicata*)

Basswood (*Tilia spp.*)

Canadian hemlock (*Tusga canadensis*)

Western hemlock (*Tsuga heterophylla*)

Mountain hemlock (*Tsuga mertensiana*)

American elm (*Ulmus americana*)

Yucca (*Yucca spp.*) and Palms (*Washingtonia spp.*)

Pecans (*Carya*, belonging to the walnut family, *Juglandaceae*)

NATIVE NORTH AMERICAN PLANTS

While the Old World passed on many of its valuable fruits and vegetables to the New, there was still much treasure to be found in the many thousands of plants native to North America. Many of them have great beauty and can be found growing in our gardens today. And there are hundreds of others yet to be tried and yet to be appreciated.

The plants growing wild in North America have grown here for thousands of years. Their presence is ample proof of their ability to survive in our climate. While plants from foreign countries must usually be tested for a period of years in various places, to find out whether they are adapted to our climate, native North American plants have long since passed their most important "tests."

Many of our native plants have been used to breed better garden varieties. For example, some of our wild azaleas have been used along with other species to produce what are perhaps the finest flowering shrubs in existence. These are the Exbury or Knaphill azaleas. Much of their beauty and fragrance comes from our flame azalea of the Appalachians, the Pacific azalea from the California mountains, and two other pink-flowering wildlings from the eastern United States.

The Exburys may survive in most regions of our country. *Some can withstand temperatures down to 40 degrees below zero and up to 100 degrees.* All require acid soil. Way-side Gardens, Hodges, SC 29695-0001, has a fine collection of native American plants, as well as many superlative hybrid creations. This time the italics are mine — I have a long-standing love affair with azaleas.

Native American Azaleas

- *Azalea canescens* — Piedmont Azalea
- *Rhododendron arborescens* — Sweet Azalea
- *Rhododendron austrinum* '*Escatawpa*' — Florida Flame Azalea

Others are: *R. alabamese*, a native of Alabama; *R. nudiflorum*, native from Maine to Florida and Texas; *R. pruniflorum*, southwestern Georgia and eastern Alabama; *R. occidentale*; *R cumberlandense*, Virginia and N. Carolina; *R vaseyi*, Blue Ridge Mountains of N. Carolina.

Growing Native Plants in Your Garden

★ **Grow the plants under conditions that resemble as closely as possible the plant's wild habitat.** Plant water-loving plants in wet places, shade-tolerant species in shade, and sun-loving plants in the sun.

★ **Be liberal with peat moss.** Gardeners have found that *sedge* peat moss (not sphagnum) does something beneficial to the soil. Sometimes peat moss makes the difference between success and failure.

★ **Purchase your plants from nurseries or seedsmen who specialize in native materials.** There are a number that do and they usually advertise in gardening magazines. Collecting wild plants yourself is often illegal and may dangerously reduce fragile populations.

It's worth remembering that native plants can stand the competition of other plants better than foreign species can. Wild plants often become more luxuriant in a garden than they appear in the wild. For example, sagebrush out west is scarcely beautiful because the plant is almost always chewed upon by livestock. Grown in a garden, the plant is a lovely, shapely, silvery-white bush of great character and beauty.

Two years ago when my son built his new home, he purchased approximately ten acres of land. Desiring a planting as nearly carefree as possible he chose such species as sugar maple, flowering dogwood, American holly, walnut, pecan, incense cedar, sweet gum, tulip tree, magnolia, pines, and western red cedar. Now coming into their third spring, they are simply beautiful, blending well with native oaks already growing on the property.

CONTROLLING ORCHARD PESTS

While native species are hardier and less subject to insect damage, problems are not unknown and you should start checking for these in early February.

Dormant Oil Spray

In addition to such measures as orchard cleanliness and attentiveness, many orchardists rely heavily on dormant oil spray, sometimes referred to as "miscible oil," to control sucking and chewing insects in the egg stage. This consists of a light-grade mineral oil suspended in a soap-water emulsion. Effective against aphids, red spiders, thrips, mealybugs, whiteflies, pear psylla, all kinds of scale insects and mites, codling moth,

oriental fruit moth, various leaf rollers, and cankerworms, dormant oil spray can be bought from garden supply houses or can be made by using the following recipe:

Dormant Oil Spray

Combine 1 gallon light-grade oil and 1 pound soap (preferably fish-oil soap) with a half gallon of water. Boil. Then pour back and forth from one container to another until blended. Dilute with 20 times its volume of water. Use immediately before it separates.

This non-toxic spray may be applied in late autumn as well as in early spring, when trees are dormant and before buds develop, while the temperature is between 40 and 80 degrees, with no freeze expected for at least 24 hours. It is useful on shrubs and evergreens, but fruit trees seem to have more enemies and need it more.

In early spring insects that hatch from eggs laid on plants the previous fall can be readily killed, because the shells of the eggs and the protective covering of hibernating scales become softer and more porous at this time. The dormant spray penetrates and makes a tight, continuous film over these, literally suffocating the organism to death.

It will also form a similar film over leaves and injure them, which is why you apply only while the trees are in a leafless state. Citrus trees, which do not shed their leaves, are given a very dilute spray, usually made with "white oils," highly refined oils that present the least chance of foliage injury.

Dormant oil sprays have a residual effect, too. An oil film covering the plant interferes with the successful establishment of any young insects that may hatch for several days after spraying.

It is difficult to apply harmful amounts of a miscible oil spray. If too much of the emulsion is applied, the excess simply runs off. A tree should for this reason be sprayed all at once, not one-half first (as when a sprayer goes down an orchard row), the other half later, after the first has dried. Always cover a tree thoroughly in one spraying.

Other Safe Methods of Orchard Pest Control

Another valuable mechanical aid to the home fruit grower is the use of bands of tar, or some sticky material, two to four inches wide around tree trunks, several feet from the ground. These prevent crawling insects (various worms and beetles) from ascending. Commercial compounds and prepared adhesive bands are available from garden supply houses.

Early day gardeners had their problems, too, and in 1898 a gardening magazine gave this advice to a correspondent complaining of a white "scaly bug" on apple tree trunks: "One of the best remedies for bark insects is *sal soda*. Make a rather strong solution and apply it by means of a bristle whitewash brush. It may be effectually applied either to ornamental shrubs and trees or to fruit trees."

In the middle of the 19th century the trunks of fruit trees that were being bothered by blights or bark insects were given a coat of clay and water. This, too, was brushed on — the mixture used being about the consistency of thick cream.

San Jose scale, which often affects apple trees, can be scrubbed off the bark with a stiff brush or a wad of burlap, yielding a yellow ooze that indicates you've killed the scale. Ladybugs are also useful in combating scale.

The codling moth is probably the most serious apple pest in the Northeast, causing practically all the wormy apples. One way of destroying them is to scrape off the loose bark in the spring and scrub the area with soapy water, thus destroying the eggs. Some gardeners maintain that if the herb southernwood is planted near fruit trees it will repel harmful moths.

For **aphids** or **plant lice,** other successful methods are: using, as a spray, water in which crushed tomato leaves have soaked; a tea made of wormwood (cover the herb with water, bring to a boil, remove from the heat, dilute with 4 parts of water, stir ten minutes and use at once); pureed onion in water; stinging nettle tea (using instructions for wormwood tea); or just soapy water. A strong jet of plain water from a hose will often wash aphids off trees and discourage their return.

Other gardeners plant nasturtiums under their trees as a trap crop to gather aphids and distract them from the fruit trees. This fascinating method of "trapcropping," in which one plant is used to lure pests away from the main crop, was practiced a long time ago, and is beginning to be explored again.

Peach leaf curl is caused by a fungus that causes leaves to pucker and twist and drop early, lowering tree vitality. If individual leaves are affected, pull them off and burn them. If the entire tree is infected, feed it generously with rotted manure or other material high in nitrogen.

Brown rot of stone fruit is also a fungal disease and very destructive to peaches, cherries, plums, nectarines and apricots, most often affecting them in wet seasons. To avoid this prepare a garlic, onion or chive tea (as you did wormwood tea). Use it weekly as a spray, starting two or three weeks before harvest.

Gathering dried, shrivelled fruit ("mummies") that remain hanging on the tree or fall to the ground, helps greatly to reduce sources of infection for the next season.

Oriental fruit moth attacks the tips of growing peach shoots and infests the fruits. Tansy planted at the base of peach trees has been reported to repel the moths.

Peach borer, very prevalent in the southern states, also attacks apricot, nectarine, cherry and plum trees, although peach is its preferred host. It is indicated by a gummy, amber-colored, gelatinous material, exuding from the tree near or slightly below ground level. This very serious pest can be removed with a knife or wire probe, or by killing them in their tunnels. Whitewash, if applied three times a season to the trunk and main branches up to three feet off the ground, has been reported as discouraging borers and may destroy their eggs. Planting garlic around the base of the trees is also helpful, but it must be planted when the trees are young and first put in the ground — after infestation has taken place it will not help much.

Japanese beetles can just about ruin a fruit tree in a few hours, eating the entire foliage and attacking the fruit as well. Watch for them and hand pick them when they appear. Milky spore disease, a pathogenic organism sold commercially, gives good control of Japanese beetles.

Plum curculio is one of the worst orchard pests but there's a rather amusing way of combating it. The entire tree or individual limbs may be jarred gently with the hand or a wooden mallet. The beetles fall on a white sheet spread beneath the tree and are then collected and burned. If you have chickens, they would find the beetles a treat.

When I was a child I remember that my father planted several trees in our poultry yard, protecting them, of course, while they were small. Peach trees are usually short-lived but those three trees not only lived but bore enormously every year, perhaps thanks to natural pest control. As they grew older and stronger, the hens used to roost up in the branches. Those trees never had any insect or fungus damage and were still in excellent health when we sold the property.

Harmless Herbal Pesticides

In addition to non-chemical measures there are several safe botanical pesticides now in use in both home and commercial orchards.

Ryania: This extract comes from a Latin American shrub and is valuable against codling moths, aphids and Japanese beetles.

White hellebore has been known for thousands of years and is good against slugs on cherries. Old timers also used hellebore (derived from the Veratrum plant)

against caterpillars and other leaf-eating pests.

Pyrethrum, the herbaceous chrysanthemum, is an age-old insecticide especially effective in the orchard for slugs.

Nicotine in the form of tobacco dust was widely used in the mid-19th century against aphids on chrysanthemums. For house plants bothered by aphids, some gardeners blew tobacco smoke through the foliage. In the orchard nicotine, the primary alkaloid of tobacco, is helpful in controlling codling moths, aphids, psylla and caterpillars on fruit trees.

Derris, an age-old Chinese discovery, can be used for control of leaf-eating caterpillars and aphids.

Rotenone is an insecticide derived from certain tropical plants, derris, cube barbasco, timbo and a few others. Devil's shoestring (*Tephrosia virginiana*) is the only native plant that contains rotenone (the roots contain as much as five percent rotenone) and it is a common weed in our eastern and southern states. Rotenone can be safely used on all crops and ornamentals, and even on cats and dogs, being especially helpful in killing external parasites such as fleas.

If you would bless someone, scatter the leaves of elder (Sambucus canadensis) to the four winds in the name of the person to be blessed.

WILD FOODS FOR FEBRUARY

Being an avid eater of greens I start looking in my garden rows for lamb's quarters, also known by such jolly names as bacon weed, muckweed, midden myles, pigweed and fat hen, along about the last of February. Once nobody but "poor folks" (who aren't so dumb as many think) paid much attention to this venerable weed. Since I was poor folks when I grew up I knew all about it from an early age. We often had a mess of lamb's quarters for lunch with my mother's delicious hot cornbread. I never felt "deprived!"

But this weed is now looking up in the world. It seems to deserve another of its many names, "All Good," for laboratory tests have revealed that it contains more iron and protein than either raw cabbage or spinach. Speaking of spinach, I usually have some in my early spring garden, which I sowed in late fall. I combine the weed and the spinach and, to me, it all tastes the same. I cook it, drain it, and add a little flour, butter, salt and pepper with a dash of nutmeg. To this I add half-and-half, making a creamy sauce. It seems downright wicked that something so good should also be helpful and healthy, containing as it does more vitamin B1 than raw cabbage and more vitamin B2 than either raw cabbage or spinach, and not be more widely used.

The young seedlings are good in salads, and the leaves, cooked and chopped or put through a meat grinder, will make a bracing, bright green soup for winter menus.

Dill is another semi-wild plant that comes up early. When I went to the Sausage Festival, held yearly in New Braunfels, Texas, I found the good German ladies there using dill as an ingredient in potato soup. I got hooked on it and have been letting it reseed itself (what do I mean, "letting" — I couldn't stop it if I wanted to) in my garden ever since. To make this delectable soup, rice cooked potatoes, adding a few tablespoons of cooked carrots and onions (chopped), minced dill, butter and enough milk to thin for soup. Heat all together, adding seasonings and serve with garlic bread.

Lamb's quarters (Chenopodium album) *is an easily recognized edible weed which likes to grow in cultivated gardens. Young plants may be boiled as greens. Indians of the Southwest like to cultivate it for its seeds.*

FLOWERS WAKE UP IN FEBRUARY

February is a great month for bulbs. In the South and Southwest those you planted last fall will start popping through. Spring bulb beds and many other plantings will benefit from a dressing of fertilizer applied to the ground and gently scratched in, just as the tips of the bulbs show above ground and as perennials begin to grow.

But if you live farther north there are bulbs that you too, can enjoy. I am the happy possessor of the 1941 edition of *Watkins Household Hints* by Elaine Allen, published by the J.R. Watkins Company. Evidently, Ms. Allen was the Heloise of her day and the book is just chock-full of what it says it is — household hints. Here are her directions for growing paper white narcissus indoors:

Narcissi of the Paper White type may be forced in pebbles and water. Choose a low bowl or other container and stand the bulbs on pearl chips or pebbles. Between the bulbs, which are placed close together, more chips or pebbles are poured. When planting is completed, the container is filled with water and put in a fairly cool place. In their early stages the bulbs may be kept either in darkness or light. They soon develop roots and shoots. After the shoots are 3 or 4 inches high, the container of bulbs must be removed to a sunny location and flowers will develop in a few weeks.

This is so easy to do, and the results so pretty, that you may want to start several containers. Don't try to reuse the bulbs a second time but you need not throw them away either. I always plant mine somewhere in the flower beds to renew their strength, form new little bulbs, or whatever it is they do underground, and eventually I am rewarded with more blooming narcissi!

Paper-white narcissus is easy to grow and gives a lovely touch of spring to your home, office, or classroom.

February Lore

Something else besides flowers is supposed to wake up in February — the groundhog. Groundhog Day is a bit of folklore that has managed to linger on. It is based on a custom that people from Germany and Great Britain brought to America. They believed that it was a time for forecasting the weather for the next six weeks. According to legend, the groundhog or woodchuck awakens from his long winter nap on February 2nd. He sticks his head out of his home in the ground and looks around. If the sun is shining and the groundhog can see his shadow, he is frightened and crawls back into his hole. This is supposed to mean that there will be six more weeks of winter weather. But if the day is cloudy and the ground hog cannot see his shadow, he stays out of his hole, indicating that spring weather will soon come.

Science has not confirmed this and, in fact, says that statistics have shown that there is no basis for the legend. But just try and tell an old timer *that.*

Predictions, possibly a bit more reliable, which have come down to us:

Spiders do not spin their webs out of doors before rain. Previous to rain, flies sting sharper, bees remain in their hives or fly but short distances, and almost all animals appear uneasy.

A thunderstorm in winter (usually in January or February) is always followed by clear, cold weather. It is not, as many think, the breaking up of winter.

If it starts to rain after seven o'clock in the morning it will continue to do so all day, and very often it is the indication of three days of rain.

When it is raining and the clouds are still massed in heavy blankets, one sure sign of clear weather is the patch of blue sky that shows through the rift large enough to make a pair of "sailor's breeches."

Pisces the Fishes (February 20 - March 20)

Worm Moon
MARCH

*Weather Lore ★ First sowing of early root crops ★
Baking a Carrot Dream Cake ★ March planting and
transplanting ★ Start an asparagus bed ★ Plant
English peas ★ Sharing the abundance ★ March
gardening chores ★ Play a little — take time off to go
fishing ★ Cattails for food ★ Taming the stinging
nettle ★ For Vitamin C eat violets ★ Wild onions
and wild leeks ★ Folklore of Easter ★ Poison ivy ★*

COULD IT HAVE BEEN AN OLD-TIMER who said, "March comes in like a lion, and goes out like a lamb?" Probably was, it's one of those homey, folksy sayings and it just happens, for the most part to be true.

I've also always loved the little jingle that goes like this:

Red sky in the morning —
    sailor's warning,

Red sky at night — sailor's delight.

When you see a mackerel sky,
'Twill not be many hours dry.

When the seagulls inland fly,
Know ye that a storm is nigh.

A ring around the moon
Means a storm is coming soon.

When it rains before seven,
'Twill clear before eleven.

WEATHER LORE

Early day farmers, who didn't have the "benefits" of our modern meteorologists, had a lot of ways of predicting the weather and a lot of them were very valid, such as, "A foggy morning is usually the forerunner of a clear afternoon." They believed that a red or copper-colored sun or moon indicated great heat. A silvery moon was thought to indicate clear, cold weather.

Let's take that one that says a ring around the moon means a storm is coming soon. An approaching depression and its frontal system show the cloud sequence cirrus-cirrostratus-altostratus-nimbostratus — white feathery clouds changing to a milky veil followed by a lowering, darkening gray pall of cloud. This sequence is a reliable indicator of rain, especially when accompanied by a falling barometer and wind backing from west to south or southeast in the northern hemisphere, west to north or northeast in the southern hemisphere. During the cirrostratus phase, a halo frequently appears around the sun or moon; the halo is, therefore, justifiably regarded as a sign of imminent rain.

For the last week or so there has been a halo around the moon — and not just a halo. The halo has been a definite rainbow, clearly showing the colors. Now I'm listening to the weather reports on the radio as I write this page — and tornados are striking all around it's scary!

This business of the "Red sky in the morning, red sky at night" is based on the same depression cloud sequence. The morning red sky is caused by the red rays of the rising sun shining on the clouds in the western sky, often cirrostratus or altostratus, indicators of rain approaching from the west. The evening red sky means that the western sky is clearing and that the bad weather clouds are passing

away to the east.

The early morning sky is sometimes deceptive. In anticyclone weather, the day often dawns with a complete cover of low gray stratus, which breaks up during the early afternoon to be followed by a sunny warm day. On the other hand, especially in the polar air stream behind a depression, cloudless skies in the early morning are often followed by cumulus and, later, by cumulonimbus with showers. Hence the saying:

Shiny morning, cloudy day;
    Cloudy morning, shiny day.

All of these things are indications, and good indications, but not to be taken too seriously for they are not, of course, completely reliable; if they were there might be no work for professional forecasters. In the early days, however, they were all that farmers and gardeners had. As we have seen, they were often valid, deriving from the long experience and shrewd observations of shepherds, farmers, sailors, and others who follow outdoor occupations.

Pisces, (watery, fruitful, with strong-rooted tendencies) is still with us in March, extending as it does from February 19th to March 21, when Aries (fiery, dry, windy and barren) takes control until April 20th. Best not to plant in the arid sign of Aries, and also best not to plant on Sunday, as Sunday is ruled by the sun and believed to be dry and barren also.

Remember Moon Signs

Nevertheless, sometimes things work out in such a way that, in the interest of making the most of an opportunity when *you* have free time, it becomes desirable to do some planting. When this happens remember what I told you about the moon's place being ruled by a different zodiac sign every two or three days. Thus, the barren sign of Aries may be weakened or over-ruled by the moon's daily place sign — such as the good planting signs of Cancer, Scorpio or Pisces. Libra and Taurus are also good "secondary" signs, should an unexpected holiday give you a chance to get in a few licks in the garden. And Aries *is* a good sign for plow-ing, cultivating, and destroying weeds.

March seems to be a bit different every year and I remember a time, several years ago, when it turned really raw, bitter cold and then was made further depressing by a sleet storm. It was, however, the "right" day and the "right" sign so my husband and I bundled up and went out and planted pota-toes. Everybody laughed at us — some said the potatoes would rot. They didn't. That year we had the biggest crop and the best potatoes we ever had.

🍎 🍎 🍎

GROWING ROOT CROPS

Directions for planting root crops often tell us to "plant as early as ground can be worked." Though southern areas may have suitable planting days in Febru-ary, March is usually the month when seeds for root crops go into the ground. Bear in mind that root crops will not do well in a tight soil — they need "their own space," especially carrots which tend to wrap around each other in a tight soil or when sown too thickly. Steel yourself to the task, and thin.

Here is a way of growing pota-toes you might like to try. Dig a trench about a foot or so deep, place your potato "eyes" in the bottom of the trench and cover with leaves and dry grass clip-pings, in alternating layers. Often such material is bagged and set out on the curb for the sanitation de-partment to haul away, so if you pick it up instead no one is going to object. You may even gather this in late summer or early fall and save it for your spring plant-ing. As they grow, the potatoes will be clean and you can reach down from time to time and get some of those wonderful little potatoes that taste so good.

In 1790, *The Farmer's Dictionary* by Isaiah Thomas offered some advice that could well be used to-day. He describes it as "a new method of planting potatoes," and continues, "After dung is spread and ploughed in, raise ridges with the cultivator; dibble in the sets along top of ridges, about as deep as ridges are above the surface be-fore ridges were made. Cover with straw or old refuse hay to a depth of about 12 inches. Nothing more has to be done, until they are taken up — they will be clean and the crop considerable."

The practice of "stealing" a crop of young potatoes early was well known and practiced by gardeners a century or more ago. A garden guide of 1871 even tells how to do it! "In April, potatoes may be tried by scraping away the earth near the collar. The largest tubers are generally near the surface, and may be removed without disturbing the plants, which should be left to perfect the smaller ones; water, if required, but liquid manure is not necessary." If you are tempted to do this be sure to tuck some extra compost around the plants you have robbed, press it down gently but well, and water.

Carrot-Pineapple Dream Cake

3 cups sifted flour (white, unbleached)
2 cups sugar (white)
2 teaspoons cinnamon
1 teaspoon ginger
1½ teaspoons baking soda
1 teaspoon baking powder
3 eggs, beaten (I like large eggs)
1½ cups cooking oil (I like sunflower oil — and be sure your oil is fresh)

1½ teaspoons salt (preferably sea salt)
2 teaspoons vanilla
1 can crushed pineapple (8¾-ounce size)
2 cups raw carrots, grated (save yourself work and put them through your meat grinder)
1½ cups finely chopped pecans
½ cup grated coconut

Mix together flour, sugar, cinnamon, ginger, baking soda, baking powder, eggs, oil, vanilla, and salt. Add pineapple and juice, carrots, nuts and coconut. Mix well. (This is a big cake so use a large bowl — I mix mine in my Dutch oven). Pour mixture into rectangular cake pan (9" x 12" x 2"), which has been sprayed with non-stick vegetable oil spray. Bake at 350° F for approximately one hour. Stoves differ slightly, so watch it a little the first time, and remove it when done. It's important not to underbake as it will be a little soggy — and if overbaked it will be dry.

I keep testing. After the first time or two you will know exactly when to remove it from the oven, as this recipe is practically foolproof. It's less expensive to make than fruit cake, and my own family likes it better.

If your family is small you might prefer to bake in two pans, serving one cake and freezing the other for later use. Since I do not put on frosting I like to decorate the top of the cake, just before baking, with rows of pecan halves. And this cake is not only good, but good for you. Especially if you will pay attention as the old-timers did to harvesting your carrots at just the right time.

Reliable Root Crops

Somehow, today, most of us seem to think of root crops, good as they are, as strictly utilitarian. Not so the early settlers, who were often dependent on stored roots to see them through a long hard winter when fresh vegetables were difficult if not impossible to obtain. Those glamorous eye-pleasers, tomatoes, corn, cucumbers, eggplant, squash, and beans, were but a delicious memory, but the roots of beets, carrots, turnips, rutabagas, parsnips, and salsify were right down there in the root cellar waiting to be brought up and used to satisfy hearty winter appetites.

We know today that root crops are very nutritious, containing many healthful vitamins and adding fiber to our diet, and creative cooks know many attractive ways to serve them. It is even possible, as with carrots, to make them into a delicious dessert. This recipe is so good that I'm going to give it to you right here. (Note: It is the easiest cake to make that I have ever found.)

Harvesting on Time

Did you know that the time of day has a bearing on the quality and the nourishment to be derived from roots? Gardeners knew this a long time ago but they didn't know why. Now scientific studies have shown that there are two very important rules particularly applicable to root crops, which remain constant at all stages of plant growth.

The first is that the vital life forces of all plants gradually return to the roots during the course of late afternoon and evening. Secondly, having returned, these vital forces remain in the roots during the hours of the night.

With daybreak, these forces again start their gradual rise back into the above-ground portion of the plant. This is scientifically measurable. It may even be compared to our own time of rest after the day's work, when our minds store and file the information we have accumulated during the course of the day. Roots, in like fashion, store the vital forces the plant has gained during the day's photosynthesis.

How can we best interpret this knowledge and make use of it? By understanding and observing these conditions, it becomes easier for us to produce healthier and more nourishing plants. Following this line on a little further it becomes apparent that we should harvest (as an old gardening manual directs) all root crops in the afternoon, when the vital life forces begin to return to the roots and the energies gathered that day are in the plant in their most concentrated form. An observant early day gardener also commented that "root crops harvested late in the day seem to have better keeping qualities than those harvested in early morning."

In early days keeping qualities were very important. It is also important to remember that root crops will keep better if harvested (dug) in the dry signs of Aries, Leo, Sagittarius, Gemini and

Aquarius — 3rd or 4th quarter.

Carrots, beets, parsnips, turnips, rutabagas and radishes can all be handled this way. Top crops, on the other hand (that is, those such as tomatoes, corn, and others that bear their edible portions above ground), should be harvested between ten in the morning and three in the afternoon for maximum quality and best keeping.

We can further utilize this knowledge of roots by planning all root divisions, root feedings (such as fish fertilizer or side dressings of compost), and root prunings (sometimes necessary through transplanting procedures) to take place during the hours of greatest root vitality. These are, of course, the late afternoon and evening hours, or very early in the morning, shortly after daybreak.

Doubling Up On Root Crops

Most of the early day gardeners had ample land, so space-saving gardening methods may not have received as much attention as now, when land is more expensive and garden plots must be smaller. But even so, many had to clear arable land by cutting down trees or clearing out stones.

Perhaps they, too, saved garden space by doubling rows of narrow-growing crops. For example, onions, which take only as much space as the diameter of the bulb, may be grown in double (or even triple or more) rows six inches apart — even closer if you plan to pull every other one for table use,

letting the rest have more space for bulbing. You may arrange mulch between the two or more rows when the plants are large enough, in order to cut down on hand-weeding. But do not make the mulch too heavy, for onions need sun and heat for bulbing.

More Root-Crop Hints

Here's another hint for planting, which I have found works well with just about all root crops. Work your soil deeply to a fine tilth, breaking up any clods and incorporating in it what organic matter you have in the form of compost. Mix carrot, beet, turnip or radish seed with sand or used coffee grounds, so you will not plant too thickly. Then broadcast this seed right on top of the ground. Cover with a thin layer, about ¼ inch, of peat moss and sifted compost. Sprinkle lightly so seed will not wash. Usually a watering can is best for this purpose, when you water the first time. For me, this method ensures almost 100 percent germination of seed. Most gardeners tend to plant too deeply, while nature most often strews her seeds right on top of the ground.

Root crops do not need as much sun as above-ground crops do — one reason why carrots grow well with tomatoes. Onions grow well with lettuce. Beets and kohlrabi do well together if you want to practice the type of companion planting I call "two-level gardening."

Carrots

Carrots were a staple in American gardens from the beginning, a

Lutz Green Leaf or Winter Keeper beets stay tender no matter how large they grow. They cook in about the same time as other beets.

must in soups and stews. And they were also grown as a field crop, providing good winter feed for cattle, horses, sheep and pigs. Today the older varieties have been greatly improved. Personally, I prefer the tender Nantes type — especially for my carrot cake.

An old gardening book gives another way of sowing carrots. "Spread 4 inches of compost and dig it in well before sowing seed. By not sowing thickly you can save seed and avoid much tiresome thinning."

As an old seedsman put it, "They can be left in bunches of four or five together. They will crowd each other like a bunch of onions but if the soil is rich enough and the weeds are kept out you will have a great yield."

Beets

Beets were known to ancient civilizations in the Mediterranean area, but as a garden vegetable they made a slow beginning in about the 14th century in England and France. Though they were not a rarity by colonial times in America, there was little choice in variety. A seed catalog of the 19th century listed four varieties, which grew to at least a dozen by the 1880's — and by that time they even had white and yellow as well as red roots.

An old proverb says, "Waste not, want not." Those thrifty early day gardeners took this seriously — even if seed was only five cents a package, including postage. An old practice, if very early beets were wanted, was to sow seed in hotbeds and transplant seedlings later to the garden after removing the outer leaves. As this suggests, beet thinnings in the garden can also be transplanted. Beet seedlings tend to come up thickly because the seeds themselves form in a cluster. So if you have the time and patience, transplanting may be a good idea.

Onions

The time the edible bulb forms is determined by the amount of daylight the plant receives, and not by the maturity of the plant. This explains why some types of onions form bulbs in certain localities and not in others. There are onions that form bulbs when receiving only 12 hours of daylight daily (Yellow Bermuda, White Creole, etc). Ebenezer and Yellow Danvers require 13 hours of daylight each day to bulb. Such types as Red Wethersfield require as much as 14 hours. Bulbing is no problem in the southern states but northern gardeners should take note of this.

Yellow Ebenezer (Gurney, Parks, etc.) is a great favorite with many gardeners as it matures early and keeps well. In Canada, McFaydens offers Yellow Globe Danvers (100 days), good for both storage and cooking.

Salsify

Salsify was something else again. This ancient annual root vegetable seems to have been among those in early American gardens, certainly appearing toward the end of the 1700's. Oddly, for so good a food, salsify was not planted widely then, nor is it now.

Salsify likes a deep soil, well dug and enriched with compost. One pound of cottonseed meal per fifteen feet of row should be added. Thin plants to 6 inches apart and give them a compost mulch when about half grown. Salsify has a beautiful ferny top, and will occupy the space all season. The roots resemble parsnips and may be left in the garden all winter, lightly straw-mulched in cold climates. Their oyster-like flavor is improved by a freeze, and a cream soup made of them tastes much like an oyster stew. Boiled, mashed, and made into fritters, an old seedsman told his customers, "they are delicious."

My mother, who was raised in the northern part of the country where salsify grew well, agreed with his comment, and she often deplored the fact that salsify would not do well in hot, dry southern Oklahoma.

Parsnips

She was also a great fan of parsnips. This vegetable, among the first vegetables to be grown in American gardens, was appreciated more by early American gardeners than by modern ones. It is an old plant, growing wild in both Europe and North America.

As an old seedsman put it, "Parsnips should be seeded early, as they need the space all summer, but one of their merits is that they can be left in the garden all winter, to be dug as needed."

My mother prepared parsnips by boiling until tender, draining and then seasoning them with butter and a light dusting of cinnamon, which blends well with their slightly sweet flavor. I grew up eating parsnips and I still love them.

Rutabagas

Quite frankly, I think rutabagas deserve a better press. They never have been popular in the United States and did not, in fact, even arrive until around the 19th century.

In his fascinating book, *Bull Cook and Authentic Historical Recipes and practices*, George Leonard Herter says that the rutabaga was the result of "a rare accidental hybridization of a cabbage and a turnip" and was first mentioned by the Swiss botanist, Caspar Bauhin, in 1620.

He goes on:

It did not become popular in Europe for a very long time, however, due to its strong flavor and coarse texture.

"By 1800," Herter wrote, "the Swedish people were raising large quantities of potatoes, which, of course, originated in America. They liked their potatoes but they didn't care too much for cabbage's poor relation, the rutabaga. Then some creative Swedish cook tried mixing boiled mashed rutabagas with one-third of mashed potatoes. To this add one-eighth teaspoon of nutmeg for two cups of the mixture and a tablespoon of grated onion (more, if you like) per two cups of the mixture. Mix in the onion and nutmeg well while the rutabagas and potatoes are hot and add butter to taste and season with salt and pepper. They call this 'Stockholm Creamed Rutabagas.' They are simply delicious.

When I read this I just couldn't wait to try the recipe. I like it and I've been using it for winter meals ever since. Those connoisseurs of good food, the French, love them prepared in the Swedish manner and I think you will too. Try it, you may like it!

After your spring crop of rutabagas are gone you might like to make another sowing in mid-summer about three months before hard frost is expected. Care for them as you do turnips or beets, but they like a richer soil than the other two. Rutabagas are annuals, but if you protect them with a six inch mulch they can stay in the garden all winter, to be dug as wanted.

Turnips

Turnips have always been a popular vegetable with American gardeners and arrived with the very first settlers, enjoying an uninterrupted association with them ever since. Obliging as to climate, and with a fairly short growing season, turnips have graced gardens from New England to Florida and moved west with the pioneers.

This venerable vegetable was feeding man and beasts in the Old World for many centuries long before it arrived in the New. Turnips came from Siberia in the first place. The spicy leaves are even more nutritious than are the flavorful roots — and the Tokyo Cross Hybrid is very popular for its quality tops for "turnip greens" in the home garden. I like to grow several varieties of turnips both spring and winter, and I like to mix the greens with Tendergreens (mustard spinach), spinach, chard, pakchoy and even lamb's quarters, on occasion.

Gardeners just love to grow "giant" vegetables, and in 1850 a

100-pound turnip was reported grown in California. Turnips, grown in the same way as beets, are very easy to grow and, like rutabagas, can be kept in the garden over the winter by protecting them with a 6-inch mulch.

The Purple Top White Globe, which is purple above the soil line, is good fresh and stores well. The small black flea beetle is sometimes a menace. Beatrice Trum Hunter, in her book *Gardening Without Poisons*, advises planting a trap crop near them of nasturtium or mustard to attract the beetles away from the turnip leaves.

Wearing fresh sweet pea flowers (Lathyrus odoratus) *attracts people and promotes friendships.*

Radishes

You may or may not like radishes, but this ancient vegetable was one of the first annual vegetables the first American gardeners raised. It was highly prized by the Greeks of antiquity and long before that by the Egyptians, who believed the radish to be an aphrodisiac. In America a seed catalog of 1884 listed 26 varieties, a good indication of their popularity.

Radishes like soil enriched with plentiful organic matter, plenty of moisture, and cool weather. Be sure to plant them under a favorable sign such as Libra, Taurus, Pisces, Sagittarius, Capricorn, or Aries, and in the 3rd quarter, otherwise you may get all tops and little root.

MARCH PLANTING
AND TRANSPLANTING

Start an Asparagus Bed

In the South and Southwest asparagus shoots start popping up around the first of March, the season proceeding northward as spring advances. This pretty and tasty vegetable discovered America along with the colonists, according to many early day records of colonial gardens, yet there is some evidence that a wild variety was already here — or perhaps it escaped from an early settler's garden, the seed carried perhaps by birds.

If you don't have asparagus in your garden, you are missing something. Since it takes about three years before you can have an appreciable amount to cut without feeling guilty, I always advise new gardeners to get with it as soon as possible. If the Romans had it, so can you.

Order your plants and try to get them in under the sign of Cancer, Scorpio or Pisces in the first quarter. A bed, well cared for, will last at least 20 years. Follow the advice of an early gardener and begin by digging a one-foot-deep trench.

Half-fill it with compost mixed with ¼ cup of bone meal per one foot of trench. Set roots 18 inches apart in the trench, and gradually fill the trench with earth as the roots sprout. Actually, although asparagus does best where winters are not really mild, it will grow just about anywhere in the United States.

The ancients believed asparagus had aphrodisiac qualities. They also thought that growing it with parsley and basil enhanced its vigor and theirs as well. Tomatoes, containing *solanine*, give protection against asparagus beetles.

It was the custom of early day gardeners to sprinkle their asparagus beds with salt each spring, on the theory that the plant's origin was the seacoast. Actually, it was the manure (hopefully well decomposed) gardeners spread on the bed each fall, and again in the spring after cutting was over, that the plants thrived on. A good, established bed will yield for ten weeks each year, starting in late March, early April, or May, depending on where you live.

As previously mentioned, it's debatable whether asparagus grew wild in America or whether, like so many other plants, it just went wild on its own. Either way, look for it in your area — it grows "wild" on several vacant lots near my home and I cut these extra goodies each spring. Best to do your exploring in the fall when you can still identify the delicate ferny foliage and mark the spot. Then in the spring you will find, at the base of the dried plants, spears and greening asparagus tips protruding through the matted grass and weeds. Often the old weeds have kept the asparagus pale, and it will be very tender.

Bountiful Peas and Lettuce

I plant my English peas in February but you northern gardeners probably will do this in March. A cool weather crop, they are best sown in the early spring, and you can do what early day Americans did — spread the harvest by planting early peas, mid-season peas, and late peas all at the same time. Peas were apparently in American gardens in the 1600's, and sometime in the 1700's edible-podded sugar peas were being grown here. Nineteenth-century seed catalogs carried many varieties of peas, including some still on the market, such as Telephone and Dwarf Gray Sugar. Those early-day gardeners had a lot of varieties to choose from, but none as delicious as the recent introduction, snap peas (Park's 1987 catalog lists Sugar Pop, Super Sugar Mel, Sugar Bon, Sugar Ann, Sugar Daddy, and Sugar Snap).

That grand old gardening lady, Ruth Stout, in her book, *How To Have A Green Thumb Without An Aching Back*, tells about her struggle to grow peas, vowing that she was just about ready to give up until she discovered the variety called Lincoln. Having been very successful, she then proceeded to recommend them to friends who also "picked them by the bushel."

If you would like to duplicate her experiment you will find Lincoln at Stokes, Gurney's, and the Lincoln-Homesteader at McFayden's in Canada.

Personally I find pea growing a bit tricky. For me they grow graciously, vine gracefully, make lovely blooms and start to bear. Then, just as I am beginning to get all excited about my hopefully big crop, mildew strikes. A sudden change in the weather from cool to warm and humid seems to do this every year. So, like Ruth, I, too, began experimenting with the varieties recommended for the state of Oklahoma by our Agricultural Experiment station and I found several varieties that now

do reasonably well for me. I nearly always get a fair crop from Little Marvel. If you are having a problem growing English peas I would suggest you contact your state experiment station and find out the recommended varieties. Depending on your area, the variety you grow does make a difference.

Start your first planting of lettuce in March and, if it comes up a bit too thick, be as thrifty as your forebears, and transplant the extras. Since lettuce grows "on top of the ground," and onions underneath, I often put the lettuce thinnings in the onion row where I have pulled onions for the table. They are compatible and get along in a friendly fashion.

Sharing the Abundance

The way I go at things, carefully conserving plants and space, you probably think I have a lot of overproduction. Yes, I do. But nothing is ever wasted. Going on the principle that "charity begins at home," I sell enough from my garden to pay for seeds, water, fertilizer, and the garden chores I cannot do myself. And, after first satisfying family needs, I give away to a lot of friends and neighbors — many of whom are elderly or ill and cannot make gardens for themselves, or have no space. Even after this, there is often overproduction of such things as tomatoes, squash, cucumbers, all rampant growers some years. It is then that I take these to the kitchen of the nearby hospital where I have worked as a volunteer "Pink Lady" in the hospital auxiliary. They know me, and they know I garden without using poisonous pesticides, so they are always happy to receive my garden produce, something they can never be really sure about in the fruits and vegetables they buy from their sources. And then there is the Salvation Army which makes up baskets from time to time for families in need.

Gardeners, from earliest times, have always been giving people, sharing with others. The pioneer spirit of helpfulness is not dead. Many times, when I have a short crop of something, my gardening friends gift me in return.

Beautiful Broccoli

March is the time to transplant those early cabbage plants you started back in February. And I hope you also started some plants of my own favorite, broccoli. It's downright criminal, in my opinion, to buy those expensive frozen broccoli spears when it's so easy to grow. Be aware that the young plants are subject to damage by both aphids and harlequin bugs. Pyrethrum powder is good used against these pests. Pyrethrum is an herbaceous perennial chrysanthemum called "the bug-killing daisy." The ground-up flowers of certain species contain substances which are toxic to many insects by acting directly on their nervous systems. When pyrethrum is applied to plant foliage in sunlight or strong artificial light, it breaks down rapidly, having a very short-term residual action. For this reason it can be used as a pre-harvest spray. That "short-term" also means that you may have to watch your plants and use the spray several times during their growing season.

Broccoli is a member of the cabbage family and the variety commonly grown in America first came from southern Europe. It is sometimes called "Italian broccoli." It seems to have been a latecomer to American gardens and, in fact, it took broccoli until the 1930's to really catch on with the American public — though records state that it was being planted in the first half of the 18th century.

❦   ❦   ❦

March Gardening Chores

Before I let you go on to the fun of hiking about the countryside and foraging for wild food, I'm going to be a temporary kill-joy and remind you of some gardening chores that should be attended to in March. Do your homework first and then you can enjoy your pleasure without feeling guilty.

★ If you have a lusting for greens March is the month to satisfy it by making first plantings of Swiss chard and additional plantings, if you have used your earlier ones of spinach and kale. Put in a sprinkling of radish seed to show where your rows are located.

★ Get with it on your perennials — hoe out those weeds before they get a head start.

★ If you like anise, seed it now. If you haven't tried anise you are missing something. The green leaves make great salads and the seeds are delicious in applesauce, cakes, bread, soups, stews and cottage cheese. Anise was beloved of our great-grandmothers and was an honored inhabitant of early American gardeners.

★ Cut back your asparagus beds and dress them with those hardwood ashes you saved from the winter fireplace.

★ Make a new seeding of basil, or bring out and replant the plants you wintered indoors.

★ Thin and cut back bergamot and mint.

★ That caraway I hope you planted last fall (see "October") should

fertilized.
rich soil and
...ves.
...r horseradish roots
...t back the stalks.
...your parsley hasn't wintered over, make a new planting.

★ Fertilize rhubarb and give the plants a light cultivation. Dust with nicotine to discourage grubs.

★ Cut back sage to encourage new growth.

★ Pull the straw covering off your strawberry bed, cut the runners, and set out new plants.

★ Divide your winter onions if they are getting too thick.

★ Do the same with berry bushes, which should be fertilized now to help them produce an early crop.

Sage

Sage came to America with a centuries-old reputation for benefiting human health and conferring long life. Old *materia medicas* noted sage tea's value as a gargle for sore throats, an oil in the leaves being the medical factor.

🍒 🍒 🍒

A MARCH WALK

With all that out of the way let's put on old clothes and walking shoes, pack a light lunch, and start out. You might even want to take along your fishing pole just in case your path leads you by a pond or stream. Fishing is likely to be most productive in the watery signs of Pisces, Cancer and Scorpio, in that order.

Fishing Secrets

Temperature, according to old-timers, has a lot to do with fishing as well. If fishing is your sport you've probably noticed that in the hot summertime, right before a cool spell moves in, bass will go on a wild feeding spree, and the same thing holds true in the winter when a warm front moves in.

That oft-quoted little poem may help you remember this:

When the wind is free from the
south
It blows the bait in the fishes'
mouth.
When the wind is from the west
The fishes bite the very best.
When the wind is from the north
Neither man nor beast should
go forth.
When the wind is from the east
The fishes bite the very least.

In March, while it's still cool, the fish are not likely to bite well until the air and water have been warmed by the sun, the best time being from noon to about 3 p.m.

If you live in a rural area, take note of whether or not cattle are grazing. If they are, fish will likely be biting as well. Nothing magical about this — it simply means that the wind tides that govern fish also govern land animals. When one is feeding, the other will be also.

A warm, cloudy, overcast day is exceptionally good fishing weather. Why? Because fish have no eyelids and are distressed by extremely bright light. A dull day lets them feed near the surface, and if you happen to be there with the right bait, that's when you get a good catch.

If you've been following the gardening practices of early day gardeners and incoporating plenty of decomposed manure and compost into your garden soil, chances are you've got a lot of fat earthworms tunneling around just beneath the soil surface. Turn a few shovelfuls and look — there's your bait! Catfish, like bass, are hungry and will take practically any bait. Those caught in the cold water of March are particularly firm and tasty to eat. When their dense, sweet meat is properly skinned, no taint of mud remains.

OTHER TREATS

Cattails

After you've caught your mess of fish don't leave the pond until you've collected a basketful of young cattail shoots (*Typha latifolia*). If you want the roots, you should plan ahead and mark specific plants so you will be able to identify them. The inner portions of the root and stem are cut into 1- or 2-inch segments and cooked in soups and stews. They are better tasting in early spring because frosts have sweetened and tenderized them. When the young stems or shoots are cut 10 to 12 inches from the root and the outer rind is peeled off, they may be added to a vegetable salad. You may even cook the very crispy young shoots of early spring and serve them as you would asparagus, complete with Hollandaise sauce.

There is a treat in store for the creative cook who would like to make bread or cakes from the pollen heads or down of this

Cattail flowers enlarge to become long brown spikes which, like the starchy roots, are edible. For dried arrangements, pick when dry and dip in undiluted shellac.

swamp-dweller. It will take about 20 to 25 good-sized pollen heads to yield a small-sized loaf of bread. It is advisable, however, to mix in an equal portion of pure whole-wheat flour, so that uniformity and adhesiveness are more easily obtained. Cattail flour, especially if made from the pollen, is reported to contain protein, sulphur, phosphorus, carbohydrates, sugar and oil.

Long before the Spaniards began civilizing the Indians with gunpowder, the red men had been using cattail in various ways. Especially in the spring, the Indians dug the starch-filled, bulbous roots and used them in making soups.

They dried the rhizomes, ground them, and used the product as flour. Records tell of hungry Virginia settlers boiling the young blossoms for soup. Indian squaws lined papoose baskets with the soft down from the blossoms. Pioneers put a wick through the strong stems and used them as candle molds.

The starch content of the roots is sufficient so that cattail flour can be used as a substitute for cornstarch.

Sweet-Flag

Since the earliest days of recorded time, sweet-flag root (*Acorus calamus*) has been used as a confection. Flag-root candy is still made in northeastern communities that perpetuate pioneer ways of living.

Sweet-flag leaves are much like those of the poisonous Rocky Mountain iris, long used by the Indians as a medicine and as a poison to dip arrowheads into, but when the blades of sweet-flag are pinched they emit a ginger-like fragrance. The flower, jutting from one side of the leaf like an ear of corn, is a light green spike. About five inches below the mud you will find the horizontal root, and it is usually topped with old leaves. You can find sweet-flag plants along the margins of ponds from Canada to Texas.

The roots collected in spring are a good substitute for some of the imported spices such as ginger or cinnamon. They are used fresh or dried as a culinary herb, and to flavor meats and fish, stews and soups. The spicy roots will also add extra zest to an herb or spice vinegar.

Stinging Nettle

Stinging nettle (*Urtica dioica*) has been called "the cursed weed" but, upon closer acquaintance, many have not found it so. "Was it not Goldsmith," asks Charles Francis Saunders in his *Useful Wild Plants of the U.S. and Canada*, "who wrote that a French cook of the olden time could make seven different dishes out of a Nettle-top?" Ah, those thrifty French cooks, trust them to know a good thing when they find it — and if it was free for the taking, so much the better.

This weed would be interesting if only because its encrusted tails of pale green, male or female flowers usually grow on different plants. This somewhat prudish separation of the sexes accounts for the plant's species name. For *dioica* means "two dwellings." The

stinging nettles have an enchanting early-morning festival when
the males gaily puff their pale
golden pollen into the air to be
caught by the females. It's worth
getting out of bed early to watch.

Nicholas Culpeper, a great ad-
mirer of the stinging nettle, wrote
in about 1650: "Nettles are so
well known, that they need no description; they may be found by
feeling for them in the darkness of
the night." But this hint of pain
merely introduces his long praise
of the weed's curative properties.
In his time, these were confined to
healing the ailments of man, because it was quite a while before
we gardeners realized that plants
can work for the welfare of one
another. Yet, in the latter context,
nettles are the most valuable of
weeds. While growing, they stimulate the growth of other plants
nearby and make them more resistant to disease (in the same way
as does the foxglove). Nettles also
improve the storing capacities of
root vegetables and tomatoes, a
quality much appreciated by people of an earlier day.

A complete plant-food liquid
can also be made by soaking a
sheaf of nettles in a vessel of rainwater for two or three weeks. At
the end of that time, the water will
contain all the plant's virtues. A
liquid fertilizer made from nettles,
either fresh or dried, is not only a
good plant food, but also an effective spray against mildew, black
fly, aphis, and plant lice, both in
the greenhouse and outside it.

The nettle's good points, however, are often obscured by its bitter ones. For the stems of this
weed are covered with stinging
hairs that, once they penetrate the
skin, pour acrid formic acid (the
same acid ant stings have) into the
man or beast unfortunate enough
to encounter the plant's defense
mechanism. The pierced area becomes swollen and inflamed, and
the victim will have as much pain
as if he had been stung by a bee or
hornet.

If you lightly touch a nettle,
    It will sting you for your
        pains.
But grasp it, like a lad of mettle —
    Soft as silk it will remain.
POEM FROM COUNTY CAVAN, IRELAND

To avoid distress when gathering (should you come upon a
patch some day when you have no
gloves), grasp the stem strongly so
that the hairs are pressed back
into the stem. Then the plant will
not be able to sting you.

Creamed Nettles

Wear gloves to gather a
quantity of nettle tops. Wash
and shake off excess water.
Strip off leaves and place in a
pot with two tablespoons of
butter. Simmer over a low
flame, stirring gently from
time to time so all will be
coated and cook equally. As
juices start to flow, add seasonings. When thoroughly
cooked and tender, strain.
Reheat the leaves, stirring in
a little more butter and some
cream. The addition of a few
chopped chives, shallots or
spring onions improves the
flavor.

Nettles are rich not only in minerals (as a source of iron, they exceed spinach), but also in vitamin C. Only *young* nettles should be gathered to eat, for in late summer the older ones develop gritty, harmful crystals.

Grazing animals will not eat nettles, but when mowed and dried, all kinds of livestock eat them avidly and thrive on them. Cows give more and richer milk and hens lay more eggs when powdered nettle leaves are added to their mash, the eggs actually having a higher food value. Turkeys fatten and baby chicks grow faster when this nutritious food is added to their rations.

Violets

The Pennsylvania Dutch (who are actually of German origin) are famous for their industry and thrift — so wouldn't you just know they would be well aware of that early spring blossom, the violet? Euell Gibbons, in his book *Stalking The Healthful Herbs*, mentions seeing the children of his Pennsylvania Dutch neighbors avidly eating violet blossoms in the spring. And their parents included violet leaves in the wild greens that they cooked and served to their families as a spring tonic.

If you would do the same, search out such March greens as dayflower, day lily, amaranth, shepherd's purse, mustard, wintercress, watercress and wild lettuce and boil them briefly along with the violet leaves. These plants should be identified during the summer and marked for picking the following spring, mixing or matching them.

Gibbons refers to the common blue violet as "nature's vitamin pill." He had both leaves and blossoms analyzed and the results proved that they were amazingly rich in vitamin C and the leaves an excellent source of vitamin A. The Pennsylvania Dutch children are wise in eating violet blossoms, for these tasty little flowers are three times as rich in vitamin C, weight for weight, as oranges.

It's good to know that the violet, unlike many wildflowers, is not harmed by picking its blossoms, for these showy flowers seldom or never produce seed anyway. Apparently produced out of sheer exuberance you may feel free to take all you want, for the more you pick the more the plant will give — an endearing characteristic shared by pansies. Later on, the plant will produce, down under the leaves, some inconspicuous blooms that have no petals and never open. These are the fruitful blooms, and they bear an abundance of seed.

Although the vitamin content was unknown until Gibbons had the violet plant analyzed, it had long had a prominent and well-established place in herbal medicine and it has been used to treat a host of different illnesses.

Gather only bright-green leaves while they are young and tender. Wash them thoroughly to remove any clinging sand and then snip them into ¼-inch shreds with a pair of kitchen shears. Add very little water and cook in a covered vessel over low heat for about 15 minutes. Season with salt and butter, and eat juice and all, as this juice is likely to contain some of the minerals and vitamins. Some of the violet flavor and even a hint of violet fragrance will be apparent in the cooked leaves.

A word of caution: Eat small servings at first to determine whether or not the leaves are laxative. After you determine your tolerance in this respect you can enjoy them as often as you like.

Juliette de Bairacli Levy in her *Herbal Handbook for Farm & Stable* writes: "The flowers and leaves, being emollient, are used in skin lotions and ointments." To make a **violet ointment,** melt 1 ounce of lanolin and 3 ounces of cocoa butter in a small stone jar. Add as many fresh violet leaves and blossoms as the melted fats will cover, set in a medium oven, 350° F, for one hour, pour through a strainer to remove the spent leaves, and store in covered jars. This remedy is reputed to aid in the healing of sores of both man and beast.

The leaves have also long been used in compresses, plasters, poultices, and ointments. To make a **violet poultice,** cover one cup of the leaves with boiling water and let stand until cool enough to apply to the affected part. Recommended for boils, carbuncles, old wounds and swellings, the warm leaves are loosely bound to the affected part and changed every few hours.

Other Wild Greens

Other spring greens appearing in March are wild onions and leeks, chicory, dock, dandelion, salsify and skunk cabbage. These should be boiled in several waters until mild-flavored and tender. Good either mixed or matched.

Many people do not realize what a spring treat wild onions can be. Watch for them to push up through your dormant spring lawn, for they will cook into a sweet potherb. Smother them in a cream sauce, seasoned with nutmeg and drizzled over with thin slivers of cheese.

Wild leeks, also of the allium family, come on a bit strong. After removal of roots and the dry outer leaves, wash the plant and plunge it into boiling water. Cook for about 15 minutes and if you would have a milder flavor, pour off the water and boil a second or even a third time. Chop and serve them in cream sauce.

Red Spider

Red spiders usually become noticeable with the onset of hot, dry weather. Observing this, an early day gardener wrote: "The spider does not like water, or a moist location, and I have been fairly successful by sprinkling my plants occasionally with water. It cuts down noticeably on the red spider population."

Another gardener of the 1870's advised spraying with a tablespoon of kerosene mixed with one quart of lukewarm water, followed by a spraying of plain water the next day. Success was reported by another gardener who said she sprinkled the ground around her rose bushes with tobacco tea whenever she saw a sign of red spider.

EASTER TRADITIONS

Easter has a way of appearing sometimes in March and sometimes in April. Old timers believed that an early Easter meant an early spring. Peoples from many lands brought their Easter customs with them when they arrived in America.

The Moravians, a Protestant religious group in Bethlehem, Pennsylvania, have an unusual custom. The trombone choir of the Moravian church awakens the people on Easter morning and members of the congregation pray and sing joyous Easter hymns as they await the dawn of Easter Day.

The German people brought with them a tradition of coloring the Easter eggs in a dye made of onion-skin broth (see box). Flowers, ferns and grasses are bound to the eggs with strips of thin cloth and they are placed in the broth and cooked as one would hard-cooked eggs. When the cloth strips are removed the result is a lovely blending of soft colors with the warm brown dye of the onion skin.

Onion-skin Broth

Onion-skin broth is very simply made. Previous to time needed save thin brown skins of onions (or ask your friendly neighborhood grocer to help you). Depending on number of eggs to be colored you should have a quart or more of skins, less if you only want to dye, say, a half dozen eggs. There really is no set amount. Place the skins in water in a fairly large saucepan and cook until you have a dark brown liquid, about 20 to 30 minutes. Leave skins in pan. Cool. Remove eggs from refrigerator and bring to room temperature. Tie flowers, ferns, etc. to egg with thin strips of cloth about 1 inch wide. Tighten strips with thread. Place eggs in cooled broth (so they will not crack) and cook just as you would hard-boiled eggs. Remove to slightly warmed water and slip off cloth. If cloth is cleansed and dried it may be reused. Do not mix red & yellow onion skins. If you want to use red skins, keep them separate.

Easter egg rolling is an Easter custom practiced in several countries. The most famous rolling takes place on the White House lawn in Washington, D.C. Thousands of persons gather to roll Easter eggs on the lawn on the Monday after Easter. President Hayes started the custom in 1879. It has been observed ever since, except for the years between 1942 and 1953.

BEWARE OF POISON IVY

Sometime in your rambles through the woods — foraging for greens, seeking wild herbs, or fishing, you are practically certain to encounter poison ivy. It is good to know that poison ivy, recognized by its three leaflets, has an excellent remedy growing nearby. Jewelweed or wild touch-me-not (*Impatiens capensis*) requires the same soil and moisture conditions as poison ivy, and so it is seldom far away. To make the lotion, boil a potful of jewelweed until the liquid is about half of its original volume. The strained juice is effective both in preventing the rash after exposure and in treating the rash after it has developed.

The lotion will not keep well, however, even when refrigerated. The secret is to strain the juice of the jewelweed into ice trays and freeze it. Once frozen, eject the cubes from the trays, place them in bags, and store them in the freezer. This way you can make a quantity at a time and always have them on hand during the spring and summer months. You can apply an ice cube or melt it and use the liquid. Several poison ivy lotions sold commercially are really extracts of this plant.

A Word on Modern Appliances

You can just bet those practical-minded pioneers would have used freezers if they had had them. Just because we are exploring old-time remedies and old-time methods doesn't mean we have to be fanatic about it! We should use and enjoy our modern appliances — just as we should plant improved seeds and plants. "Be not the first to accept the new — nor the last to discard the old."

Aries the Ram   (March 21 - April 20)

Pink Moon
APRIL

April is a green, wet month ★ Time to transplant ★
Plan weeding and watering strategy ★ Dowsing ★
Pond building ★ An Oklahoma spring ★ Mushroom
hunting ★ April chores ★ Seasoning herbs ★ Dyeing
eggs ★ More about Easter customs ★

APRIL SHOWERS bring spring flowers, but they also bring something else — weeds. Even so, when the Moon is in the barren sign of Aries, March 21 to April 20, it is a good time to destroy noxious weeds and unwanted growth. And no time is better for this purpose than during the last quarter of the moon or the first three days of the new moon. It is also a good time to turn sod or plant fenceposts.

Experienced gardeners did not plow their gardens until the sign of Aries and then waited until Taurus (April 20 to May 21) to plant their main garden as well as their farm crops. Taurus, the bull, was believed to be an earthy, moist and productive zodiac sign, and a fruitful constellation under which to plant. The bull was thought to be strong yet characterized by feminine productivity as well.

Such crops as broccoli, barley, cabbage, corn, lettuce, chard, kale, endive, oats, rye, spinach, and other leafy vegetables may be planted during the first quarter of the Moon under Taurus.

During the second quarter you can plant beans, peas, squash, and tomatoes.

The third quarter is favorable to beets, carrots, parsnips, potatoes, radishes, rutabagas, turnips, onions, and bulbous flowering plants.

Under the fourth quarter no planting should be done. The time is better given to mowing, preparing soil, or even repairing fences.

WEATHER FORECASTING

Human Barometers

As far as weather predictions are concerned, early day folks set a lot of store by their aches and pains. Many people troubled with rheumatism or neuralgia acted as barometers for the small community, predicting a change in weather by "feeling it in their bones."

Was this really possible? Perhaps. Julius Fast in his interesting book *Weather Language* tells the story of an indomitable 72-year-old lady gardener, bent almost double with arthritis, who says, "So I'm bent over. I'm nearer to the ground, and it's easier for me to weed. And I'll tell you what: I can tell any weather change better than that funny guy on television."

When the author asks her her secret, she confides that it is "a matter of pain" — if she feels a stabbing pain in her hands on a cold day, she knows that in exactly three hours it will turn warm. Likewise, if the pain hits on a warm day, she knows that in eight hours it will turn cold.

When she gets such a "message" from her hands, Anita knows to cut down on anything physical. "You have to learn to live with arthritis," she says. "You have to learn your limitations and how far you can go. My body sends me a message that no doctor can equal."

Julius Fast goes on to say: "I asked a rheumatologist of my acquaintance about Anita's acute weather sensitivity, expecting her to laugh. But instead she nodded

seriously. 'Yes. Weather language is what it is. Most arthritics have that ability, though some are not aware of it. The weather has such a direct effect on them that they become what the Germans call *wettervogel* — "weather birds." They can tell us when a warm front or a cold front passes over, and they can tell it in advance. I have one patient who can tell me exactly how severe any storm is going to be, and always well in advance of that storm.'"

So, score one again for the old-timers who could tell "in their bones" when there would be a change in the weather. In April, those changes can happen quite often.

Predicting the Harvest

Which brings me to something else old farmers believed. They watched the temperature, believing it determined harvest time. If April daytime temperatures were 75° F or above, they felt reasonably sure that beans, beets, chard, cucumbers, kale, lettuce, okra, onions, peas, spinach, and summer squash would be ready to harvest six to eight weeks after planting.

If temperatures were in the 80's they counted on harvesting sweet corn, limas, carrots, potatoes and melons in ten to twelve weeks.

I live in a most unpredictable climate — we can have a very warm winter and then have a big snowstorm in May. The weather sashays back and forth between hot and cold so fast that sometimes it makes your head spin. I usually grow my own tomatoes so I can have the exact varieties I want at the times that I want them. Generally I set out a few as early as March, putting them under "hot caps" and giving them additional covering if we have a really cold spell. If I'm lucky this first dozen or so will bear early. If I lose them I have lots more and I just keep on planting. I set out my main-crop tomatoes in early April along about Easter time (which can come in either March or April). Figuring like the oldtimers that an early Easter means a warm and early spring, I find this to be as good a date as any. Transplanting, like planting, is best done under the watery signs of Cancer, Scorpio and Pisces, moon increasing. Or, in a pinch, you can use one of the secondary signs such as Taurus.

🐛 🐛 🐛

TIME TO TRANSPLANT

When it comes to transplanting, there's lots of good advice to be had from those who were performing this pleasant chore a long time ago. The introduction of the peat seeding block has simplified transplanting today. We simply plant the seeds in the blocks and when the seedlings are moved to the garden, the blocks go right along. The unsuspecting little plants scarcely realize they have been moved and, being undisturbed, suffer no transplanting shock.

The eggshell seeding I told you about earlier on was an early version of the peat block, and so was this handy little idea, suggested in the 1890's but known for years before that. Here is the strategy. "A safe plan is to sow about five seeds on reversed pieces of sod about 4 inches square. On planting in the ground insert the sod with the growing plants, and firm the soil in the usual way." In early days gardeners sometimes referred to transplanting by the quaint term "after-planting."

Another bit of advice ran like this: "Transplanting is most apt to be successful if done just at evening, or immediately before or during the first part of a rain, about the worst time being after a rain, when the ground being wet, it is impossible to sufficiently press it about the plant without its baking hard." This is just as true now as it was then — don't transplant after a hard rain.

More good advice: "If there is not as much soil on the roots as you desire, make a 'puddle' of thick muddy water in a pail, washtub, or half-barrel, get a handful of plants and dip the roots in this muddy water." This also holds true when transplanting ornamental shrubs or trees — puddling the roots keeps the air away from them while you are doing your transplanting.

The famous old seedsman, Joseph Harris, once commented on

the custom of yanking at plants after transplanting, to see if they were set firmly: "A man may press the soil so firmly around the stem, the plant would stand quite a pull while in fact there might be a hollow space about the roots. [That hollow air space could be very detrimental.] This is like leaving your feet bare and trying to keep them warm by putting on a pair of garters. The proper way, of course, is to press earth well about the roots and then to water thoroughly."

Then, as now, plants sometimes drooped after being moved — and one gardener, way back then, had a remedy we can use today. "A good way to revive newly set plants," she wrote, "is to place a flower pot close to the plant, press it down in the earth, and fill it with water, which will gradually filter through the hole in the bottom and moisten the ground at the roots of the plant."

An early 1879 gardener apparently took her transplanting very seriously and intended to do it no matter what. Here is her advice for plants ordinarily hard to transplant. "Take them up in winter," she said, "when the ground is frozen hard, by digging up a clump of earth with an axe, and put the plant where it is wanted to grow. It will awaken in the spring and not know the change."

Watering

Coping with the problem of getting water to our plants when and where it will do the most good is nothing new. Watering is best done, as you might expect, in the moist signs of Cancer, Scorpio, Pisces or Libra, for it is held that plants absorb water best when they receive it in a watery sign.

An experienced nurseryman of 1879 gave this advice on deep watering of garden plants. "Beside each at the time of planting, sink a piece of 4-inch drain tile as deeply as the plant's roots reach, resting the bottom end of the tile on a brick or flat rock, and covering its top end, reaching slightly above ground level, with a rock. Filling the tile with water twice a week is usually often enough, and fertilizer can be added to the water when needed. For larger plants, use a 6-inch tile. If you cannot obtain tile, a length of old downspout would serve the same purpose as the tile."

Notice, he says to sink the pieces of the tile as deeply as the roots reach. How deep? Here is my answer: *Shallow-rooted crops* — those having their root systems within the top foot of soil — include cauliflower, cabbage, celery, sweet corn, lettuce, onions, potatoes and radishes.

Medium-rooted crops — those that root in the top two feet of soil — include snap beans, carrots, cucumbers, eggplant, pepper, peas and summer squash.

Deep-rooted crops — those with roots in the top 2 to 4 feet of soil — include artichoke, asparagus, cantaloupe, pumpkin, tomato and watermelon.

Gardeners a century or two ago didn't have to put up with water pollution as we know it today, nor did they have the problem of acid rain. Yet, though their water was comparatively pure, they still held the belief that rainwater was the proper water for plants. For this there seems to be some scientific reinforcement. At the Agricultural Research center in Apopka, Florida, it was found that faucet water containing even minute amounts of fluoride caused tipburn and spotting of the leaves of some plants. These happened to be ornamental plants, but this does not rule out the chance of injury to some others. The study also found small amounts of fluorine present in perlite and in sphagnum moss.

Benefits of Melted Snow

In the matter of watering here is something I would like to quote from my own book, *Planetary Planting* (published by Astro Computer Services, San Diego, California).

> Now rainwater is good, very good — but melted snow is even better. The Russians have an old folk saying, 'Snow in the fields, corn in the granaries.' And Soviet scientists have found this to be true: the more snow the better the harvests.
>
> The experiments were carried out in the Siberian Botanical Garden. Here cucumbers and radishes were watered with melted snow, and it was found that they grew twice as fast as the control plants supplied with ordinary water. Similar results occurred in experiments with wheat.
>
> Why is melted snow better for plants than ordinary water?

Well, it's like this: They found that snow contains about 40 percent less *heavy water*, or deuterium oxide, than normal water. Deuterium (whose symbol is D), is a heavy isotope, a form of hydrogen but slightly different. When combined with oxygen it does not form the water molecule, H_2O; instead, the molecule D_2O is formed. Normally, about one water molecule in every 6,000 is found to be a heavy water molecule. But, somehow, in a way we do not understand, the formation of snow removes many of these heavy water molecules.

And just what's wrong with heavy water? The scientists have discovered that D_2O slows down some chemical and biological processes. So, when heavy water molecules are removed, plants seem to grow faster.

Perhaps this is why climates that have heavy snowfalls and short summers can still mature plants — the plants simply grow faster in the limited time at their disposal. Houseplant gardeners take note: Save some water from melted snow and use it on your houseplants — the warmed water could be very beneficial.

Benefits of Tepid Water

The case for tepid water was stated in an old gardening magazine: "Where a vigorous growth of foliage is desired, or if we should wish to increase the size of the flowers, it is always an advantage to use warm water, instead of that direct from the well or cistern. Water may be warmed for this purpose by allowing it to stand in vessels or tubs exposed to the sun during the heat of the day." Today a metal drum in the garden, kept filled with rainwater from a downspout if possible, can furnish tepid water, and a few plants growing around it will provide a suitable screen for appearances' sake."

Take note that a well is mentioned. With "city water" like everything else going up in price, lots of people today are drilling wells to provide irrigation for their gardens, lawns and flower beds. Generally speaking, this clear, pure water coming out of the ground is very seldom detrimental in any way to plants and trees. And well water is mighty handy to have if

rainfall is insufficient or doesn't come at the right time.

Pill Bugs Are Real "Pills"

In large numbers, often attracted by moisture, these little nasties can be very destructive. An 1880 gardener said he inverted a flower pot in places where he had young things planted, going around every two or three days with a pail of scalding water and destroying the hundreds of bugs which gathered under the pots, which also attracted slugs.

Another gardener reported using the same idea with the addition of potato peelings and cabbage leaf scraps under the pots as a lure.

WATER DIVINING ("DOWSING")

If you would like to have a good, handy water well in your future, do what the old-timers did and look up a dowser. Since I am myself a dowser, and both my son and my granddaughter have this ability as well, I firmly believe in water dowsing. This ability is more common than most people realize, simply because they haven't tried it. You may be a dowser, too.

My son has two excellent water wells on his property, located by dowsing friends. Unknown to each other, and at different times, each one took his divining rod (a forked willow branch), and began walking over the land. Each one came within a few inches of the same

spot and then the rod bent sharply down.

The driller moved in and began drilling a test hole, finding nothing until he passed into an extremely hard sandstone formation at 155 feet. He struck water of such abundance at this depth that he went thirty feet more, still in the formation, setting perforated casing. He was of the opinion that he might have struck an underground river. He told my son that he had been drilling wells for thirty years or more and he had seen only two other wells of equal capacity. The clear, cold water is good tasting, with no trace of iron or salt.

A year later, when we decided

to drill another well, we did the dowsing ourselves and found water production equally as good.

Dowsing (water witching or water divining) is probably as old as man's need for water. It is a gift certain people have that enables them to find underground sources of water. The dowser can determine where the water is, as well as its depth and volume. There is no trickery or chicanery involved.

Why, it might be asked, doesn't everyone have this gift? Why only certain people? I honestly don't know. Wild animals in the bush can "smell" a waterhole miles away. Perhaps the ability to dowse is the vestige of some such animal instinct that only a few civilized people still possess. Perhaps this is why it is often referred to as *radiesthesia* — a sensitivity to the radiations that emanate from everything around us, including people, minerals, water, and so on. The whole phenomenon of dowsing interested Albert Einstein, who believed that some day electromagnetism might be found to hold the answers. (Remember what I wrote in February, about using magnetism in the garden to gain added production?)

With dowsing, either you have the gift, or you don't. It has been said that about one in ten possesses it — the other nine often being ready to accuse the one who has it of being a fake. Folklore has some fascinating answers surrounding the subject. "The power is inherited from mother to son or from father to daughter." Our own experience would seem to bear this out, since I, my son, and

my granddaughter share the ability. Another — "Only a chosen few are handed this gift of divination from above...or from the Devil below." I sincerely hope we received ours "from the good place!"

Would you like to try? The rod you use can be as simple as a forked branch or as complex as electronic gear. The pendulum, that ancient magic device, is a popular dowsing device in Europe. Personally, I favor the forked willow branch.

Cut a branch and remove all small twigs. It should be pliable so that it bends rather than breaks when the end is pulled down. A branch of any tree that meets these requirements will do. Joseph Baum recommends in *The Beginner's Handbook of Dowsing* that the rod have the diameter of a pencil and be about 18 inches long, but it can be thicker and longer.

Grasp the branch by the tapering forks, palms up. Rest your clenched fists on your hips. Let the tip of the branch point straight out, slightly higher than level. The forks should be held firmly enough to prevent the tip from bending down as a result of gravity.

Holding the rod properly, walk slowly over the area to be dowsed. Keep your feet close to the ground, just avoiding a shuffle. If you are a dowser, and you pass over an underground water supply, the end of the rod will suddenly be pulled downward to a vertical position. The pull can be so strong as to rupture the bark or even break the rod at the point where you are holding it. If your eyes were closed you might even imagine that someone had actually taken the end and forced it down.

When the rod has signaled the spot, put in a stake or marker at the Point of Greatest Pull. If you approach the spot from different directions you might find that this point varies slightly. If this happens place a stake at the Point of Greatest Pull along each of the directions from which you approach. The place to dig for water would be at the center of these stakes.

These directions are, of course, somewhat of an oversimplification but they will give you a pretty good indication of whether you are a dowser or not.

★ ★ ★

BUILDING A POND

Since water — and plenty of it — is so essential to gardening and farming, I'm thinking it would be of interest to those of you who have enough land to consider building a pond. Believe me, it was an essential part of the homestead of early American gardeners and farmers, often their only source of water. And a pond is not to be discounted even today.

When my son bought the site for his new home a year or two ago there was a deep depression on one portion of the land. Because of this, and the fact that it would cost a young fortune to fill in the low place, this particular parcel of land had been passed up so often that the owner was willing to sell at a very attractive price. My son's friends warned him against buying it but he kept his own counsel. Shortly after his home was built, he proceeded to dig out the area still deeper instead of filling it in. The result was a very attractive pond, now well stocked with fish. Two willows have been planted at selected locations and tulips, daffodils, iris and day lilies bloom profusely each spring on the banks. The whole makes a lovely picture to be viewed from the windows of his dining area.

Many farms come with an old pond, natural or manmade. These traditional farm ponds, however, part of the rural fire-fighting equipment and the water troughs' supply system, are located close to the barn. Often the barn is halfway up a hill, with the pond below it, and runoff from the barn area may make the water unsuitable for swimming. A second pond thus never hurts.

Contact your local Soil Conservation Service or Agricultural Extension Service and discuss pond building with them. They can help you decide on the best location, size, and layout. Check up on any government assistance that might be currently available to help you pay for pond development. Since in many cases ponds are vital in flood control as well as for general land development, the government will in some cases offset part of your expenditures. Always remember, though, to check these deals for attached strings. Some government fish-stocking plans, for instance, call for your ponds to be open to the public as recreation areas during parts of the year. This may or may not be fine with you. The point is, make sure you know what you're getting into. The government has a tendency to give it to you in one paragraph and take it away in the next.

A pond can be built at the head of a spring or in an easily dammed gully with a small, trickling stream, but don't try to dam up a stream of any size — it's difficult to do. Even if there's no direct source of running water on your property you might be able to build a "sky pond," fed solely by runoff. This is the type my son built. In the summer when it gets low he fills it from one of his wells.

If you plan to stock your pond with fish, it should be deep. This is worthwhile, for a fish crop can be harvested regularly just like any other crop on the farm. Better a smaller, deeper pond than a larger shallower one. A flat, pancake-like pond loses immense volumes of water through evaporation, and may even turn into a swamp in summer.

Pond life in general needs clear water, not silt. This means land leading down to the banks should be planted with a good deep-rooted cover crop like clover that will assure a runoff as clear as the rain itself, with only a few nutrients added through ground seepage. My son uses a hybrid type of Bermuda grass that stands up well, assisted by a watering system, under our hot southwestern sun. He left undisturbed the native oaks, pecans, cedars, redbud and dogwood that occupy the portion of his land nearest to the pond. This has invited the homesteading of wildlife, rabbits, squirrels, all kinds of birds, including wild ducks, and, to our amazement, just recently a beautiful ring-necked pheasant!

🌻 🌻 🌻

AN OKLAHOMA SPRING

April is the time of year when the pink of the redbud draws the eye irresistibly to wooded hillsides. This pink is completely different from the luminous thin shine of peach petal. At first it is almost red, but in its prime, when all the redbud trees stand forth, it is exactly the pink you get when you pour thick country cream over a piece of fresh raspberry cobbler and the juice and cream run together and blend.

Hills that were just recently colorless almost to invisibility now look suddenly like a party table. You long for a giant spoon so you can reach far out and scoop up and eat this delicious pinkness!

The glossy, heart-shaped leaves, at first a bit brownish and inconspicuous, will not open until the pink flower has played its part on the stage of spring.

Complementing the redbud, the hills are touched now with the thin pale gold of new sassafras leaves and bursts of wild white plum like sudden chords of music. Then, adding to the spring symphony, the dogwood begins to put out its flowers, each petal warped and scorched on one edge as if someone had rescued it from the fire just in time. As the redbud fades away for another year, the dogwood will come into full, rapturous white, suddenly covered with glory. Now and then take time out from your busy everyday life and enjoy the splendor of *your* spring.

Mushroom Madness

When violets, redbud and dogwood begin adding color to the brown earth, morels poke up their wizened heads to survey the landscape. Sponge mushrooms, also called miracle plant or morel (*Morchella esculenta*), are one of nature's very best spring offerings.

It is well to remember, however, that mushrooms do not grow in exactly the same place every year. Old patches are bare, and new patches appear in the woods, as if mushroom seed had been washed out in a gentle rain and left there to sprout when the water subsided. I have lived many years at my present location, but it wasn't until two years ago that I suddenly, one spring, discovered morels growing happily in my yard. The following year nary a morel did I find. Morels, shaped like Christmas trees, seem to be liked by just about everybody — and they are so easily identifiable that once seen, it is hard to make a mistake.

The experienced mushroom hunter knows to look for the mushroom's mate, and also to look under the little humped-up mounds of dry leaves for the mushrooms playfully hiding there. Mushroom hunting is a kind of

madness to which one surrenders completely — for the real, dyed-in-the-wool enthusiast it has almost as many thrills as going on an African safari.

Last spring my friend and guide, who had spotted a good patch, offered to take me with him. His jeep went over rough country but I gamely bounced right along making no comment. Getting to the creek along which the morels grew was just about as much fun as hunting the little treasures. When we did reach the creek, which was about eight inches deep, running briskly and pretty darn chilly, it was just natural that the mushrooms would be growing on the other side.

But no little 30-foot creek was going to stop us fearless hunters. So we waded in and, sure enough, on the other side was just what the mushroom lover wanted to see — tons of fallen leaves, loose soil rich in organic matter, and dozens of little golden morels peeping their heads up through the cover.

When you start to pick, mushroom madness takes over completely. After each find, however large or numerous, you think: "Just one more," and go on hunting.

Not only are mushrooms extremely tasty and fun to find, they are also quite nutritious. Raw mushrooms contain only 60 calories per pound and they are excellent suppliers of lecithin, a nutrient essential for memory functions. It also minimizes cholesterol deposits in the bloodstream.

The smell of mushrooms is delicate, but quite distinct. It is some-what as if a cup had been emptied of pineapple juice and let dry unrinsed out; somewhat like smoked wild fowl; slightly like the smell of fresh wet wood. Morels taste best when they have been sliced, dipped in a batter of egg, milk and Worcestershire sauce, rolled in flour and corn meal and fried.

A Word of Warning

Don't play "toadstool roulette." When you gather mushrooms be sure you can recognize the edible variety. My friend warned me that another variety of morel appears each fall that is extremely hazardous to one's health. This mushroom should not be confused with the safe morels that grow in the spring time.

Indians down on the plains used mushrooms freely, for there were only a few, easily identified species. These, notably the boletus, they fried, baked, or simmered into soup to which meat had been added. If there was no meat, a soup of fresh mushrooms and wild onions are equally savory.

But the Indians of the Rocky Mountains area did not use mushrooms to any extent and there is virtually no reference to them in the journals of the early explorers who partook of their hospitality. The reason is simply that there were too many mushrooms. Some species made delightful eating, but some, almost indistinguishable, were fatally poisonous. The result was that numerous tribes forbade the use of mushrooms unless they were approved by the medicine men and, we are told, a few tribes forbade their use altogether.

❦ ❦ ❦

APRIL GARDEN CHORES

Fertilizing

Even in the late 1900's compost was coming into fashion and a great variety of fertilizers were being used, some of which we have now lost sight of. As a matter of record, factory-made fertilizers were in existence more than a hundred years ago but then, as now, there were also natural ones that many gardeners used. Standard advice usually given was, "Fertilize liberally before plowing or harrowing."

The three important elements of fertilizer were also well understood, as stated over fifty years ago in the Farmer Seed Company's catalog: "Nitrogen produces early, rapid, and succulent growth of plant. Potash hardens plant growth and throws the vigor into fruit or flower. Phosphoric acid aids in nutrition, influences maturity and color. Lime releases inert plant foods, rendering them available for feeding roots."

Hardwood Ashes

Even those gardeners who could not afford to buy fertilizers had some things available to them, such as hardwood ashes, as practically everybody burned wood for heating purposes. An old seed catalog described them as indispensible for all crops needing potash, and of high value for cabbages, potatoes, onions, strawberries, fruit trees, corn and beans.

They were cautioned, however, that ashes might cause scab in potatoes. The recommended application was one pound of ashes for each 10 to 20 square feet.

While hardwood ashes were usually specified, those of soft woods were also considered of value "if they have not been leached by rain." Old English farming advice from the late 18th century advocated the collection of all ashes — those from burning brush, rubbish, weeds, and so on — to be kept dry until spring seeding time. Then the ashes were to be mixed with soot and the whole thing put through a sieve.

What plants and trees benefit by an application of wood ashes? Almost all plants. Those that need potash — fruit trees, vegetable root crops, hydrangeas, carnations, roses, peonies, and so on — are especially benefited.

It has been recorded that the Indians also knew the benefit of ashes, and certain tribes saved the ashes from their campfires and spread them over their garden plots in the spring. Samuel Deane included in 1790, among ashes for fertilizing, "coal ashes, top-dressing for cold, damp soils."

Coal ashes actually have little fertilizer value, but they do improve the mechanical condition of the soil and, to a degree, are of some value against cutworms. If a one-inch layer is placed about the bases of plants, cutworms will have difficulty in attacking them.

Bones

Bones were also available and a lady gardener of the 1880's stated that she gave her house plants bone dust once a month, preparing this herself. "I burn all the bones I get," she said, "then pound them fine."

However, burning the bones was not always recommended. George W. Park, founder of Park's Seed Company in 1868 gave this recommendation in May of 1886: Put bones and ashes in alternate layers in an old barrel, moisten the whole with water and place in a dry situation for several months. Fresh wood ashes must be used, and the compost kept continually moist." This is a good method but should not be used to feed acid-loving plants.

The same holds true of an old English method given by John Monk in 1794: "Mr. Paget recommends, instead of being at the expense and trouble of grinding the bones, to mix them in a heap with lime, which will in a short time reduce the bones to powder." Unslaked lime was used.

Bone meal, as it was made and used in Victorian England, was a far different product from the bone meal of today. Every dedicated gardener of that era had a bone grinder in his potting shed or garden house. Fresh, raw bone, with scraps of meat clinging to it, was ground and used immediately as a fertilizer. It included the marrow, blood, meat scraps, and valuable minor elements in addition to uncooked phosphorus. Now *that* was fertilizer!

Other Natural Fertilizers

An experienced gardener of the post-Civil-War era noted: "Coffee grounds are excellent fertilizers. I have seen seedlings growing vigorously in the pure grounds and thriving equally with those planted in good earth."

As previously mentioned in "February," coffee grounds may be mixed with fine seeds to facilitate sowing and to prevent seeds from being sown too thickly. Most root crops — carrots, beets, turnips, and so on — will sprout well in coffee grounds. They are also excellent in the compost heap and may often be had for the asking from places where much coffee is served. Another freebie.

An old-fashioned fertilizer for house plants was water in which crushed eggshells had been soaked for 24 hours. Eggshells contain calcium — sometimes I simply crush the shells and dig them into the pots I keep my houseplants in. Don't do this with acid-loving plants, however, such as gardenias or azaleas, because calcium (lime) is harmful to them.

That famous Indian fertilizer, fish, was also widely used. Too costly today, or unobtainable in many inland areas, fish have been replaced by fish emulsion. This liquid plant food contains nitrogen, phosphorus and potassium. It is mixed with water. Look for it under "Gardening Aids" in seed catalogs.

Greensand, available today from a few natural-fertilizer companies was also widely used. It is found along the New Jersey and Virginia coasts, among other places, and was valued as a fertilizer by the first half of the 19th century. It is a granular, half-soft marine deposit, an olive-green iron-potassium silicate, also called glauconite, containing about 6 percent of potash. Its use is reputed to give "luxurious harvests" in an old report of *Geological Survey of New Jersey* published in the 1840's. If you live in the seaboard states you may still be able to find it.

Of course animal manures were, and are, one of the best possible fertilizers and they were a standby years ago; there was so much available. Composting of manures was considered good gardening practice, although in certain farming operations fresh manure might be spread upon the land to be plowed in at once. Today, when fresh manure is harder to come by, it is a good practice to mix it in the compost heap with other materials, such as leaves, grass clippings, wood chips, ground up weeds, sawdust, seaweed (espe-

cially good if obtainable), and even mud or ditch scrapings.

Leather, being of animal origin, has also been added to the list of fertilizers, and hair, if obtainable, for the same reason. In just about every locality there is something, if one searches, which can be composted and used on the garden. Where I live cotton hulls and pecan and peanut shells may often be had for the hauling away. During the summer and in the fall months, grass clippings and leaves are often put out on the curb for the sanitation department to pick up — and no one cares who takes them. In wine-making areas there is grape pomace. In some seasons you can find spoiled hay, made unusable for animals by a sudden rainstorm while it was still in the field. Just do a little research and I'm sure there will be something you can use for building that all-essential compost heap. Best to start your compost operation in the 4th quarter under Cancer, Scorpio or Pisces.

🍂 🍂 🍂

APRIL FORAGING

April is the month to look for the first rosy-green shoots of **poke,** if you live in the South or Southwest — those of you who live farther north may have to wait until May.

Poke (pocan, ink berry, pigeon berry) comes up in rich fields, by roadsides, and under trees. You will usually find it in the same place year after year. The part

used is the young shoots, about 5 to 6 inches tall. An old recipe for cooking goes like this: "To cook stalks not over 4 inches long, lay them in cold water for one hour. Tie loosely in bundles and put them in boiling water and boil ¾ hour until tender. Drain and lay them on buttered toast, dust with pepper and salt, cover with butter and serve."

If you are lucky enough to have a cellar, the fall roots, transplanted and forced in a box of rich garden soil, will give you a plentiful supply of blanched shoots during the winter months.

Because the mature leaves, roots and inky berries are said to be poisonous, only the young sprouts, those no taller than six inches, should be cooked. They are easy to gather on a bright April day and cutting them early does not injure the plant — it simply sends up more shoots. Mark your pokeweed during the summer for cutting in the spring.

Pokeweed tastes a little like asparagus combined with spinach, and most cooks say to boil it through two or three waters. Since I like the "bite" I just boil it one time, drizzle on the butter, season lightly and have a feast of poke greens entirely to my liking.

Rebecca Parker in *Horticulture* magazine recommends adding a handful of young horseradish leaves, "if a sprightly flavor is desired," and serving with vinegar. The parboiled leaves may also be combined with an equal amount of cress, pepper grass, dandelion, or mustard and all cooked together in just enough water to avoid scorching. When done, add six or eight minced spring onions, which have been sautéed in bacon drippings, and season to taste. Garnish with the grated yolk of a hardboiled egg just before removing from the heat to serve.

My mother, who was born in Indiana, used to tell me lots of stories about plants and herbs she had gathered and sold when she was a young farm girl. Apparently **chamomile** (or camomile) tea was as popular in an earlier day as aspirin is now. If you had a headache you drank a cup of chamomile tea.

Chamomile Hair Rinse

Ladies of long ago were very partial to using chamomile flowers as a rinse for blond hair and indeed it does bring out attractive highlights. Use about 4 tablespoons of the dried flowers to about a pint of water. Boil 20 to 30 minutes and strain when cool. Hair should be fresh washed and free from oil. Pour rinse over hair and catch in a basin, so rinse may be repeated several times — do not rinse hair with clear water after using. Your hair, as an added bonus, will be scented like sweet clover. The flower heads mature over a long season and the plant is easily grown.

❀ ❀ ❀

How to Make Chamomile Tea

1. Warm a pot of china or glass.

2. Place green-dried, crushed herb leaves in teapot.

3. Pour boiling water over herb leaves.

4. Allow to steep, covered, for 5 minutes.

5. Sweeten tea, if you prefer, with a little honey.

NATIVE HERBS FOR SEASONING

For those on a salt-free diet it may be of interest to know that native herbs can be used as seasoners to perk up otherwise bland dishes:

Herb	Part Used	Use
Wild allspice	Fruits	Vinegar, coarse meat
Angelica	Leaves, roots, seeds	Soup, stew, starchy vegetables
Bayberry	Leaves	Soup, stew, good salt substitute
Sweet birch	Leaves and twigs	Vinegar, soup
Wild carrot	Seeds, leaves	Soup, fish, good salt substitute
Catnip	Leaves and flowers	Sauce, substitute for peppermint
Chamomile	Leaves and flowers	Cooked cabbage and broccoli
Sweet clover	Leaves, flowers, fruits	Soup, stew, powder
Sweet flag	Roots	Fish, meat, substitute for ginger or cinnamon
Wild garlic	Whole plant	Soup, salad dressing, sauce
Wild ginger	Root	Vinegar, substitute for ginger
Horseradish	Root	Vinegar, soup, stew, coarse meat and fish
Juniper	Fruits	Vinegar, soup, stew, venison
Masterwort	Leafstalks, roots, seeds	Soup, stew, cooked vegetables
Mountain mint	Whole plant	Substitute for other mints
Nasturtium	Whole plant, seeds	Salad, pickle
Wild onion	Whole plant, seeds	Soup, dressing, sauce
Pepper grass	Leaves and fruits	Herb salt, soup, stew, salad, vinegar
Peppermint	Whole plant	Jelly, soup, lamb, potato
Sassafras	Leaves, bark	Soup, stew, cooked vegetables
Sheep's sorrel	Whole plant	Salad, cole slaw, puree
Shepherd's purse	Whole plant	Herb salt, soup, stew, salad
Spearmint	Whole plant	Same as peppermint
Tansy	Young leaves	Vinegar, cookies, substitute for sage
Wormwood	Leaves and flowers	Vinegar, discreet substitute for tarragon
Watercress	Leaves	Salad

* * *

DYEING EGGS

I once wrote a craft book called *Egg Decorating,* in which I explored every possible method of dyeing eggs. Although the tradition of coloring eggs at springtime can be traced as far back as 5,000 years, to the ancient Persians, it is the Pennsylvania Dutch who generally credited with reviving the tradition and developing it to a fine art. As previously mentioned, the Pennsylvania Dutch are really of German descent.

The Persians and later the ancient Egyptians exchanged colored eggs to celebrate the return of spring and as tokens of good will. The eggs were often colored bright red to signify blood and the life force.

Later the Greeks adopted the custom and used colored eggs during their spring festivals as a sign of fertility and the regenerative power of nature. During Cleopatra's reign, around 50 B.C., Egyptians and Romans colored eggs as part of their spring festival.

The custom was dying out in Europe when the Pennsylvania Dutch brought it to the New World in the 1700's. By 1880 they and the Ukranians were just about the only ethnic groups in this country who still observed the quaint festivity in any number.

A hundred years ago, according to the historians, most Easter eggs were colored by boiling them with onion skins for yellow, alder catkins and hickory bark for shades of brown, madder root for red, and various materials such as coffee, walnut hulls, green wheat and beets for other colors.

Each year some enterprising women would come to William M. Townley's drugstore in Newark, New Jersey and buy a few cents' worth of dyes, such as indigo, logwood and gamboge (an orange-red gum resin, derived from certain trees).

Many, however, considered coloring Easter eggs a time-consuming, messy nuisance, and turned the chore over to others. In April, 1881, the Lebanon, Pennsylvania Daily Times carried this notice:

> Mr. C.R. Fisher, the North Ninth Street dyer, is just now kept busy coloring Easter eggs, which he does in a scientific manner. For five cents a dozen he changes the natural color into purple, yellow and red. Judging from samples shown us, it is certainly the better part of wisdom to take your hard-boiled eggs to his dyeing establishment for coloring. The sum charged is a trifling compared to the trouble saved.

Townley conceived the idea of packaging his dyes, and by 1879 one of the oldest existing businesses in the United States was founded, named for the Pennsylvania Dutch word for Easter, PAAS.

* * *

Tips on Coloring Eggs

There are many herbs, barks, flowers, leaves, vegetables, etc. that can be used for dyeing eggs naturally. Some people use beet juice or even coffee grounds. In Russia the Pasque flower, Anemone pulsatilla, which imparts a green color, has been used traditionally to color Paschal or Easter eggs. In England, furze or gorse, a shrub with yellow flowers, has been used. I find it great fun to experiment. I also find that it is best, if possible, to use very white eggs. Another hint is to use clean rainwater — city water may have chemicals in it which will keep the vegetable dyes from working well. Generally speaking, eggs dyed with natural materials are safe to eat.

If one wishes brilliantly colored tie-dyed eggs it is also possible to use Rit, Putnam or other commercial dyes for this purpose. They should be treated, however, as simply for decorative use and never eaten. But these commercial dyes will give amazingly beautiful results.

Ferns, leaves, flowers, grasses, etc. used to tie on the shells to make patterns should not be gathered too far in advance. Not only will they wilt but their natural colors — as with dandelion, pansies, grape hyacinth, violets, etc. — will transfer more beautifully to the eggshells if they are fresh. And, believe it or not, much of the color does transfer.

Do not be too disappointed if some eggs do not dye well. This is usually caused by the content of the shell, which may differ because of different feeding practices. Just use these up as you would ordinary boiled eggs and try again.

★ ★ ★

Taurus the Bull  *(April 21 - May 22)*

Corn Planting Moon
MAY

Time of Blackberry Winter ★ Planting time ★
Popcorn ★ Moon signs ★ Gardening tools ★ Finding
and marking Bayberry bushes for candle making ★
Year-round soap ★ Old-fashioned jelly recipes ★
Pickles ★ Butterflies and other beneficial insects ★
Attracting hummingbirds ★ Flower wines ★ Daylilies
★ Beauty secrets ★

MAY, IN THE GARDEN, is one of the most pleasant times of the year. As I've mentioned before, however, it can be quite unpredictable. From *The Flower* comes this little verse:

Grief melts away
  Like snow in May
As if there were no such cold
  thing.

Like warm Indian summer in the fall, snow may occasionally be expected in May. This period of cold usually happens around May 10th and they even have a name for it — it's called "blackberry winter."

Almost any farmer can describe blackberry winter. It's that cold spell that comes in May about three weeks after spring fever. It comes when blackberries are in bloom and does sometimes actually drop a few (or a lot) of snowflakes into the white flowers. (You should mark the bushes so you can find them later when they may be overgrown by grasses and weeds — blackberry jam is great on toast, pancakes, waffles and just about everything on a cold winter's day.) Fortunately, the cold doesn't bite through to the hard, green, incipient berries nestled behind the petals. And seldom does blackberry winter last more than a week.

But it is most sincerely cold. If you happen to be plowing a cornfield, you had best wear the flaps down on your winter cap and put on all the coats you wore through the real winter. Once blackberry winter is out of the way, you can happily proceed with the rest of the delightful season.

PLANTING TIME

In early May, while the zodiac is in the earthy, moist, productive, feminine sign of Taurus (April 20 to May 21), it's important to get your seed into the ground. Avoid the first day of the new moon, but during the first quarter it is good to transplant broccoli, Brussels sprouts, cabbage, and cauliflower. You can also plant Swiss chard, sweet corn, endive, lettuce, and spinach.

Since Taurus rules the neck, many old-timers believed that leafy "neck vegetables" should be planted on the waxing Taurus moon. During the second quarter of the moon under Taurus, it is good to plant (or replant) snap beans and summer squash; and plant melons, late squash, cucumbers, pole beans, black-eyed peas, limas and okra. Tomatoes, eggplant and peppers should also be set out.

Apple-blossom time is traditionally the time for planting early corn and successive plantings may be made until the fourth of July. There are two schools of thought regarding corn. Some Moon-signers think of it as a "neck vegetable," while others call it "stem fruit." Followers of the "stem fruit" school think corn should be planted in the second quarter of the moon. The *Llewellyn Moon Sign* book advises planting corn in the first quarter under Cancer, Scorpio or Pisces.

★ ★ ★

Popcorn

While we are on the subject of corn, let's talk a little about popcorn. Plant popcorn under the same signs as for sweet corn, but if you plan to plant both types in your garden, be sure to plant several rows of sunflowers between them. Corn is wind pollinated and it would be a small disaster to have the two types mix.

No one knows who deserves the credit for "discovering" popcorn, but popcorn lovers are grateful for the discovery. It was probably an accident — one day one of our ancestors held an ear of corn over a fire, heard it make a funny noise and saw a "little white flow-

Rabbits Away!

Of course the best defense against rabbits in the garden is a 2- to 3-foot-high wire fence anchored in the ground — but this is not always practical. Or maybe it's your flower beds they are visiting at night. Oldtimers knew a thing or two about rabbits and how to foil them, and one way that was often successful was to spread human hair around plants to keep them away. You might contact your friendly neighborhood barber shop and ask their help. Another good way to deter rabbit depredations is to sprinkle blood meal around plants or small trees.

er" mysteriously grow on its side.

There is evidence that popcorn may have been the first type of corn raised for human consumption. Ancient clay and metal poppers have been found in many parts of Mexico, South America and the southwestern United States. Ears of popcorn 5,600 years old were found by archeologists in the Bat Cave in New Mexico in 1948.

Corn was not known in Europe until its introduction by Christopher Columbus after his return from the West Indies. He found the natives of the New World not only eating popcorn, but also wearing it in decorations like corsages. In 1519, Cortez found the Aztecs using popcorn as an important food, as a decoration on ceremonial headdresses, and as ornaments for the statues of their gods. Some Indians tossed kernels into the fire to predict their fortunes, predicting the future from how many kernels popped and in which direction they flew. Even today, it is a part of the life style in Guatemala, occupying a quasi-religious position in the social and political lives of the people.

Popcorn also occupied a social position in the lives of the settlers in the New World. Social leaders gave popcorn parties, inviting their friends to a gala afternoon eating popcorn, just as they gave tea parties.

In 1885 Charles Cretors of Chicago invented the first popping machine, powered by steam. He also developed the wet popper — popping corn in oil. Until then it had always been dry popped.

Perhaps the best known version of popcorn is Cracker Jack, which was a big hit at the 1893 Chicago World's Fair. The creator of this confection, F.W. Rueckheim, a German immigrant, hadn't given his product a name; he simply scooped the molasses-coated popcorn and peanut confection out of a barrel. The story varies, but in 1896 a salesman tasted the delicacy, smacked his lips and announced, "Now that's a crackerjack!" The name stuck. Later that year Cracker Jack appeared packaged in individual boxes that sold for a nickel, a price that didn't change for more than half a century. In 1912 people began finding prizes in their Cracker Jack packages, a tradition now considered as American as apple pie and, well, popcorn. Almost everybody in the United States grew up with popcorn.

If the pop-ability of your corn is not what it should be, chances are it's too dry. Popcorn rarely gets too moist after it is packaged. Place the too-dry popcorn in an airtight container with one teaspoon of water for each 10 ounces liquid measure of kernels. Shake the container several times a day for 2 or 3 days before using. Or, place a damp paper towel in the container and skip the shaking. One teaspoon of water per 10-ounce container, or one tablespoon per quart of kernels, will raise the moisture approximately 1½%.

Someone once said "the way to a successful movie theater is to find a good location for a popcorn stand and build the theater around it!"

❦   ❦   ❦

MORE MAY MOON-GARDENING

After the moon is full, the sign of Taurus is particularly favorable for the planting, or additional planting, of potatoes, carrots, beets, turnips, sweet potatoes, salsify, onions and peanuts.

During the fourth quarter it is good to fertilize, sidedress with sawdust, compost or mulch, thin, and cultivate.

The sign changes on May 21, when Gemini takes over with his twin characteristics: dryness and barrenness. This is the time to destroy unwanted plant life, trim, weed, and cut timber and fence posts. Any needed cultivation may also be practiced.

Timing to destroy or harvest is just as important as timing to nurture life. Destroying weeds under the Twins gives the benefit of both timing and rhythm, for living things on earth constantly swing between life and death.

Tools

To accomplish successful gardening you will need at least a few basic tools. Most of the gardening jobs we do today had to be done a century or two ago, and the hand tools used had been well thought out by that time. There was more variety then, however, within classes of the old tools. Many were made by the gardeners who used them, almost as if every gardener had his own idea of what a spade or a weeder should look like.

Most gardeners made good use of several hoes, narrow ones for cultivating and broad ones for breaking sod. Another hoe, that came into later use was what Deane (Samuel Deane, publisher of *The New England Farmer or Geological Dictionary*), described as a pronghoe; if it had two prong-like blades it was called a bidens (a tool that dates back to ancient Rome), and if three, a trident. The operation was described like this: "It is easily struck into the ground; and as the tines are six or seven inches long, it will stir the ground to the same depth that a plough does. It is useful in taking up strong-rooted weeds, and opening land that is crusted, or become too compact."

Another hoe of sorts came into use later, perhaps for gentlemen gardeners, since it was a kind of walking stick with a 2-inch-wide chisel blade on the end. It was called a spud, and was used to cut weeds as one walked the garden grounds.

Still another type called a "zapetino" sounds like something still known today. It is described as having a small hoe blade at one end and two prongs at the other. It was sometimes made with an eye for the insertion of the handle, and sometimes with a shank to drive into the handle. With one end of this instrument, weeds were cut up in gardens; with the other, roots were drawn out and the ground loosened to a depth of five or six inches.

The dibble was a stick to make a hole to set a plant, and was sometimes tipped with metal.

Wheelbarrows were in constant use, and many of them were homemade.

Ploughs were also pretty generally used and Deane describes them as "the most important of all the tools used in husbandry."

Digging tools were numerous, many of them homemade or made to order by the gardener. They included crowbars, then called crows, mattocks, and spades. For digging drain-tile lines, spades were made in highly specialized shapes of great variety, including triangular and sugar-scoop.

Early American gardeners also had the rake, probably an idea borrowed from the English. While wooden rakes were common, metal kinds were also used. John Monk, in his *Agricultural Dictionary* of 1794, describes one called a spring-tooth: "These rakes are in high repute; and it is the general opinion that one person will do more with this rake than four with the common wood rake....by the lower class of people they are called hell-rakes, on account of the great quantity of work they dispatch in a short time....The teeth screw in and are fastened with screw-nuts."

Row markers, mostly homemade in varying styles, were also in common use.

In the 19th century the wheel-hoe and allied tools appeared on the garden scene, many of which are still in use today. When we were first married my husband and I made our first garden with a wheel-hoe. He worked long hours and often arrived home after dark. The evening meal over, he would tie a flashlight to the wheel-hoe and go out and plow the garden. The next morning I would go out early and hoe the plants where he had missed. It was a family joke that he had cut the hoe handle short so I could do this more comfortably.

With the wheel-hoe the machine age was being ushered in, the average American quickly becoming enamored of machines' speed and efficiency. An early day gardener said of his $11 combined seeder, wheel hoe, cultivator and plough: "You can't buy mine for $100 and leave me without one." A third man remarked of his wheel hoe: "Why, my 5-year-old boy could push it anywhere," but a smoother customer had a different idea: "My wife can use it as well as I."

★ ★ ★

Bells to Beat Birds

Birds often get to fruit before you do so maybe you can beat them at the game with this device. A bell was fastened to a post set in the garden, and a cord from the bell ran to the house kitchen. Whoever happened to pass the cord gave it a yank, ringing the bell and scaring off any birds feasting on the cherries or apples. Garden hose cut in short lengths somewhat resemble snakes and these may be hung in trees to frighten birds — change their placement on limbs occasionally.

THE VERSATILE BAYBERRY

The ingenious pioneers and colonists used plants for other things besides food. One such plant was the wide-ranging bayberry or waxberry (Myrica), also called wax myrtle or sweet gale. These tender and hardy evergreen shrubs and small trees are still grown for their decorative value; one, M. rubra, is cultivated for its edible fruits.

The bayberry of eastern North America is M. pensylvanica, sometimes known as M. carolinensis. It is an extremely hardy shrub that occurs naturally from Nova Scotia to Florida and Alabama, and is well adapted for growing on poor, dryish soils in exposed locations, especially near the coast. Although deciduous, this bayberry holds its foliage well into the fall or early winter. The leaves are pleasingly aromatic. The fruits (berries) are densely covered with grayish wax and are very attractive. This wax is used for making bayberry candles and in early days was highly prized.

The wax myrtle, M. cerifera, grows wild in damp or wet sandy or peaty soils from southern New Jersey to Florida and to Texas and Arkansas, and is hardy north of its natural range. It is evergreen and attains a height of 35 feet. The fruits are covered with grayish white wax. This shrub is also sometimes called bayberry, candleberry, or tallow shrub.

Candlemaking

Candlemaking was once a necessity for colonial households and it is still practiced. The fragrant bayberries were used to make Christmas candles, as the green wax has such a pleasant odor. A bushel of berries will give about four or six candles.

The pioneers used wicks made of rolled cotton, silky down from milkweeds, cattail stems, or tow string. These were slipped over a candle rod and dipped in the melted wax. The wax clung to the wick and hardened. The dipping continued until the candles had become thick enough. Later, tin molds were used and as many as six, eight, or more candles could be made at once. The melted wax, or sometimes tallow, was poured into the molds and then allowed to cool around the homemade wicks.

Soapmaking

Soapmaking was another task often performed by the early American housewife. Every spring enough soap was made to last a year. Wood ashes saved during the winter were put into a barrel. Water was poured through the ashes and allowed to trickle out through a hole near the bottom. This brown liquid, or "lye," was then boiled in a large kettle with fats and grease saved from the year's cooking and butchering. The mixture was cooked slowly until it thickened to form a soft, jellylike, yellow soap.

★ ★ ★

MAY FORAGING

...y no means
...y a bounti-
...ttlers. All
...rries and fruits
...there for the taking — and
for those who look, many are still
available today. I make jelly every
year from wild blackberries and
dewberries. And I always look
forward to making jelly from wild
plums — their bittersweet, somewhat acid flavor is very different
from that of the cultivated species
and very much to my liking.

Fruit Jellies

Early day housewives did not
have Pen-Jel, Certo and Sure-Jell
but they managed just the same to
get a delicious product. Pectin is
that substance in some fruits that,
when heated and combined with
fruit acid and sugar, causes the
substance to congeal or "jell."
Not all fruit contains this substance but pectin may be extracted
from fruits that are known to contain it, such as apples, plums,
quinces, etc.

PICKLING TIME

One year my cucumber vines
became distressed and the leaves
turned almost white — the vines
did not die but growth slowed. An
older gardener told me he did not
know what caused this but had
seen the condition before and advised me to spray them with sugar
water. I dissolved a half cup of
sugar in warm water and put it in
my watering can, adding enough
water to fill the can, and proceeded to sprinkle the cucumber
patch. This treatment not only
"cured" the vines but bees, apparently attracted by the sugar,
came buzzing around in great numbers. As a result my vines set more
cucumbers than I knew what to do
with. At the time I did not have
the following recipe which I found
pinned inside an old recipe book.
Apparently it was a clipping from
a newspaper of 1893 and given by
Mrs. F.M. Worth, Greenville, N.Y.

Lazy Wife Pickles

"I am sure all housekeep-
ers who try this recipe for
cucumber pickles will often
use it because it is so simple
and easy. Mix together a gallon of vinegar, two-thirds of
a cup of water, a cupful of
sugar and a cupful of dry
mustard. Mix well and put in
a stone crock. Pick as many
cucumbers as you wish, a
dozen or a hundred. Wash
well, then pour boiling water
over them. Let stand until
cold, take out and put into
the prepared vinegar. Fresh
cucumbers may be added
from time to time, the vinegar being well stirred each
time. These will be crisp,
tender and of fine flavor."

BUTTERFLIES AND OTHER INSECT FRIENDS

May is the month when those gorgeous big yellow butterflies, the tiger swallowtails, take over. They are the largest butterflies that northern New England has and they usually turn up around the middle of the month, brightening meadows, gardens, roadsides — just about everywhere you look.

I became a butterfly chaser very young. I was a sickly, skinny child and my father came up with the idea that if I had a butterfly net I would get out of doors (instead of keeping my nose in a book most of the time), and get some healthful exercise. His idea worked, but what he didn't foresee was that I would get into frequent hot water because in my enthusiasm I took the heads off my mother's zinnias trying to make a catch.

Tiger Swallowtails

I became so interested that I started to read all about butterflies and found out some exceedingly interesting things about the tiger swallowtails. They are one of those marvels of the insect world which have two or more forms arising from the same lot of eggs in a way that science has as yet not adequately explained.

The splendid tiger swallowtail is an example of this "dimorphism" and of especial interest because its extra form is confined to one sex and to only the southern part of the butterfly's geographical range. The species occurs over a large part of the North American continent, being found from ocean to ocean and from Canada to Florida. North of approximately the fortieth degree of latitude there is but one form of the insect — the familiar yellow-and-black-striped butterfly everyone has seen visiting the lilac blossoms in May or June. South of this, however, some females take on an entirely different appearance, being almost wholly black with the hind wings touched with lines of blue and bordered with crescents of yellow and orange.

Like wasps and bees, butterflies are excellent pollinators. They are seldom present in sufficient numbers for their caterpillars to be harmful — with the exception of the imported or white cabbage butterfly.

The curious thing is that a female butterfly may lay a dozen eggs, some of which will develop into the usual yellow form and the rest into the black form, both groups being of the same sex. The black form is so entirely distinct in appearance that the two were originally described as separate species, and they were long considered such, until breeding experiments determined the precise condition. The different appearances must have evolved for protective coloration, butterflies tending to utilize backgrounds that blend with their coloring.

This species is also of interest for another reason. The caterpillar has a remarkable resemblance to the head of a serpent, which is thought to have a real protective value in frightening away attacking birds and other enemies.

The cardinal can live as comfortably in town as in woodlands, nesting in thickets or small trees. Its diet consists of seeds, wild fruit, grain, and many types of insects.

Enhancing Your Environment

Anyone who has a garden can exert influence over the ecology of the neighborhood far beyond the borders of his own domain. Even those who are city dwellers with a terrace, a balcony, or a well-set window can often add to the health of the cycle and the strength of links within the connecting chain of all that is live and natural.

That birds are both receivers and forwarding agents of this ecological influence has been of growing interest for many years. What is less known is that you can also attract butterflies to your garden, and surely there are few more beautiful sights to see among the flowers. Furthermore, butterflies, along with bees and other insects, are great pollinators and, with the exception of the white or imported cabbage butterfly, butterflies seldom occur in such numbers that they cause a problem. There may be a profuse hatch-out but butterflies are so frail, and have so little in the way of a defense mechanism, that great numbers quickly perish, birds and other hazards taking their toll.

Different climatic regions house different varieties of both birds and butterflies, yet some of these varieties travel very far indeed. Many migrate; some reproduce in one area and winter in another. Wherever they are born, or live, or fly to, however, birds and butterflies need nourishment.

The flower garden has been a cherished part of household gardening in America during the past two centuries. Although grim necessity had to come first in the early gardens of the New World, flowers for flowers' sake quickly followed. And when the westward trek began, flower seeds were squeezed into the jammed storage quarters of the pioneer wagons, to spread their delicate beauty across the continent.

Planting for Winged Guests

If you have meadowland, as well as a formal garden, you may want to plant wildflowers. Parks Seed Company, Plants of the Southwest and Applewood Seed Company all have highly dependable collections of wildflower seeds that will attract butterflies.

Flowers for Butterflies

Many butterflies can see red and butterfly flowers are often brilliantly colored — deep pink, scarlet, bright blue — and are generally very fragrant. Butterflyweed (*Asclepias tuberosa*) is a spectacularly vivid orange. Its cousin, the common milkweed (*Asclepias speciosa*) has silvery pink flowers and is the specific host plant of the regal monarch butterfly. Other excellent butterfly plants of the West are indigobush (*Amorpha fruticosa* and *A. canescens*), dogbane (*Apocynum androsaemifolium*), shrubby cinquefoil (*Potentilla fruticosa*), and cutleaf coneflower (*Rudbeckia laciniata*).

Hawkmoths

Hawkmoths or hummingbird moths are often mistaken for hummingbirds (more about the hummers later), as they are about the same size and have the same ability to hover before flowers with their wings beating rapidly. They generally are active in the evening and many of the flowers they prefer are white or pastel, powerfully fragrant, and open as the sun goes down.

One of the best, and one I planted all around our outdoor barbecue, is Moonvine, preferably white and deliciously scented. Entertaining with a barbecue is an old western custom, and our friends were always delighted to watch the quick turn with which the moonflowers unfolded (as well as the steaks fragrantly cooking on the grill). Later, as the evening wore on, the hawkmoths enlivened the garden scene.

The many lovely scented evening primroses (*Oenothera* species) are also classic examples of attraction, as is the rugged wolfberry (*Lycium pallidum*).

You have very likely also seen the striped hawkmoth (*Hyles lineata*), which is widespread and is active during the daytime from mid-May through the summer. It has broad white stripes in the forewings and pink buff hind wings. It shows a marked preference for blue flowers, visiting such species as *Iris missouriensis*, bluebells (*Mertensia franciscana* or *M. virginica*), and purple vetch (*Vicia americana*) in the mountains, and periwinkle (*Vinca minor*) and carpet bugle (*Ajuga reptans*) in our gardens. The caterpillars of this moth were considered a delicacy by some Southwest Indians and were eaten on ceremonial occasions.

Yucca

One of the most interesting "character" plants of the West is the yucca. From the small soapweed (*Yucca augustifolia*) to the eerie Joshua tree (*Yucca brevifolia*), they are all excellent landscaping subjects. Their large, lilylike, and very beautiful flowers are visited by a little moth, the yucca moth — their sole pollinator. She lays her eggs in the ovary of the flower where the developing larvae feed on some (but not all) of the seeds. This intricate mutual relationship ensures that both the moth and the plant will complete their life cycles.

Butterfly Breeding Grounds

If you plant flowers that butterflies delight to feed upon, you need not be afraid that your garden will be overrun with caterpillars, because for the most part the flowers on which they feed are not the flowers on which they breed.

But you may also want to provide them with breeding grounds, in your garden or elsewhere. Sometimes our gardens have weed patches that we didn't plan on. If you happen to have a clump of stinging nettles in its midst, you likely have a butterfly breeding ground going there. Many butterfly varieties lay their eggs on these plants, so that when the caterpillars are born they can start munching on their favorite food. Thistles are also great favorites, chosen by mother butterfly. Again, the climatic region and the variety of butterfly will determine which butterflies and which plants you may have.

Garden flowers that butterflies love run heavily to yellow and purple. Thistles are mauve, clover is mauve to purple, goldenrod and dandelions are yellow. In the garden you may translate this to lilacs, marigolds, buddleia bush (also known as the butterfly bush) and wallflowers, alyssum, sweet William, sweet rocket, the beautifully scented phlox flowers, candytuft, and mignonette.

Butterflies prefer the simpler old-fashioned blooms, often strongly perfumed, to the man-perfected hybrids that have been bred away from their normal, natural development. This makes a butterfly-attracting garden far easier to tend because the simpler, old-time flowers are less exacting than a selection of "show" flowers. They can be fun as well, if you want a garden you can relax in and enjoy without spending too much time and energy.

Flowers provide food (nectar) for bees too — and bees are also essential in the natural chain of life. Their defense mechanism may make them somewhat less popular than birds and butterflies, yet they play a necessary role in life on this planet. So if you have a garden, you'll welcome them into it and be glad to see them helping the pollination along. Having been a keeper of bees myself, and shared with them their store of honey, I can say unreservedly that I like and appreciate bees — even if one occasionally loses her way and gets tangled in my hair or defends herself if I chance to step with my bare foot on the clover blossom she's visiting.

Bees have favorite colors and one of them is the blue blossom that appears on borage, the herb used in summer drinks, in salads as a condiment, and in the preparation of pickles. Borage grows well in sunny, dry places, and will resow itself from year to year.

ATTRACTING HUMMINGBIRDS

While we are on the subject of attracting beauty to the garden, let's also consider the hummingbirds. Fifteen different species of tiny, iridescent hummingbirds flash through western gardens (the ruby-throated is the only hummingbird widespread in the East). They are easily attracted by planting bright red flowers, which they home in on from great distances. Like most birds they have excellent color vision (birds are also attracted to cherries and strawberries), but once in your garden they will visit flowers of any color in search of nectar and small insects.

Hummingbird flowers have much in common. They are long and tubular, often borne sideways or drooping rather than upright, and contain abundant nectar. The hummers hover before the flowers and insert their long bills and tongues for the nectar, all the while whirring their wings more than 3,000 times a minute.

Good flower choices for hummingbirds also provide season-long color: red columbine (*Aquilegia elegantual*) and Indian paintbrush (*Castilleja integra*) bloom in the spring, scarlet bugler (*Penstemon barbatus* and other penstemons) and skyrocket (*Ipomopsis aggregata*) in the summer, and hummingbird trumpet (*Zauschneria latifolia*) in the fall. Some species, such as Indian paintbrush, scarlet hedge-nettle (*Stachys coccinea*), and autumn sage (*Salvia greggii*), begin blooming in early spring and are stopped only by fall frosts.

FLOWER WINES

May is also the month when you can begin making flower wines. No one knows who the first winemakers were. We do know that the Egyptians knew how to make wine early in their civilization. Wine had a more practical reason in its beginning than the mere pleasure of drinking. Ancient peoples had little pure water to drink, and they learned that alcohol formed by fermentation protected fruit juice from spoiling. The people who drank this fermented juice did not get sick as often as those who drank the impure water. And this reason for wine drinking continues down to our day. Many peoples, especially in the Latin countries, use wine instead of water for drinking.

In most colonial households

the making of wines and brandies was carried on as a matter of course and no housewife worthy of the name would be found without her blackberry cordial or peach brandy, especially in times of illness.

The first rule of making wine in your home in the United States is to secure a permit. Each fiscal year (July 1–June 30) you must write to the Treasury Department for an Internal Revenue form number 1541 entitled "Registration for Production of Wine for Family Use." The IRS permits a household head to make two hundred gallons of wine each year after the duplicate of Form 1541 has been filled out and returned. Home winemakers must also promise not to sell or make wine in partnership.

In making wine you must also observe scrupulous cleanliness. Although fruits, blossoms, and commercial yeasts cause fermentation, sterile procedures must be followed in order to restrict the growth of yeasts that secrete sour enzymes.

Wine goes through several fermentation periods — with the fruit, after the fruit has been strained from the juice, and in containers or bottles lightly corked.

Rule of thumb for the use of sugar in winemaking is to use two-and-a-half pounds of white sugar per gallon of liquid. You may need to utilize more sugar for tart fruits; pale flower petals need less. Sugar, in part, determines the alcoholic content of the wine. (Two-and-a-half pounds of sugar per gallon

will usually produce 14 percent of alcohol by volume.) But after 16 or 18 percent alcohol by volume has been achieved, alcohol destroys yeasts and stops fermentation. Your wine will be too sweet if you use too much sugar.

A thermometer is an important tool in winemaking — you should keep fermenting temperatures in the 60°–80° F range. Later, when you store your wine, it is best kept at 50° F.

Metal containers react to the acid in wine, so use earthenware, enamel, glass, stone or wooden vessels.

You can clear wines by letting them settle and siphoning off the top wine; or you may crumble an eggshell into the liquid, and then pour through a cloth or coffee filter.

Containers used in wine storage should be well sealed, because air spoils most wines and corks shrink.

Wine may be made from many flowers, berries and edible fruits. Do not use unknown fruits or flower petals, however, as some may be violently poisonous. And be sure that those you use have not been sprayed with insecticides.

Honeysuckle Wine

When the May evening is heavy with the scent of honeysuckle, who could resist its charm? Moreover, in many areas, especially in the south, honeysuckle grows wild so there is often an abundance of blossoms for the taking — another freebie. It also rambles freely around old homesteads, or possibly on your own garden fence, for honeysuckle is a rampant grower.

Start your honeysuckle wine making by picking approximately one gallon of the flowers, and then cover the blossoms with one gallon of boiling water. Simmer for twenty minutes, cool, strain, and discard the blossoms. Then add enough boiling water to the remaining liquid to make one gallon.

Stir in two-and-a-half pounds of sugar, two cups of white raisins, two lemons thinly sliced and one package of yeast that has been dissolved in one cup of water. Bruise two ginger roots (I find these in my local supermarket), each about

an inch long and toss these in.

Cover the mixture and let it ferment for about two weeks, stirring daily. Strain the wine at the end of this time, pour into bottles, and cork lightly. Watch carefully and when the bubbling ceases (in about two months) it is time to seal each bottle with paraffin.

Field Daisy Wine

Daisies are another gift of the month of May and they, too, make a delightful flower wine, topaz to amber in color with a delightful sparkle.

Gather four quarts of field-daisy blossoms (*Chrysanthemum leucanthemum*) and cover with a gallon of boiling water. Let stand for twenty-four hours. Press out the daisies and boil the liquid gently with two thinly sliced lemons, two oranges, and three pounds of brown sugar, for about twenty minutes.

Cool and add one-half box of raisins, a two-inch piece of bruised ginger root, tied in a tiny cheesecloth sack, and one package of softened yeast. (Yeast softens best in a small quantity of warm water.)

Allow fermentation for about two weeks in a covered stone crock. When fermentation ceases, strain and bottle in sterilized jars and cap lightly. In about two months you can bottle permanently, seal and store.

From Marion Harland we have this recipe for **Elderberry Wine:**

8 quarts of berries
4 quarts boiling water, poured over berries

Let stand for 12 hours, stirring now and then. Strain well, pressing out all the juice. Add:

3 pounds of sugar to 4 quarts of juice
1 ounce powdered cinnamon
½ ounce powdered cloves

Boil five minutes, and set away to ferment in a stone jar, with a cloth thrown lightly over it. When fermentation is complete, rack it off (draw it off) carefully, so as not to disturb the lees (sediment or dregs). Bottle and cork down well.

THE DAY LILY

The day lily is a plant of more than ordinary stamina, ease of culture and freedom from disease. It is at home in many types of soil and accommodates itself to many different temperatures, growing equally well in the sands of Florida, the red clay of Alabama, or the loam of Iowa. New England's acid soil merely deepens the color of the flowers compared with those produced in the alkaline soil of Texas. It is happy in the sub-zero temperatures of Canada, the mild climate of California, or the high heat of Arizona. Its seeds are easily raised, and its roots have the tough constitution of horseradish, running under the ground and multiplying readily.

Day lily tubers and blossoms are both edible. The fresh crisp tubers are delicious eaten raw like radishes or chopped into a salad.

It is called a "day lily" because that's what it is! Each lovely blossom's life is limited to one day. Its botanical name, *Hemerocallis*, means the fleeting pleasure of a day, from the Greek *hemera* ("day") and *kallos* ("beauty"). Its trumpet blooms are typical of the lily family.

There are now some day lilies that open and bloom late in the day, and it is well worthwhile to plant these scented beauties for a garden you wish to enjoy in the evening.

Almost every part of the day lily is edible, especially palatable with pork and soy sauce, as you might expect from its Chinese origin. Roots, buds and flowers — there are highly enjoyable recipes for each part of the plant.

Dig up a spadeful of root from a clump and remove the small tubers, somewhat resembling small sweet potatoes, that nestle underneath. If you have raided a garden colony be sure to replant the older

Day Lily Buds

Boil the green buds (no stalks) for a few minutes and serve them with herb butter. To make herb butter add to ½ cupful of creamed butter, ½ tablespoon of finely chopped or minced parsley and 1½ tablespoons of chopped savory. Mix together with a teaspoon of lemon juice and season to taste.

tubers at another site, perhaps on the edge of your vegetable plot where they will thrive and continue to produce more of the little vegetables.

These tiny tubers are sweet to the taste, having a delightful flavor resembling broad beans with a background of whole sweet corn. Moreover, although the blossoms come most freely in late May and early June, the tubers are available throughout the year as long as the ground is not frozen. The buds and flowers are culinary pleasures whether fresh or dried. For any and all of these reasons you may want to make room for the plant as a permanent vegetable tenant, just as you do asparagus and horseradish.

OLD-TIME BEAUTY SECRETS

Back in 1907 a thoughtful older brother gave his young sister a book he knew she would cherish — *The Woman Beautiful*. She did, and in time the book came to me. Specially recommended to make the skin soft, white and supple, when it has become red, dry, rough or tanned from exposure to wind and sun, is this recipe for:

Elder-Flower Cream

3 ounces almond-oil
5 drachms white wax (In the Apothecaries' Weight table, 8 drams equals one ounce)
5 drachms spermaceti (A wax once obtained from the sperm whale, used in toilet creams)
1 ounce lanoline
1 drachm oil of bitter almonds
3 ounces elder-flower water
1 ounce witch hazel

These ingredients were gently mixed together, warmed, and perfumed with a half drachm of violet extract.

The American elder or elderberry (*Sambucus canadensis*) is a large, coarse shrub growing to 12 feet in height, flowering in Oklahoma in late May but farther north in June. These recipes are given here so that you may mark the shrub when it is in flower and know it later when the dark red, nearly black berries are ripe in late August. The plants grow wild in moist places, but if planted in your garden should have a site where drainage is good, as the plants do not grow well where the soil is waterlogged during the growing season.

Grandmother had her beauty secrets, too, and here is one of her best; to prevent wrinkles. Strain barley water through a fine cloth, adding a few drops of oil of balm of Gilead. Place in a bottle and allow to stand for about ten to twelve hours, shaking the bottle from time to time until the balsam is entirely mixed with the water. This mixture will improve the complexion and preserve the appearance of youth. If used each day it removes wrinkles and gives the skin a surprising lustre. Wash the face before using.

I have a number of old beauty books giving recipes for cosmetics for softening the skin, and barley water is mentioned in all of them, for this as well as other uses. It is good inside as well as out and was often given in times past to soothe crotchety infants suffering from stomach disorders. This works well for older people too.

Cologne Water
60 drops oil of lavender **60 drops oil of bergamot** **60 drops oil of lemon** **60 drops orange-flower water** **1 pint of alcohol** Cork and shake well.(See "Sources of Supply" for ingredients.)

Something I've been predicting for a long time; this caught my eye in the March 31, 1986 issue of U.S. *News and World Report:*

INSECTS THAT THWART PESTICIDES

Ever since the development of modern insecticides to control farm-crop predators, bugs have been racing to stay ahead of the chemicals. Now the beetles and budworms appear to be winning.

A study published March 14, 1986 in the journal *Science* confirms that more than 260 insect species "have developed resistance to all major classes of insecticides and will develop resistance to future insecticides as long as present application techniques and use patterns prevail." Genetic mutations from pesticide exposure enable the insects to resist the chemicals. Because many new pesticides contain powerful toxic substances, the study recommends new insect-control methods. These include natural biological and genetic manipulation as well as better crop rotation.

Gemini the Twins      *(May 23 - June 21)*

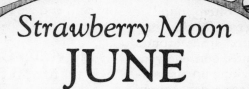

Strawberry Moon
JUNE

Cutting trees and fence posts ★ Hatching chicks by Moon Sign ★ Preserving early vegetables ★ Insects we should appreciate ★ Saving "thoroughbred seed" ★ Preserving "heirloom seed" ★ Seed savers exchange ★ Corn and the pioneers ★ Roses of yesterday ★ Rose recipes ★

UP UNTIL JUNE 21ST the airy, barren, dry, and masculine sign of Gemini rules. This is the best time for pulling weeds, destroying noxious growths, and turning sod, especially during the fourth or last quarter of the moon.

JUNE CHORES

Potatoes should be hilled up under the sign of Gemini (May 23 to June 21), and it is important that this be done before they bloom. Hilling is accomplished by hoeing the dirt up around the base of the plant in order to cover the root as well as to support the plant. Potatoes growing too close to the surface will sunburn, turn green where exposed to the light, and taste bitter. Should this accidentally happen be sure to pare off every bit of the green, as it is somewhat poisonous to the system as well as distasteful.

Potatoes grow best buried in loose soil but avoid working the earth around them while they are blooming — you will likely have very lush, lovely plants but few potatoes.

Zodiac gardeners believe that Cancer (June 21 to July 22) is the most productive sign of all for planting. In southern regions you can still make second or third plantings of many vegetables in June with a good chance of having them mature before really hot, dry weather strikes. Farther north many gardeners are just putting in their main garden.

Cutting Trees and Fence Posts

Early settlers often found it necessary to cut trees around their homes. A cleared space around the cabin prevented unfriendly Indians from sneaking up and surprising the homesteader. Knowing when to cut trees so they would not sprout was therefore a practical necessity, and cutting was generally done under the sign of Gemini.

Most fencing was of wood, barbed wire not having yet come into general use. Cutting in Gemini was believed to keep the posts from either sprouting or rotting. In Oklahoma there are many stands of Osage orange (*Maclura pomifera*), or *bois d'Arc*, often written "bow'd'arc" and called "bowdarc," hedge apple, or mock orange. These were originally planted as fence posts — possibly under the wrong sign, for they sprouted and grew into large trees. They get their common name from the fruit, which is globular, 2 to 5 inches in diameter, and somewhat resembles a rough green orange.

Clever farm ladies slice the fruit, dry it thoroughly, and make dried flowers out of it, often coloring it with vegetable dyes. I have seen these displayed at craft shows and county fairs, and they are beautiful.

Wood from the "bowdarc" is a beautiful deep orange color and the Indians used it for making bows. My husband, who loved archery, once made a bow of Osage orange and I well remember my part of the job, which consisted of steaming each end five hours so that it might be appropriately curved. The bow turned out well and we used it for many years.

Hatching Chicks by Moon Sign

Knowing when to set eggs is an important part of Moon-sign lore. In early days there were no hatcheries as we know them today. Eggs were set under hens and things were done in the natural way. Here is advice from Llewellyn George, author of *Powerful Planets*, and founder of Llewellyn Publications. Eggs should be set on such a date that 21 days later they will be hatched when the moon is *new* and in a "fruitful" sign.

Chicks hatched in new of Moon grow faster and are hardier than those hatched in 'old' of Moon. They come out of their shells all on the same day, are strong and alert.

Chicks hatched in new of Moon and in a 'fruitful' sign will mature rapidly and be good layers, while those hatched in old of Moon and in a 'barren' sign will not show such good results. They straggle out of their eggs on different days, are weak and sluggish compared to those hatched in New Moon.

Chicks hatched when Moon is in Gemini will be restless, active, cluckers and fliers, big eaters, but not good layers. Hatched in Leo or Virgo their productiveness will be only of ordinary degree.

Hatched in new of Moon and in sign of Cancer is best of all, for they will mature quickly, be domesticated, maternal and very productive. Hatched in Scorpio or Pisces (fruitful signs), they will be good layers.

He adds: "Poultrymen who observed these laws of Nature soon had prizewinning stock and sold hatching eggs at highest prices to others who want well bred stock."

How are you going to know when to do or not do all this? The *Llewellyn Moon-Sign Book* (see Reading List) is published annually and gives the appropriate dates for setting eggs for chickens. It also gives the incubation period for eggs of other domestic fowl — turkey, Guinea hen, pea hen, duck, goose, pigeon, and canaries.

American Astrology magazine in its "Farm and Garden" section also gives monthly information on correct time to set chicken, turkey, duck, and goose eggs. This section also carries much valuable information in its "Planting Guide" on what to do when on each day of the month. There is detailed information on flower and vegetable gardens, seeding for hay and lawns, harvesting and pruning, slaughtering animals for food, freezing and canning, making wine and sauerkraut, weaning animals and changing feeds, making preserves, jellies and pickles, soap, paint, laying shingles, and setting fence posts. They make it easy for you to do just about everything under the right sign in all farming and gardening operations. The early settlers and farmers who had

to figure everything out for themselves would have just loved this.

Why paint, for instance, under a dry sign? Because if you do, the paint will dry well and any necessary successive coats go on smoothly and well. Paint applied when the sign is moist will not dry well, may blister and peel, making it necessary in a short time to do the job all over again, with the added chore of scraping to get off the flaky paint.

Grafting is also best accomplished under the sign of Cancer, with Scorpio and Pisces coming in a close second.

June Abundance

Early-planted vegetables of home gardens begin to pay off in June. Now we can enjoy radishes, lettuce, green onions, peas, summer squash, greens, and beans — the abundance sometimes stunning us by the celerity with which it comes about — seemingly almost overnight.

Really efficient, dedicated gardeners endeavor to manage their planting by "staggering." This is done by planting specific vegetables, or replanting them, every few weeks to insure continued fresh produce over a long period of time. A sort of "floating crop game" is played. They also like to practice "catch-cropping," which means that quick-growing crops are sown and harvested before the time when late crops must be planted. Thus you may harvest lettuce and plant late cabbage (for sauerkraut) in the same ground — or plant turnips after the main crop of potatoes has been dug. After potatoes I also like to plant field peas, crowders, black-eyes, and others of the same family. By now the weather has turned really warm, which black-eyes love, but there is still sufficient moisture in the ground to help them to sprout.

Sweet potatoes and peanuts are also excellent for use as catch-croppers, both liking warm weather and growing well.

Preserving Early Vegetables

Preserving vegetables for winter use was very important in the early days before freezers and even before canning jars became widely used. Green string beans were picked when young and tender, placed in a layer about 3 inches deep in a small wooden half barrel or keg. They were then sprinkled with salt an inch deep, and another layer of beans was put in, followed by a layer of salt, alternat-

ing until the keg was full and being sure the top layer was salt. The whole was then covered with a piece of board, cut to fit inside the barrel or keg and a heavy weight placed upon it.

The salt drew out the moisture and made a brine. When the beans were wanted for use they were taken out and soaked in water, the water being changed several times to rinse out the salt. They were then cut and boiled as when fresh.

Carrots, beans, beet roots, parsnips, and potatoes were often covered with dry sand or earth in the cellar, being placed in wooden boxes if they were available. Turnips for later use were kept in the same way, while others were simply placed in a heap on the cellar floor and used first. Turnips sprout easily and the sprouts were cut off and used as salad greens. It was considered important not to wash root crops until ready to use, but instead to leave them covered with the earth that remained about

them when taken from the ground.

Potatoes were carefully watched and any sprouts coming on them were cut or rubbed off. Some farmers believed that a light sprinkling of lime on the potatoes would help to keep them from sprouting and give them a longer storage life.

Celery could be kept all winter by setting it in boxes filled with earth, and keeping it in the cellar where it grew and whitened in the dark. Leeks could also be kept this way.

It was considered best to store onions by stringing them and hanging them in a dry place. When I harvest my onions in late June, I place them on discarded window screens, elevated on bricks, which allows free circulation of air both above and below. I cut off the tops and place them on the screens. I find I am often using the last of these in late January. Many are still firm.

Those that sprout, yellow or

Ant Traps

Ants themselves may not be pests but they are fond of "honeydew" (a sweet fluid secreted by aphids or "greenflies"), and certain species of ants keep these tiny "cows" to milk them — often transferring them from plant to plant. An 1840's gardener heated the fleshy side of a bacon rind and placed it on the ground under a stone. When covered with ants it was plunged into hot water. Boiling water poured down the entrance to an antbed will often be effective. An 1870's ant trap was a flowerpot inverted over the ant hill — when it became well populated it was plunged into boiling water. Sulfur sprinkled on affected plants was also effective, but this should not be applied to garden vine plants such as squash, as it may kill them. Another weapon was a chalk line drawn around a plant — thought to be especially effective for fruit trees espaliered against a house wall. This was reinforced by another broad band of chalkline made on the wall near ground level.

white (red do not do well), are planted in my fall garden. If the fall is not too dry, I often have green onions to put on my Thanksgiving table which are large enough to eat, four to six onions growing out of each bulb I have planted. The rest I leave in the ground all winter, giving me table onions very early in the spring. One year I experimented and left a few in the ground. They grew into fairly large bulbs, repeating the cycle. A good onion never dies — it doesn't even fade away.

★ ★ ★

BENEFICIAL INSECTS

By June a lot of insects are competing with you for the garden produce. But before you start out on a foray of indiscriminate slaughter it's a good idea to know what you are killing. Insects are not all bad — even some of the "bad" ones have good points. Others, like most of the butterflies, do not exist in sufficient numbers to have any great nuisance value — with the notable exception of the imported or white cabbage butterfly.

Pollination is vital — without it, most crops would not mature — and insects are the chief pollinators. (Corn is an exception as it is wind-pollinated. Hummingbirds and other birds help pollination of certain plants, and even bats are known to be helpful.) The pollen usually available in flowering plants provides the protein food required by many insects, particularly bees, and many kinds of bees in particular depend upon it to supply their young with protein, lipids, vitamins, and minerals.

Supplemented with nectar (often converted to honey), pollen is a necessity for bees, and they have evolved many remarkable structural adaptations to help them collect and handle pollen. Plants too have changed in complicated ways to take advantage of the visits of bees and other insects. The reason for this is simple. Like the early colonists, those who adapted survived and produced seed: the rest died.

Here is a rough grouping of insects that show strong attractions to certain types of flowers:

Insects attracted to pollen flowers. Syrphid flies, colorful soldier flies, pollen-feeding beetles, and many pollen-collecting bees are often seen on poppy, rose, potato, elderberry, and similar flowers that provide pollen but no nectar. Moths, butterflies, and hummingbirds, interested only in nectar collection, are not usually attracted to these.

Insects attracted to flowers with exposed nectar. Short-tongued bees, flies, and many kinds of wasps are frequent visitors to the flowers of carrot, maple, saxifrage, euphorbia, poison-oak, and

1 CLAWS
2 STINGER
3 ABDOMEN
4 HIND WING
5 FRONT WING
6 THORAX
7 SIMPLE EYES
8 COMPOUND EYE
9 ANTENNAE
10 FRONT LEG
11 MIDDLE LEG
12 POLLEN BASKET ON HIND LEG

Worker Honey Bee

grapes. The flowers are usually inconspicuous, but it is easy for these insects to obtain the nectar. Years ago I learned the wisdom of picking my black-eyed peas early in the morning. Wasps, which are their pollinators, are less active at that time and there is less danger of getting stung. I have a very healthy respect for wasps.

Insects attracted to flowers with partly concealed nectar. Syrphid flies, short- and long-tongued bees, honeybees, and a few butterflies are attracted to the moderately showy flowers of stone fruits, strawberry, raspberry, cactus, buttercups, and cruciferous plants.

Insects attracted to flowers with concealed nectar. Many sorts of bees, wasps, and butterflies are attracted to the generally conspicuous flowers of currant, blueberry, onion, melon, and citrus. Although the nectar is hidden, there is often a copious amount.

Insects attracted to social flowers. A large variety of both nectar- and pollen-collecting insects, including long- and short-tongued bees, showy butterflies, and colorful beetles, are frequent visitors to the conspicuous composites such as dandelion, sunflower, and aster. The showy "petals" are actually sterile flowers used to attract insects to the many tiny fertile florets of the central disk. The nectar is usually hidden in narrow corolla tubes and the insects usually have to force their tongues past the stigma and stamens to reach the nectar.

Flowers adapted for bees. Only medium- to long-tongued bees can operate the sometimes complex mechanisms protecting the pollen and nectar of legumes, mints, sages, violets, delphinium, iris, etc. These flowers are sometimes visited by butterflies and moths for nectar, but the insects generally do not operate the pollinating mechanism. Some flowers, such as purple clover, have nectar so deep that only bumblebees can reach it. Others have tough mechanisms requiring large powerful bees for pollination. Sometimes bees will bite holes in the flower tubes to "steal" nectar without pollinating.

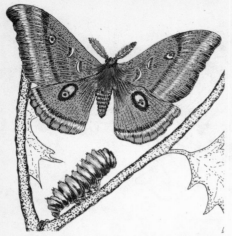

Moths pollinate flowers by night just as butterflies do by day. The cecropia *has a wingspan of up to 6 inches.*

Flowers adapted for butterflies and moths. Large, conspicuous, strongly perfumed flowers with nectar at the base of long narrow corolla tubes or spurs are visited principally by butterflies and moths, although some are also utilized by long-tongued bees and flies. Hummingbirds and honey birds are important pollinators in tropical areas. Examples in this group include honeysuckle, trumpet flowers, tobacco, phlox, and many orchids.

Food Crops That Require Insect Pollination

A partial list of crops known to require or benefit from insect pollination includes almonds, apples, cherries, cranberries, cucumbers, cantaloupes and watermelon, and strawberries. Lima beans, buckwheat, celery seed, mustard, rape, and sunflower are other seeds we consume that result from pollination. A large number of seeds used for propagation require insect pollination also. Some of the more important ones are alfalfa, asparagus, cabbage, broccoli, cauliflower, carrot, clover, onion, radish, rutabaga, and turnip.

In your own garden, visits by honeybees and other bees to your fruit trees, holly trees, pyracantha shrubs, cucumber, muskmelon, watermelon, squash, blackberry, raspberry, and strawberry patches are to be greatly encouraged.

There are other "good" insects in your garden such as ladybugs, useful against aphids, and praying mantis — considered so helpful in eradicating aphids, leafhoppers, chinch bugs, crickets, locusts, beetles, flies, and tent caterpillars that their egg cases are often bought by gardeners to be placed here and there in their gardens, to hatch out in the spring and go to work.

I would even say a good word for garden spiders, especially those large, beautiful, golden ones that spin their webs on my okra plants in the fall. I always leave them there for they catch grasshoppers, as do other garden spiders working on the ground and around my compost heap. I always practice mental communication, saying to the spider, "If you leave me alone, I'll leave you alone." We seem to arrive at mutual respect, each keeping our distance, and I've never had any problems.

In my two previous books, *Carrots Love Tomatoes — Secrets of Companion Planting with Vegetables* and *Roses Love Garlic*, on companion planting with flowers, I've gone thoroughly into the subject of insect pests, so I will not repeat that information here.

SAVING "THOROUGHBRED" SEEDS

What I think might now be of interest to you is the end-result of all that pollination — *seeds*. Aside from those seeds we eat, there are those that must be replanted the following year.

While I strongly advocate buying proven and tested seeds and high-producing hybrids, there are some occasions when it is important to save seeds from your own plants.

Years ago, Llewellyn George suggested that he and I try to put together our bits of knowledge of moon-planting and give some idea of what would happen if several lunar factors were combined in one plant. From this came his rule for developing "Thoroughbred Seed":

"To do this seed is saved for three consecutive years from plants grown by the correct moon sign and phase to breed into the plant the desired characteristics.

You can plant in the First Quarter phase and in the sign of Cancer for fruitfulness; the second year plant seeds from the first-year plants in Libra for beauty; and in the third year plant the seeds from the second year plants in Taurus to produce hardiness.

In a similar manner you can combine the fruitfulness of Cancer, the good root growth of Pisces, and the sturdiness and good vine growth of Scorpio. And don't forget the characteristics of Capricorn, hardy like Taurus, but 'drier' and perhaps more resistant to drought and disease."

If you want to experiment, this idea can be adapted to many vegetables, flowers, and even shrubs and trees.

Virtues of Old Varieties

There are other reasons for wanting to save seeds. A book, *The Heirloom Gardener*, by Carolyn Jabs, published by Sierra Club Books, says to the home gardener, "You too can become a seed saver, to halt the tide of disappearance." We are discovering too that many of the old-time seeds had a lot of vim, vigor, and vitality, and being closer to their wild cousins they also had insect and disease resistance that some modern varieties lack. I mentioned to you that single flowers, generally speaking, were easier to grow and often more fragrant than the newer double varieties. The same thing may be true of vegetables in some cases.

The home gardener is given a great challenge, also, to take part in finding and saving seeds of varieties that may be on the verge of extinction. The names of some of these are enough to make gardeners perk up and take notice. "Garnet Chili potatoes, Mortgage Lifter tomatoes, Early Tennis Ball lettuce, Black Afghan carrots, Bloody Butcher corn, Lemon Cucumbers." Miss Jabs even mentions a melon called the Alma Glen, which was "so delicious that it brought prosperity to the entire town of Alma, Illinois."

The Seed Savers Exchange

A very active role in the conservation and preservation effort is being played by the Seed Savers Exchange, 203 Rural Avenue, Decorah, Iowa 52101, a nonprofit citizen's group of vegetable gardeners. In its brochure, the Exchange says,

> We are particularly interested in contacting other gardeners who are also keeping seed of vegetable varieties that are: family heirlooms; not available commercially; traditional Indian crops; garden varieties of the Mennonites and Amish; outstanding foreign varieties; mutations, extremely disease or insect- or drought-resistant; very hardy; rare or unusual or unique; of exceptional quality.

Kent Whealy, director of the Exchange, has written a book, *The Garden Seed Inventory*, listing all non-hybrid vegetable and garden seeds still available in the U.S. and Canada. Among these is one with the interesting name Moon & Stars Watermelon. This was nearly extinct but its seeds are now available through Exchange members.

The general rule for saving seeds of, say, a certain type of squash is to grow only one variety, or to grow it in an isolated place so it cannot crosspollinate. Even so, your neighbor down the road may also be growing squash of a different variety and the bees will visit both plants. As soon as seeds are ripe they should be gathered, and those kinds not harmed by drying should be spread out on papers to dry in a well-ventilated room. In the case of soft-berried fruits, the seeds are first squeezed out of the pulp, the larger seeds being rubbed in a handful of sand before spreading them out to dry. When they are quite dry, the seeds are packed and stored in a dry, cool, frostproof place.

Plants of the Southwest (1812 Second St., Santa Fe, NM 87501) has this to say in their catalog:

> Learning how and when to collect seed is mostly a matter of careful observation. Annuals which can be up from seed and flowering in six weeks set seed very rapidly. A month or so after bloom you should be watching. Perennials will usually not bloom the first year, but from the second year on your efforts will be rewarded.
>
> If you want to keep seed such as vegetable seed for next spring or wildflower seed to send your grandma for a Christmas gift, don't keep it in plastic. The seed might be moist, and mold can destroy it. Seed in our dry Southwest should be stored in paper bags through which air can pass. If you live in a damp climate it is best to keep seed, once thoroughly dried, in a tight moisture proof jar.

All this is good advice. I have also been successful in keeping seed over a fairly long period of time in my refrigerator. Remember to collect only a small proportion of the seeds produced by a wild plant, so as not to threaten its survival.

★ ★ ★

CORN AND THE PIONEERS

We have seen how corn saved the early colonists; it was also to play a large part in settling the West. Most of the corn the Indians were growing was like our field corn today — intended to mature on the stalk and then gathered when dry, for winter storage. Sweet corn, for eating fresh, was also grown by Indians, but few colonial gardeners knew sweet corn until about the time of the Revolutionary War, and it took another fifty years or more for it to start becoming somewhat familiar in household gardens. By the 1880's, seedsmen were offering up to about 20 varieties, calling it "sweet," "sugar," or "table" corn, and popcorn also appeared in their listings. At this time, white corn was outnumbering yellow by five to one. (Today, in a typical listing, yellow sweet corn will outnumber white by two to one or more.)

Many early pioneers took a supply of corn meal and at least one cow when they traveled to their new homes on the frontier. Wild game and wild berries added to their food supply, and they could get along.

But corn, however, was their main food. Corn meal was used in some form for every meal, as mush, pone, johnnycake, hoecake, or corn bread. It was the way these were cooked that distinguished them from each other. Generally speaking, the only one of these dishes that contained anything besides corn meal, salt, and water was corn pone, which had small pieces of sliced bacon in it and was baked in the hot ashes of the fireplace. Hoecake was cooked on a hot griddle. When it was baked on a smooth board before the fire it was called *johnnycake* — a word some believe to be a corruption of "journey cake."

Johnny Cake

1 teacup sweet milk	1 teaspoon soda
1 teacup buttermilk	1 tablespoon melted butter
1 teaspoon salt	white corn meal (use as needed)

Mix ingredients, using enough meal to enable you to roll it into a sheet ½ inch thick. Spread on a buttered tin or in a shallow pan, and bake forty minutes. As soon as it begins to brown, baste it with melted butter five or six times until it is brown and crisp. Break, do not cut up, and eat for luncheon or tea, accompanied by sweet or buttermilk.

NATIVE AMERICAN CUISINE

Despite primitive conditions and few cooking utensils, Indian women were scrupulously clean in their cookery. Back in 1977, I did a great deal of research for an Indian cookbook I was writing at the time and became friends with Mrs. Neoma Rainwater (Choctaw-Chickasaw). In 1976 Mrs. Rainwater, retired dietician at the Carter Seminary for Indians, was chosen "Woman of the Year," by the Ohoyohoma Society of Indian Women. Mrs. Rainwater gave me a number of Indian recipes that she had updated to reflect modern cookery methods.

When the pioneers came into Indian Territory (the future state of Oklahoma) they brought with them huge iron wash kettles. The Indians were not long in seeing their virtues as cookpots. They were particularly useful at the Indian gathering known as "Pashofa," and the food cooked in them was also called *pashofa*. A huge quantity was made, but here is a "meal-sized" version worked out by Mrs. Rainwater:

Pashofa

1 pound cracked corn (White cracked corn can be bought at many grocery stores)

2 quarts water (add more as needed)
1 pound fresh lean pork (meaty backbone)

Wash and clean corn. Bring water to boil and add corn. Cook slowly, stirring often. When corn is about half done, add fresh pork. Cook until both meat and corn are soft and tender. The mixture should be thick and soupy. Cook about 4 hours. Add *no* salt while cooking. It is the Indian custom for each individual to season this food according to his own taste. If back bone is not available, use fresh pork, such as pork chops, chopped small.

Shuck Bread (Bahnaha)

This is the favorite recipe of C. David Gardner, Principal Chief, Choctaw Nation of Oklahoma.

4–6 cups corn meal
3–3½ cups boiling water

1 teaspoon soda
1 teaspoon salt

Add just enough boiling water to meal mixed with soda and salt to make a stiff dough. Roll dough into corn shucks, folding to hold, and drop into rapidly boiling water and boil for 10 minutes. For easier handling, soak shucks in warm water to soften and make pliable.

JUNE FORAGING

Blue Elderberry (*Sambucus Mexicana*). The Indians call it "the tree of music," as they make flutes from the branches that are cut in the spring and then dried with the leaves on. When thoroughly dry, they would bore holes in the branches with a hot stick. The long shoots were used for arrow shafts.

The berries were used in several ways — as a drink and also dried and stored for winter. The flowers were used fresh, externally in a decoction for an antiseptic wash for skin diseases, and taken internally to check bleeding of the lungs. The inner bark yields a strong emetic. This plant is found from California to western Canada.

Blue Curls (*Trichostema* — Mint family). Sometimes called "vinegar-weed." The wooly blue curls, T. *lanatum*, is a shrub, but most other species of this genus are herbs. It has blue or purple flowers (rarely white) and hairy leaves. The name vinegar weed comes from the penetrating and acrid odor of the foliage of all species.

Indians made a decoction of leaves and flowers for colds, ague, and general debility; a bath of this decoction was taken against smallpox; leaves were chewed and put in the cavity of an aching tooth. It is a major honey plant.

One of its greatest uses, however, was to stupefy fish. In the early days there were no laws concerning fish and game; you took what you needed to survive any way you could get it. But fish and animals were killed for food — not for sport or just the "fun" of killing something.

Another plant used to stupefy fish was Turkey-Mullein (*Eremocarpus setigerus*). The leaves contain a narcotic poison, the foliage being used by the Indians to stupefy fish and also to poison their arrow points. Yet the plant — like foxglove, also poisonous — had its good side. A poultice relieved internal chest pains and a decoction of leaves in warm water helped asthma and fevers.

Wild Lettuce (*Lactuca*). Sometimes called Prickly Lettuce, the tender shoots are edible but seldom eaten uncooked. They are best steamed (or pressure cooked) or included in vegetable soups. It is believed that our cultivated lettuce is derived from this wild species.

Nasturtium (*Trapaeolum majus*). Nasturtium is sometimes called Indian Cress. This plant is now most often cultivated in gardens. Both the leaves and the seeds are used. Leaves and flower petals mixed with other greens add a spicy taste to salads and sandwiches.

Here is an old recipe using nasturtium seed.

Take the green seed after the flower has dried off. Lay in salt and water two days, in cold water one day; pack in bottles and cover with scalding vinegar, seasoned with mace and white peppercorns.

Sweeten slightly with white sugar. Cork and set away 4 weeks before you use them. They are an excellent substitute for capers.

How much white sugar, the recipe does not say. So many of the recipes given in old cookbooks had a fine disregard for amounts to be used. Since most cookstoves were fueled by wood, no temperatures could be very well given. Cooks just did their cooking "by guess and by gosh," using experience and studying how their particular stove functioned. Most of them got pretty good at it.

Greens for the Taking

Pigweed (*Amaranthus blitum*). June sees an abundance of amaranth — now widely acclaimed for its high nutrition and health-giving qualities. Both the young leaves and the seeds are eaten. The leaves may be served uncooked in salads or cooked as pot herb spinach. Young leaves of amaranth are vitamin packed, comparing favorably with carrots or beets, and are delicious eaten uncooked as salad greens. Cook as you would spinach, serving either with butter or with oil and vinegar.

As an additional food source the Indians used the shiny black seeds, sometimes parching them and grinding them into meal which was either baked into cakes or included in porridge.

Burdock (*Arctium Lappa*). The first year burdock produces a rosette of large, ground-hugging, dull green leaves. The roots of the first year's growth, collected in spring, are a good source of food. The stems of the first year's growth with their "elephant-ear" leaves are collected in late June. They may be prepared by steaming in the same way as asparagus, in as little water as possible. Serve with butter and seasonings or with herb vinegar or lemon juice.

Chicory (*Cichorium intybus*). Chicory is sometimes called wild endive and both the early leaves and the roots are used, the leaves in early spring and the roots in summer.

The leaves may be eaten uncooked in a salad, using as seasoning a little vegetable oil and herb vinegar, or they may be steamed or made into a soup. The early spring roots were sometimes cooked and eaten as a warm vegetable or cut up and cooked in a soup or stew.

Chicory root, which has no caffeine, has made coffee (New Orleans style) famous. See "July."

---

*The scent of fresh basil (*Ocimum basilicum*) will promote sympathy between two people.*

---

*The leaves of orange bergamot (*Mentha citrata*) slipped into the wallet will attract money.*

ROSES OF YESTERDAY

What would June be without roses? I simply cannot imagine it without these lovely and useful flowers. The New World had the wild rose (Rosa californica), but it was a somewhat scraggly bush, about 3 to 6 feet high. Growing along stream and river banks it had pretty, light pink flowers and bright red hips (fruit). Father Font of the Anza expedition (1746) speaks of gathering and eating them right from the bush. Of course it was not known until much later that the hips are especially rich in vitamins A and C — even richer than oranges.

The Indians seem to have learned about its good qualities by experimenting down through the centuries. They made a tea from the tender root shoots for colds; seeds were cooked for muscular pains (vitamin C is especially good for such pains); leaves and hips steeped and drunk for pains and colics. The old straight wood was used for arrow shafts. Spanish Californians made jelly from the ripe fruit and ate hips, softened by the first frost, raw from the bush. The leaves and petals were astringent and used in perfume. Petals, peppermint, lemon peels, and linden leaves were made into a tea for arthritis or dyspepsia; the petals were also believed to dissolve gallstones.

According to Peter Beales, author of Classic Roses, a gorgeously illustrated book published by Holt, Rinehart, and Winston, there were other native species on the American continent as well. These included the clear pink R. virginiana, a tidy plant with attractive, light but rich green foliage. Like most of the American species it flowered slightly later than those the early colonists brought from Europe. There was also R. palustris (swamp rose), R. setigera (prairie rose), and R. carolina (pasture rose), with small, clear pink petals.

From the more temperate parts of the American continent might have come two relatively thornless, pink species, the large-flowered R. blanda and the smaller-flowered but equally interesting R. foliolosa, with its unusual, grass-like foliage.

Wilhelm Miller, a landscape architect from Chicago, wrote in the American Rose Annual in 1917:

"About ninety per cent of the commonest landscape problems can be solved with the aid of nine

Are Mealy Bugs Mealing Up Your Roses?

Spray them with a "hellebore" solution, being sure that you use white, or false, hellebore, not really hellebore at all but derived from the Veratrum plant. True hellebore, a constituent of the Christmas rose, is toxic. Small caterpillars on roses were also attacked by sprinkling the plants with soot, sometimes mixed with white hellebore.

species of wild roses." Six of these were the American species already mentioned; the other three were R. *rugosa*, R. *multiflora* and R. *wichuraiana*, all from Asia. Perhaps not "all" can be solved — but at least the landscape can be made more interesting.

> Roses do best if planted in the first or second quarter under Cancer.

Rose Companions

Colonial ladies had their rose gardens as well as their gardens for vegetables and herbs. In the old days these were mostly kept separate — now we know that mixing them up is helpful in keeping down insect populations and in controlling disease. There's nothing better for roses than having garlic or onions planted around them, a fact known and practiced for centuries by the rose growers in the famous Kazanlik Valley in Bulgaria, whose principal product is Attar of roses, still the most valuable essence known. Garlic does not change the odor of the rose, but enhances and strengthens it. Chives, shallots, and ornamental alliums may also be planted with roses with good effect.

Tomatoes are also good planted with roses, and a spray made from tomato leaves is helpful in overcoming black spot. Parsley is helpful against rose beetles; onions repel rose chafers; mignonette as a ground cover helps preserve moisture; lupines increase soil nitrogen

and attract earthworms; marigolds control nematodes, and geraniums or milky spore disease repel Japanese beetle. An infusion of elderberry leaves in lukewarm water is believed to control caterpillar damage and is also recommended for blight.

"Old Roses are for Loving"

Would you like to grow some of the really beautiful, fragrant, and useful old-time roses that graced colonial gardens and were the pride and joy of the "lady of the house?" You can — Roses of Yesterday and Today (802 Brown's Valley Road, Watsonville, CA 95076), has practically all of them and they are described in their attractive catalog, "Roses of Yesterday and Today." Will Tillotson, founder of the company, once said, "The new roses are for admiring, the old ones for loving." This is still true and always will be, but the old roses have other qualities, too. They are not only for loving, but they are also beautiful and durable and mingle perfectly with newer varieties. They have practical as well as sentimental value, for many are completely hardy where winters are severe and summers hot; they are excellent for all sorts of landscaping effects. All the roses in Tillotson's catalog will thrive almost everywhere in the United States — and many of the hardier ones with care will thrive in Canada. The huge climbers need little care after they are well established, except to cut out canes every couple of years. Others, while needing a bit more care than the climbers, will still thrive and do well with less care than hybrid teas and other modern roses.

Let's begin with that lovely old rose, American Beauty, a hybrid perpetual introduced in 1875 and still popular. Growing 4 to 5 feet tall, it flowers repeatedly. This large, full-bodied and heavily perfumed rose was the darling of the Gay Nineties, and typifies the era when Lillian Russell reigned in the theater and Diamond Jim Brady dined and wined her extravagantly. For those too young to remember, the flowers are a live rose, shaded smoky carmine, so distinct a color that this shade of rose has long been popularly called "American Beauty." There is even a lovely lipstick, carried by the cosmetic company, Anita of Denmark, in a shade called "American Beauty Red." I put some on this morning!

In 1909, Climbing American Beauty was introduced and it has all the good qualities of the original, but will grow 12 to 14 feet — a well-established plant providing an almost unbelievable number of blooms.

Other Great Old Roses

Austrian Copper (R. *foetida* bicolor), was first introduced to the rose world in 1590 and has just one annual flowering. It is an early bloomer and the most brilliantly colored of all roses — the one-inch single blossoms, orange on upper side of petals, yellow on reverse, literally cover the plant. It is very hardy, growing in Illinois, Wisconsin, and Minnesota without winter protection.

Mildew

Home remedies for mildew possibly recognize mineral deficiencies of plants. Some people have thrown a handful of rusty iron nails around the roots of roses and claim that the practice has kept the plants healthy and free of insects and mildew. My own father-in-law was once gifted with a beautiful, healthy wisteria plant. In its new location the blossoms were snow white, resembling white lace. Wanting to restore it to its original color my father-in-law dug a lot of rusty iron nails into the soil about its roots and in time the plant resumed its normal purple color again.

It is sensible to stay out of the garden when it is wet. At such times plants are tender and bruise or break more readily, making them vulnerable to mildew and rot. Certain fungi and bacteria that produce plant diseases thrive on moisture and move from leaf to leaf during rainy periods.

Diatomaceous earth, which originates from ancient deposits of many tiny marine creatures, is a valuable source of minerals and trace elements. It can be mixed with water and sprayed on both sides of leaves of roses, citrus plants and others against aphids, red spiders and on tomatoes to combat mildew.

The apple rose (Rosa pomifera) *is a handsome shrub which, being tolerant of almost any soil, can be grown in any garden. It likes a sunny place, not too exposed, and not too near trees or shrubs that will rob it of nourishment. The large fruits are a rich source of Vitamin C and useful for making wine or rose hip syrup.*

Marechal Niel — *Noisette* (1864) grows 8–10 feet and flowers repeatedly. This is one of the great roses of all time. The perfectly formed buds of unfading pale yellow open to show the beauty of the double, pendant flowers. The unforgettable fragrance is described as a blend of orris root and English violets, the true old tea-rose odor. It is somewhat tender and temperamental, however, and likes warmth.

Musk Rose. This rose is so ancient no one really knows when it was first planted in gardens, but it is still a delight, blooming annu-ally in a great mass with an unforgettable mysterious fragrance. For those who would grow old roses the scented single white flowers are priceless.

Rosa damascena trigintipetala. Introduced sometime prior to 1850, this rose is also known as Kazanlik, for it is grown extensively in the Kazanlik Valley, Bulgaria, to make attar of roses. It takes approximately 1,200,000 blossoms to distill 2¼ pounds of the essence. Semi-double, rose red, 3½-inch flowers with stiff yellow stamens, the petals are wonderful to dry for potpourri.

Oil of Roses

Another centuries old oil treatment for the skin is oil of roses, made by steeping rose petals in a bland oil (mineral oil is fine). An old recipe directs: "Place a sufficient quantity of rose petals in a crock, cover with water and put in a warm place. As the oil rises to the surface collect it on a piece of dry cotton wool and then squeeze into a bottle." Actually this is attar of roses, the most rare and costly fragrance in the world. Another collecting method is to chill the water, congealing the oil so that it can be picked up like bits of butter.

Wearing a wreath of amaranth (Amaranthus hypochondriacus) *confers invisibility.*

Rose Recipes

Potpourri

For the beginner, this is a basic and simple recipe that gives the general idea of how potpourri works.

2 parts (2 cups) dried rose
  petals
1 part scented geranium
  leaves

1 part sweet basil
a few cloves (7 or 8 for 2
  cups of rose petals)
1 nutmeg grated

The petals and leaves should all be dried before they are mixed together. This mixture can also be reduced to a powdered state by crushing the leaves. Since one of the ingredients is in powdered form anyway, use silk or close-woven fabric if you wish to bag the potpourri. Otherwise, keep it in an open, wide-necked container.

Red Roses Conserve

Let your roses be gathered before they are quite blown, pound them in a stone mortar, and add to them twice their weight in double-refined sugar and put them into a glass close stopt up but do not fill it full. Let them stand three months before you use them, remembering to stir them once a day. John Nott, cook to the Duke of Bolton, *The Receipt Book of John Nott,* 1723.

Drying Rose Petals

To dry rose petals, lay them on tissue paper or wire screening, placing them in an airy room but keeping them away from sunlight. Depending on variety and moisture content drying will take several days. Spread them thinly, and when dry mix them with cloves using just a few so their fragrance will not overpower that of the rose petals.

Simple Rose Water

1 teaspoon rose extract   12 tablespoons distilled water

Measure the liquids carefully. Use only distilled water as ordinary tap water may have a chemical taste. Mix both liquids thoroughly and pour into a sterilized bottle with a cork or screw top. Store in a cool, dark place.

Rose Wine

Growing on my garden fence I have a rose called Seven Sisters, which I rescued from an old homestead. When I found it one one of my own rambles it was rambling all over the stones of the broken chimney. It has just one blooming in the spring — but what a blooming! The delicately beautiful small pink buds are grouped in clusters all over the climbing plant and provide me with sufficient numbers of petals to make rose wine.

Pour one gallon of boiling water over 3 or 4 quarts of lightly packed rose petals, add the cut-up rind of 2 oranges and 3 pounds of sugar. Boil for 20 minutes; cool, strain, and add a package of yeast dissolved in warm water and the juice from the oranges and 4 or 5 peppercorns (white). Let all ferment in a covered crock for about 2 weeks. Strain, discard petals, and bottle in sterilized jars, corking lightly for about 3 months or until the wine has finished working. Seal each bottle with paraffin.

For those of us today who find it so easy to run down to the corner drugstore for cosmetics and medicines, these formulas seem almost too time-consuming to bother making. But centuries ago every house of any importance had a "stillroom" where the mistress mixed formulas, often carefully copied by hand and handed down from generation to generation, for beauty preparations, herbal teas, medicines and even cleaning products for the household.

Cancer the Crab   *(June 22 - July 22)*

Thunder Moon
JULY

Moon changes ★ Plant late vegetables ★ Indian
customs ★ Beekeeping ★ French and Spanish culture
★ Chicory ★ Pralines ★ Growing peanuts ★
Medicinal herbs for pets ★ Feeding farm helpers ★
Gooseberry Fool ★ Berries ★ Insects sing in July ★

THE MOON'S CHANGES — that is, the time of the coming of the New Moon, first quarter, Full Moon and last quarter — are all significant points in predicting the weather — and, of course, have much influence on all gardening operations, moon-sign followers believe.

This is refined even a bit further by those who have studied this believing that the nearer the Moon's change is to midnight the fairer the weather will be for the following seven days. Vice versa, the nearer the Moon's change is to noontime the more stormy the weather will be for the same period of time.

The equinox is the time of year when the center of the Sun is directly over the equator. The word equinox means "equal night." The word "equidies," or equal day would have been just as fitting, because during an equinox the days are the same length as the nights all over the world.

The Sun crosses the equator twice a year, and so there are two equinoxes. The spring, or *vernal*, equinox occurs around March 21, as the sun moves north. The autumn, or *autumnal*, equinox comes around September 23, as the sun moves south.

Storms that arise during an equinox are sometimes called equinoctial gales. During this period the Sun is traveling north or south faster than at any other time of the year. In a week it moves over 2½ degrees, or half the distance between the two pointers in the Big

MOON CHANGES

IF THE MOON'S CHANGE OCCURS BETWEEN:	THE WEATHER WILL BE:
Midnight and 2:00 A.M.	Fair
2:00 A.M. and 4:00 A.M.	Cool and stormy
4:00 A.M. and 8:00 A.M.	Wet
8:00 A.M. and 12:00 Noon	Changeable
12:00 Noon and 2:00 P.M.	Rainy and blustery
2:00 P.M. and 4:00 P.M.	Mild and showery
4:00 P.M. and 8:00 P.M.	Windy but fair
8:00 P.M. and 10:00 P.M.	Clear but colder
10:00 P.M. and Midnight	Fair

Dipper. This change in the Sun's position produces such variations in the pattern of warm and cold air masses that violent storms often result.

The time from the end of the vernal equinox to the beginning of the autumnal equinox is longer than the interval between the autumnal equinox and the following vernal equinox. This difference amounts to seven days each year, or six days in leap years. It is caused by the elliptical shape of the earth's path around the sun. The earth moves faster when it is nearer the Sun. Around January 1, the earth is nearest the Sun, and about July 1, it is farthest away.

Some old-timers believe that if the Full Moon and the equinox meet, violent storms will follow, and spring weather will be unusually dry.

🌱 🌱 🌱

PLANT LATE VEGETABLES

Cancer, the fruitful, watery zodiac sign, extends from June 21 to July 22. Cancer is one of the best planting signs, and plants seeded under this sign will breed true and even. They will sprout and mature quickly, and most likely the fruit will be juicy, succulent, and delicious. Because of this, however, they will store poorly. Use and enjoy them as they ripen. If you have an over-abundance, trade, sell, or give them away.

The fiery, dry, barren, and masculine sign of Leo takes over from July 22 to August 23. Do no planting during the last week of July — but this is a good time to get out your "grubbin' hoe," get the weeds out of the garden, and thin the late crops of root vegetables — beets, parsnips, turnips, and rutabagas.

In my southern zone onion tops have fallen over long ago but in more northern areas they may be just beginning to fall. To prevent neck rot, break the onion stalks so they lie level to the ground and harvest them in the old of the Moon. The auspicious time is during the third and fourth quarters under Leo — if possible, a week or so after they are broken. In mild climates they can be left on the top of the ground fully exposed to the sun for a few days to dry completely. If you live in a hot climate it is best to put them in filtered shade. Take them up if wet weather threatens.

Give your tomato, pepper, and onion plants an extra boost by heaping compost around them. This will keep their roots cool and moist and help them endure the heat of the sun and produce longer. Tomatoes need not be exposed to the sun to ripen well — like grapes, it is the sun on their leaves that causes the fruit to ripen. Indeed, if exposed to too hot a sun they may turn white from sunscald on the exposed side.

July is the time when you will probably have more squash than you know what to do with. Though pumpkins and squashes originated in tropical America their usage spread widely and they became basic foods of the North American Indians, ranking next to corn. Possibly because of their abundance, they were also a valuable trade commodity.

≫→   ≫→   ≫→

Indian Ways

The Indians prepared squash by baking it whole in the ashes of their fire pits. They ate it all, including seeds and shells. Sometimes it was simmered into a subtly sweet stew, flavored with squash blossoms. These lovely blooms are still considered a gourmet dish, particularly if prepared by the Zuni who select only the largest male flowers to fry, serving them as an appetizer at the beginning of a meal or to season stews or soups.

It has been traditional with the Cherokees since time immemorial to plant squash, beans, and corn together, because of a legend that they were the Three Sisters. This practice is still continued. We now know that the protein of squash, beans, and corn, though individually incomplete, is equivalent to that in beef when the three are eaten together.

I have known and loved the Indian people all my life, spending my school days in the Convent of St. Agnes. This convent, built in the days of Indian Territory, educated the daughters of chiefs and important tribal members.

The Indian way of life, particularly among the hunting tribes, was often a matter of feast and famine. Indigestion was often prevalent and many, various herbal treatments were described in books of Indian medicine. It is well to remember that behind the window dressing of gestures, dances, and incantations, the medicine man often had a vast storehouse of real knowledge about curative plants.

The purpose of rain dancing is not to have "instant" results, but to have sufficient rain during the entire growing season. The shamans set the date of the dance by astrological calculation.

The early Indians gave great feasts. Few among us understand or properly appreciate their tremendous generosity, their desire to share, which was not forced upon them but given willingly. Among the Northwest Coast Indians these feasts were called "potlatches,"; among the Plains tribes they are often called "pashofas."

At a recent Thanksgiving *pashofa* held at the ranch home of Buster Ned in the Yellow Hills of Southern Oklahoma, a story was told of another feast held some fifty years ago. The time was in the 1930's Depression days, when the government was trying to get rid of surplus cattle to aid the bankrupt farmers.

"A cow was given to each Indian family," Buster recounted. "My father killed his government cow and called in the area Indians for a big stomp dance and feast. They visited and danced and played stick ball but in a couple of days the beef ran out and the people began to leave.

"Another Indian said, 'Don't go home. I have a government cow at my house.' He got the cow and they butchered it and the festivities went on. When this beef was gone another Indian brought in his government cow and this went on until the stomp dance and feasting lasted two whole weeks."

Great stamina those old-time Indians had!

★ ★ ★

Moon-Planting

Some farmers believe that the last planting of corn should be made in early July. Planted at that time, the ears of corn will reach outward from the stalk and try to grab the New Moon, in this way being more easily fertilized by falling or blowing pollen. If corn is planted during the second quarter of the Moon, the ears are said to hang close to the stalk in fear of the larger Moon; thus the corn silk will not catch the pollen and fewer grains will mature.

Never plant corn and tomatoes close together; the corn earworm and the tomato worm are the same pest. When the silks start to turn brown it is time to put a few drops of mineral oil on them to keep out the earworm. If this is done too early, however, it may prevent fertilization and the ears will not fill out well.

Cucumbers should also be scheduled for early July, during the first quarter, as they may not

mature in some areas if planted later. Fertilization of cucumber flowers by insects is thought to be affected by the Moon. When the Moon is a new sliver, the bugs rest at night and fly by day. With the waxing moon the nights grow brighter and the winged pollinators are so worn out with nighttime reveling they no longer visit the cucumbers by day. This means it's best to plant so that the cucumbers will flower during the New Moon.

Cucumbers bloom about four weeks after planting; so, if planted early in the first quarter of the Moon, they will bloom during the following month when insects are starting their daytime visits again.

Remember that cucumbers, like squash, put on male flowers first. The female flowers come later on the same plant, and in a short time you can usually see a little knob back of the blossom if they have been fertilized. This is the blossom that will bear the cucumber.

New Potatoes

July's garden produces many food treasures, among them little new potatoes. My husband used to gather up bags of leaves in the fall and heap them up in a long row on one side of the garden. In the spring we would make a hole in the leaves, dig a few inches into the earth below and put in a bit of sprouting potato, just barely covering it. The potatoes would come up through the leaves, which were thick enough to cover them and keep them from turning green. Most of the potatoes grew in the leaves with their roots in the soil, and when we harvested them they were huge and so clean they did not need washing.

We simply could not resist robbing some of the plants early for we had a taste for the little new potatoes, boiled in their baby skins, drained, salted, peppered, and gently mounded on a plate, drizzled with butter and topped with a big plop of sour cream. Fit for a king!

BEEKEEPING

The history of beekeeping goes back thousands of years. The people of the Stone Age, who ate honey that they stole from wild bees, learned to make crude hives, so the honey would be near their homes. They probably made the first beehives out of hollow logs with sticks inside to support the honeycombs. Later, farmers in Europe built straw "skeps" that looked like baskets turned upside down.

Colonists probably took honeybees with them from England to Virginia in 1622. Swarms of them escaped from their hives and built new nests in the woods. The settlers also took beehives with them as they moved westward.

Most beekeepers now provide standard hives for their bees. The hives are made up of several removable drawerlike "supers," or sections. Inside the supers the bees build their honeycomb on movable frames that hang ⅜ inch apart. Bees can pass through this "bee space" to all parts of the hive, and the beekeeper can move the frames about. Each super holds 10 combs, and each comb contains about 6,600 cells.

Hiving a Swarm

My husband had kept bees as a boy, and when we married he already had the equipment. After we had settled a while in our new home we decided we would like to keep bees. So we got everything unpacked and one spring we set up the hives. One day when I went out to the garden about noontime I noticed that a swarm of bees had settled on a young fruit tree. This is something that often happens as they seem to like small trees as a landing place.

I was terribly excited — here was a swarm for free. I went in the house and put on the veil and gloves (several sizes too large), grabbed up an extra super and bravely went out to hive my swarm. I was not afraid. When bees swarm they are "drunk" on honey and relatively docile and I had already recognized them as "three-banded Italians" — gentle bees, if bees can ever be called gentle.

Following the directions in the book I shook the tree gently. They obligingly fell down into the super I had placed beneath them. I could barely wait for my husband to come home, but alas, "pride goeth before a fall." By the time I got back to the garden the hive was empty.

Once the swarm has landed somewhere, it stays there for a time and sends out scouts to locate a new home. Apparently the scouts had come back, delivered their message and taken the swarm elsewhere. My husband explained all this to me very carefully.

A few days later, another swarm came through. This time I was seven days older and considerably wiser. I hived the swarm as I had done the first time, but this time I picked up the super and carried it several yards away down to the other end of the garden. Apparently when the scouts returned they were confused and could not find the swarm, for the bees stayed in the hive and went to work.

Later, when we robbed the bees — carefully leaving them enough for winter — we had jars and jars of beautiful golden honey. Having grown our own peanuts as well, we roasted them, ground them up, mixed them with honey and had ourselves a yummy spread. And, oh!, how our two kids loved this homemade peanut butter!

The old-fashioned straw skep (sceppe meant basket in Old English) is still used for a beehive in Europe, where wood is in short supply, but seldom in North America. The disadvantage of the straw skep is that when the beekeeper wishes to harvest the honey, the bees must be destroyed. With a box hive, the beekeeper can remove frames full of honey without harming the bees.

Honey for Health

Honey is not only good but good for you. Old-time doctors mixed honey with infused sassafras bark and gave it to their patients as a pickup for "burned-out blood." This was considered particularly effective as a spring tonic.

Another remedy for aches and pains in the joints consisted of a pinch of caraway seeds sprinkled into a cup of boiling water in which a tablespoon each of honey and lemon juice had been dissolved.

For coughs and colds the doctor recommended an extract of pine and honey. Strawberry leaves, boiled and strained, were made into a tea, sweetened with honey and given for liver complaints. Sweet basil tea with honey was thought to clear the throat and sinus congestion.

A nervous headache could be alleviated with a pinch of rosemary floated on a teaspoonful of honey. An old almanac describes bergamot tea with honey as a soother for motherly nerves to be taken at 4 p.m., "with the feet up."

Using Honey

A beauty preparation of glycerine and honey with a sprinkle of rose extract was used for chapped hands by early day housewives. Honey was also used in many face creams. Of course, honey is used in every conceivable way in various foods. It is a natural accompaniment to baked beans — so make them following your favorite recipe and dress them up with a bit of honey.

FRENCH AND SPANISH CULTURE IN NEW ORLEANS

Much of our culture comes from the early colonials who settled in New England, but they were not by any means the only early settlers. France sold Louisiana to the United States in 1803 when Thomas Jefferson was President and New Orleans was already a large and thriving city. Louisiana was settled predominantly by French- and Spanish-speaking peoples who brought their own culture with them. Even today, Louisiana has many laws dating back to the Napoleonic code, rather than to the laws of England as the rest of the states do.

More than 200 years ago, a few surviving bands of homeless Frenchmen — all that were left of approximately 16,000 who had been driven ruthlessly by the British from their farms and families in Nova Scotia (then known as Acadia) — found sanctuary in southern Louisiana, among people of their own French tongue.

It was 1764 when the original twenty of them, ragged and hungry, struggled to Louisiana. For the first time in their years of wandering and hardship, they were treated kindly. They were given land, cattle, ammunition, guns, provisions, and sympathy. The next year 120 more came; later, still more, and by 1788 over 4,000 of these hardy Acadians had settled contentedly and permanently on Bayous Lafourche and Teche. Evangeline, immortalized by Longfellow, was among them.

Their descendants are known as "Cajuns," a familiarity that time and a dozen different tongues have taken with the original word "Acadians."

Today not only the Acadians, who have created an agricultural paradise in southwestern Louisiana, are known as Cajuns, but also all the trappers, fishermen, truck farmers, and dwellers of the bayou country. It has come to be a general term for all the hardy inhabitants of the swamps and bayous.

(The term Creole, on the other hand, describes white descendants of French or Spanish settlers of the Gulf States — although in colonial days, any white person born in South America was called a Creole, from the Spanish *criolla* meaning "native to the place.")

Okra

Many people in the North do not care much for okra. Southerners, however, love it. I could eat it for breakfast, lunch, and dinner and never grow tired of it. It is a plant of Africa, a kind of hibiscus.

Okra is an annual, growing to a height of two to eight feet and bearing rounded, fine-lobed leaves and beautiful green-gold flowers. The pods are from 4 to 6 inches long and are best used while young and very tender. Some species have pods exceeding a foot when fully grown. My own favorite is Gold Coast, sold by the Reuter Seed Company in New Orleans.

Okra and Vegetables

Pan fry about ¼–½ pound ground beef. Add salt and pepper. Add coarsely chopped celery, onion, and green pepper (about 4 or 5 stalks of celery, one large onion and one green pepper). Add equivalent of one can of stewed tomatoes, or fresh if available. Add ¼–½ cup small elbow macaroni not previously cooked. Simmer gently on low flame and add more stewed tomatoes or a little water if mixture cooks dry. Add okra slices (about ¼" thick), 1 or 2 (or more) cups as desired. Aunt Rhody always put in a lot. Continue simmering until macaroni is just tender and also okra. Dish looks most attractive if okra is still slightly green.

Chicory

There is nothing quite like coffee, New Orleans style, made with a chicory blend. First of all, however, let's remove some misconceptions.

Chicory is not a coffee substitute. It is a coffee *flavorer*, and just how much of that flavoring is added depends on the person or the locality. It is generally conceded by the best chefs that the finest coffee is made with a 10 percent chicory content.

But down in the bayous, the fishermen and trappers like it with 25 percent or even more chicory. That's when it gets thick as molasses, is black as sin, and will almost support a spoon standing upright in the middle!

Chicory is a vegetable, similar to a carrot in appearance. The chicory is dried and ground and looks exactly like coffee. In fact, although it contains 10 of the 24 chemical ingredients of coffee it has no caffeine — so you can safely add chicory if you cultivate the taste for it. My dentist used to offer me a cup of chicory coffee when I had an early morning appointment. I always felt it strengthened me for the ordeal ahead.

The charm of chicory is the bold, distinctly different taste it gives to coffee — a taste that first annoys, then tempts, and finally turns you into one of those ardent devotees who think pure coffee is dishwater. Your dyed-in-the-wool chicory fan goes in for those little demitasse portions without cream or sugar. He'll drink them all day long, and much prefers concluding a business deal over what he calls a "small black."

Pralines

It may take you a while to become accustomed to chicory coffee, but just about everybody loves pralines. This confection originated in France and was brought to New Orleans by nobility fleeing revolution. The word *praline* seems to have been purloined from the name of the man who popularized the original sugar-coated *almond*-delicacy in the salons of Paris, the Duc d'Praslin.

In Louisiana, however, the almond was replaced by the paper-shelled pecan. The praline has survived flood, war, plague, and politics. Its popularity has never waned.

Pecan Pralines (Pralines aux Pacanes)

½ pound freshly shelled Louisiana pecans (1 pound unshelled)

1 pound brown sugar
4 tablespoons water
1 tablespoon butter

Chop the pecans — some into fine pieces, others into halves, and others again into quarters. Set the sugar, and just enough water to melt it, on to boil. As it begins to boil add the chopped pecans and the butter.

Stir constantly till the syrup begins to thicken and turn to sugar. Then take from the stove and turn out on to a marble slab to dry. Some cooks prefer to drop the mixture by tablespoonsful on to the slab.

GROWING PEANUTS

Peanuts, which grow so well in the South where they are often put in as a late or second crop, will also grow in the North, even in southern Canada, if the right variety is chosen. The right variety is Early Spanish (110 days) — available from Park, Henry Field, Farmers, Burpee and others in the States, and from McFaydens in Canada.

The large-podded Virginia peanut grows well in the southern states but takes longer to bear (120 days) and may not mature well farther north.

The peanut, of course, is not a nut but a pea, being related to the pea and the bean. But while it blossoms much the same, it develops its pods underground. It is a rampant grower and the crop can be greatly increased by burying the runners, leaving just the tips above ground. These runners will then produce a good but smaller crop than the parent plant.

I always covered these runners myself because I knew exactly how to do it, but one year when I was pregnant with my second child and not feeling very well I asked my husband to do this for me. I forgot that he was a New Yorker and not accustomed to growing peanuts. I should have explained. Wishing to please, he did indeed cover the peanuts — completely. I did not discover it until about a week later when I stumbled out to the garden one morning. That year we had no peanuts — the plants were ruined. It was my turn to explain to him, very carefully, as he had done for me about the bees and their scouts. Again we made peace and escaped having a barn burner!

Peanuts are attractive plants with sweet-pea-like blossoms. Here we see a plant with root, blossom, and underground nuts. (1) Blossom cut lengthwise; (2) Ripe nut; (3) Nut cut lengthwise; (4) Seed; (5, 6) Germ. Recent experiments have shown that peanuts planted in rows running north and south take up water more efficiently — something astrologers have known all along.

☙ ☙ ☙
MEDICINAL HERBS FOR PETS AND POULTRY

Herbs and herb lore have fascinated mankind since the dawn of time. Much of our early knowledge was gleaned by watching the plants that animals turned to, instinctively knowing which herbs would be helpful to them when they were ill. It is not by chance that dogs eat couch grass, cats love catnip, and many animals both wild and domestic eat garlic.

Poultry

Old-timers had a remedy for coccidiosis which can be used just as well today. This ailment of the intestines is quite common in poultry, particularly if there is overcrowding, insufficient exercise, and lack of green food. Feed dandelion greens and young stinging nettles chopped together to prevent or cure coccidiosis in baby chicks. Older chickens may be given flaked garlic cloves for about 10 days. Exhausted chickens may be given drops of warm honey, which frequently acts as an immediate restorative.

A free-ranging farm hen is usually free of worms, which are often the result of artificial rearing, crowding, and inadequate diet. Remedies vary with the type of worms present — roundworms, tapeworms, hairworms, gapeworms, or pinworms. Give flaked cloves of garlic, or two or three drops of oil of eucalyptus in a little milk, to each hen.

My husband was at one time employed in the Swift and Company hatchery and we kept a flock of chickens. More than once when we were raising chickens I have seen these simple remedies work.

Cats

Phoenician traders, carrying Egyptian cats on their ships (to catch rats and mice), probably brought the first domesticated cats to Europe about 900 B.C. The crossing of Egyptian cats with European wildcats produced the domestic cat of Europe. European explorers, colonists, and traders brought their domestic cats to the Americas during the 1700's. These animals became the ancestors of most of the cats that live in the United States today.

I love cats and I have always kept at least one, and often several. They have their problems, too, however. If you suspect that your cat has worms, evidenced by a dull coat, inflamed eyes, coughing, and vomiting, you may find that garlic tablets, good for both dogs and cats, are an effective remedy. American scientists have determined that garlic contains a substance (crotonaldehyde) which is effective against diseases of the nose, throat, and intestine, being especially useful as a febrifuge (fever remedy) and vermifuge. It is also a fertility herb, and animals, both wild and domestic, seek it eagerly.

Ticks are eight-legged, hard-shelled arachnids, similar in appearance to spiders. A cat allowed outdoors may have ticks burrow into its skin, where they feed on blood, causing the animal to become anemic. They can often be loosened from the cat's skin by soaking in vinegar, or covering with an oily or greasy substance which stops the tick from breathing. Vaseline is good for this. Vaseline or petrolatum is a by-product of crude oil.

Rotenone

Rotenone powder is the best thing I have ever found for fleas on both cats and dogs and it may be used with safety, but don't get it in their eyes. Rotenone comes from the roots of several species of trees, especially the lonchocar-pus from Latin America. Devil's shoestring in the States also contains a high percentage of rotenone. This powder is also effective against a number of garden pests such as the spittlebug, potato and tobacco flea beetle, aphid, spider mite, chinch bug, harlequin bug (often particularly destructive on broccoli plants), imported cabbageworm, carpenter ant, pea weevil, mosquito, and housefly.

The effect of rotenone on insects is to slow down the rate of their heart action and breathing. Little is known of the fundamental basis for its effectiveness. When you are using the dust be careful not to breathe it. If you do, it will make you feel dry and uncomfortable, but otherwise there is no evidence to show that it is harmful when used in normal concentrations. It is always a good idea to wash hands and face after using any insect spray or powder.

Bugging the Bugs

Grandmother didn't have much in the way of household sprays but she knew that planting tansy around doorways would keep out ants. And strips of cucumber laid here and there would offend them enough to make them go away if they found some other way of getting in. When outdoors she dabbed camomile tea on exposed skin as an insect repellent. For keeping moths out of clothes closets she hung them with sprigs of rosemary or wormwood. These were also put in storage chests for clothes. Sage, tansy and spearmint were used to chase flies, rue to repel flies, fleas and some other insects. Pennyroyal discouraged flies, fleas and mosquitoes. Actually pennyroyal's name is a corruption of the Latin pulex for flea, and "royal" meant a relief or defense.

Try putting pennyroyal on your cat's collar to keep her free of fleas.

SUMMER CUISINE

In July there are so many things to do you just don't have the time to worry about them. In July the wheat is combined, the hay mown, raked, and baled, and the corn spray-weeded or cultivated and laid by. There is always excitement. Will there be time to get the last load of baled hay into the loft before the storm breaks from a tumultuous, dark-blue, Rip-Van-Winkle-thundering sky?

Feeding Farm Helpers

In the old days when farmers helped each other it was customary for the homemaker to serve them their noon meal. In July this was no great problem, for the vegetable garden was yielding abundantly, wild fruits and berries could be made into pies, and just about every farmhouse had chickens.

Blackberry blossoms are beloved of bees. The foliage is eaten avidly by all animals and the astringent fruits are refreshing and tonic.

Berry Delights

July is a month of berries. Black raspberries are diminishing, but red ones are taking their place, and blackberries soon follow. Already the first apples can be picked, to unburden the tree and make into pale-green applesauce.

Blackberries

You can just bet your great-great-grandmother was watching those blackberries to make sure she was on hand to get them when they ripened. Wild creatures, even snakes, like berries, too. Here in the Southwest, I have more than once seen the big, hairy spiders called tarantulas cut off a berry and roll it into their hole under the ground.

If your grandmother didn't get those berries, there wouldn't be any blackberry cordial and this was depended upon as a medicinal beverage in most colonial households.

Elderberries

While Elderflower Wine was also made from flowers earlier in the spring (see "May"), it was July that the berries usually ripened and that great favorite, Elderberry Wine, could be made.

Gooseberries

Gooseberries are also a fruit of July, and their prickly, sour fruit, suitably tamed with sugar and spices, makes one of the most delectable pies known to mankind.

Less Common Berries

There are a number of delicious and usable wild berries, growing in many parts of the United States and even into Canada and Alaska, that were used in an earlier day but have, seemingly, been forgotten about now.

Dewberries (*Rubus trivialis*) grow well and wild here in Oklahoma and I have my own secret places where I pick them every spring, places my son found when he was a teenager and loved to hike around the countryside looking for a good place to fish. They are a well-kept family secret. I like dewberries (also called running or ground blackberries) better than blackberries because they are sweeter, less acrid, and much larger than their black cousins. They make wonderful wine and jelly.

The **cloudberry,** (*Rubus chamaemorus*), or **baked-appleberry,** grows in wet areas and in acid peats from the arctic regions southward through New England. A most helpful booklet, *Wild, Edible and Poisonous Plants of Alaska* is obtainable from the Cooperative Extension Service, University of Alaska, Fairbanks, AK 99775-5200. The publication is No. A-00028, and it gives both pictures and descriptions of wild berries. (Cost is $3.25 including postage.)

The cloudberry ripens in the States and southern Canada in July, but if you live in Alaska you may have to wait until early September. The fruit is collected in quantity by the Eskimos, who prize it highly. The fresh berry is a good source of vitamin C, the antiscorbutic vitamin. When frozen immediately after picking and kept frozen until ready for use, the berry retains much of its vitamin C value. The fruit, oddly, is red when unripe and amber-colored when mature. The Eskimos preserve them by burying the seal poke, keg, or barrel containing them in the frozen tundra or by storing them in ice cellars.

Cloudberries (and what a lovely name!) are delicious either eaten raw or made into jam.

An Earful on Earwigs

Earwigs seldom exist in large enough numbers to be really harmful but if you have problems remember you can trap them with simple devices just as your grandparents did. They are attracted to hay, paper, or moss stuffed into inverted pots set on top of sticks or stakes. Or rags and paper can be placed under bushes where earwigs are apt to be found. Earwigs crawl into cooler earth in the heat of the day; therefore, check the trap materials early in the morning.

Another effective trap is based on the knowledge that earwigs favor small dry places to lay their eggs. They breed in April and are most active at night.

Elderberry Wine

8 quarts of berries	**4 quarts of boiling water poured over the berries**

Let stand 12 hours, stirring now and then. Strain well, pressing out all the juice. Add, to each 4 quarts of juice:

3 pounds sugar	**½ ounce powdered cloves**
1 ounce powdered cinnamon	

Boil 5 minutes and set away to ferment in a stone jar, with a cloth thrown lightly over it. When it has completed fermenting, rack it off carefully, so as not to disturb the lee. Bottle and cork down well.

Blackberry Cordial

1 quart of blackberry juice	**¼ ounce allspice**
1 pound white sugar	**¼ ounce cloves**
½ ounce grated nutmeg	**1 pint best brandy**
½ ounce powdered cinnamon	

Tie the spices in a thin muslin bag. Boil juice, sugar, and spices together 15 minutes, skimming well. Add the brandy and set aside in a closely covered vessel to cool. When perfectly cold, strain out the spices and bottle, sealing the corks with paraffin.

Gooseberry Fool

Gooseberries, being a threat to pines because they host blister-rust disease, cannot be enjoyed in all states. But if you have them there was another delectable dessert grandmother had "up her sleeve." Here's a recipe that's hard to find nowadays in modern cookbooks.

1 quart gooseberries, ripe	**4 eggs, separated**
1 tablespoon butter	**meringue of whites**
1 cup sugar	**3 tablespoons sugar**

Stew the gooseberries in just enough water to cover them. When soft and broken, rub them through a sieve to remove the skins. While still hot beat in the butter, sugar and the whipped yolks of the eggs. Pile in a glass dish, or in small glasses, and heap upon the top a meringue of the whipped egg whites and sugar.

All-Purpose Berry Jam

Here is a good basic recipe for making jam that can be used for many fruiting berry bushes: Wash and crush 4 cups of berries, mix in 3 cups of sugar, and boil slowly in a large, heavy pot for 10 minutes. In my opinion, the secret of successful jam or jelly making is to work with small quantities.

Use a large pot for jams and jellies boiling high in the pan. When they start boiling down (that is, when you can see ¼ inch or so distance between the boiling surface and the high mark on the side of the pot where the liquid was at first), start testing for the jellying point.

To test for the jellying point, dip a spoon into the boiling jam or jelly. Tilt the spoon until the liquid runs off. Watch the drips. When the jellying point is reached, the last two drops will run together, then flake, or just skid from the spoon.

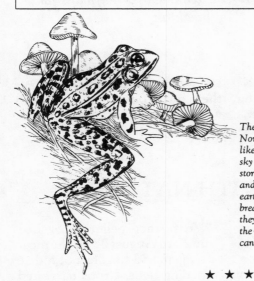

The leopard frog (Rana pipiens), most common in North America, is bright green with black leopard-like blotches. Frogs have been said to fall from the sky like rain. This happens when a strong wind-storm sucks up small creatures that live in ponds and carries them quite a distance before they fall to earth again. Tadpoles have tails, no hind legs, and breathe underwater through gills. As they mature they grow legs, lose their tails, and finally develop the wide mouths and long, sticky tongues. Bullfrogs can live for more than twenty years.

★ ★ ★

I love the insect noises of July. I've always had a friendly feeling for crickets. And I love to go to sleep at night lulled by the shrill cry of the cicada or harvestfly. They make a lot of noise but are seldom found in enough numbers to be damaging. I even love the big noise of the tiny tree toads. Summer is a good time to be alive, to work, to rest, and to sleep.

✸ ✸ ✸

Leo the Lion  (July 23 - August 22)

Green Corn Moon
AUGUST

In tune with Nature ★ Green Corn Moon ★ Corn relish ★ Molasses ★ Fishing by the Moon ★ Stone fruits of August ★ Seeding pansies ★ Occult properties of herbs ★ Vital rain forests ★ Companion planting ★ Dyeing with herbs ★ Puffballs for breakfast

MOON-SIGN GARDEN-ERS consider timing and rhythm very important for successful crops. Planting, cultivating, eradication of pests and weeds, and harvesting all have their own zodiacal sign and fall within the rhythm of the Moon's phase.

IN TUNE WITH NATURE

People who garden by the Moon believe that a counterpoint zodiac rhythm exists in the daily Moon place sign and that by working in accordance with the sign, phase and daily place sign, a balance with Nature is achieved. The Bible would seem to bear this out.

> *"Let there be lights in the firmament of the heaven to divide the day from the night, and let them be for signs, and for seasons, and for days, and years."*
> GENESIS 1:14

We further believe that Leo (July 22 to August 23) is the most lofty, firm and steadfast of zodiac gardening signs. Crops harvested under its fiery, barren, dry, masculine characteristics are thought to keep better and longer.

Fruit, one of the best gifts of the month of August, packed in nettle hay will ripen faster. This is especially desirable with Kieffer pears, often picked green, and packed in dry nettle hay. This weed also deters fermentation, keeps fruit free of mold, and bestows upon it good keeping qualities.

Stinging nettle, grown near other plants, has a number of helpful attributes, changing the properties of neighboring plants and making them more insect resistant. The iron content of nettle also helps plants withstand lice, slugs, and snails during wet weather. Mint and Tomatoes are strengthened when stinging nettle is grown nearby. (For more on stinging nettle, see "March.")

Grains, beans, and herbs to be dried should be gathered and prepared for storage under Leo and during the Moon's last quarter. If possible, canning should be done during the dry zodiac sign of Leo.

Late cucumbers should be pickled and late cabbage krauted under Leo if you would have a firm and zesty product. August is a cornucopia spilling out its abundance of lima beans, beets, pole beans, Brussels sprouts, chard, squash, okra, and tomatoes. Pumpkins begin to shape up and really look like pumpkins.

Green Corn Moon

Indians knew August as the time of the Green Corn Moon, an appropriate name. For now field corn was sure of itself, and late sweet corn ready to be roasted in its tender inner shucks, or boiled six minutes in salted water, then salted and peppered, bathed in butter and enjoyed. Those who do not grow their own corn never really have a taste thrill like this — for corn is best just as it comes into the milk stage. Five minutes from the stalk and into ready-prepared boiling water and quickly out again is a taste never to be forgotten. Once plucked, corn loses its sugar quickly and the longer it sits around the less desirable it becomes.

Weather Sign

If corn shucks are thick and tougher than ordinary, there's a tough winter ahead.

Cabbage is one of the most nutritious of vegetables, high in vitamins C and A. An old gardening book advises that cabbage may be stored in a cool cellar (35–40° F) with a dirt floor by hanging it, roots up, from a nail in the ceiling. Cabbage made into kraut should be covered with grape leaves, which will firm it and add bacteria for fermentation.

AUGUST RECIPES

Cantaloupes ripen in August and so do watermelons. The Indians used melons of all kinds in many ways and the early day homemaker learned much from the Indians.

The Florida Seminoles made a relish using corn, watermelon rind, and red and green peppers, which was well liked by all who tasted it. This is their original recipe, updated slightly so that more modern ingredients can be used. Plan to make it in late summer when watermelons, red and green sweet peppers and corn are abundant and less expensive.

In August you can also dry late Corn for keeping. Holding the fresh-picked ears by the stalk, plunge each one into unsalted, briskly boiling water. Cut the kernels from the cob, cutting as close to the cob as possible.

Working with small quantities, spread the Corn one layer deep on white butcher's paper, cover with cheesecloth (securely) and place in the sun. About three days of hot sunshine will remove most of the moisture and "set the sugar." Place in a warm dry place, like your attic, and let the kernels complete their cure. When thoroughly dry, store in sterilized jars with tight lids. For winter use the dried Corn should be soaked overnight, then cooked.

Corn Relish

2½ cups whole kernel corn, cut from the cob, also scraping from cob as much of the milk as possible

1 cup watermelon rind, finely chopped (carefully remove the green outer skin and any red flesh on the inside of the rind)

¾ cup of red sweet peppers, finely chopped

¾ cup of green sweet peppers, finely chopped

1 large onion grated as fine as possible

1 teaspoon black pepper

2 teaspoons salt

2 teaspoons sugar

½ cup white vinegar

½ teaspoon cinnamon

1 teaspoon coriander seed

5 teaspoons cornstarch

Preheat oven to 275° F. Cover all ingredients except cornstarch with water in a large cookpot. Bring to a boil and boil for 10 minutes, stirring in the cornstarch while mixture is boiling. Remove and put aside what you want for immediate use, placing in refrigerator or cool place. Put remainder in Mason jars, filling to within ½ inch of top. Place jars in a shallow pan of warm water in preheated oven and process for one hour, or process in a pressure cooker.

Molasses

Molasses contains about 69.3 percent carbohydrates, 25 percent water, 2.4 percent protein and 3.2 percent ash or mineral. A pound has a high energy value of 1,290 calories. It is an excellent source of iron, a good source of seven other minerals, and six of the B vitamins. "Blackstrap" is most nutritious.

Indian Pudding

As the early colonists learned much from the Indians, so did the Indians learn from them. Using their own Indian meal, they traded for Molasses and made a very tasty pudding.

½ cup corn meal	2 teaspoons ginger
½ cup cold water	1 teaspoon cinnamon
1 quart milk, heated	1 teaspoon salt
½ cup molasses	1 cup cold milk
¼ cup brown sugar	

Preheat oven to 300° F. Add corn meal, mixed with cold water, to warm milk. Cook about 20 minutes in double boiler, stirring often. Add molasses, sugar, ginger, cinnamon, and salt. Pour into oiled baking dish. Bake 30 minutes. Add cold milk and bake slowly (without stirring) for about 3–4 hours longer.

)))

FISHING BY THE MOON

In the month of the Green Corn Moon there are days when you almost feel you could cook the corn in the steaming August heat. By noon the days are parboiled, but the early mornings are dew drenched and cool, if you get up early enough. That's the time to get your chores out of the way, so you can have some afternoons free. In short, August is a wonderful month to go fishing. "All work and no play makes Jack a dull boy" to quote a maxim from *Poor Richard's Almanac*. So pack up your bait, your gear, and your lunch and start out.

The best fishing signs are Cancer, Scorpio, and Pisces. But if you can't go on those days, there are also the second best signs of Taurus, Libra, and Capricorn, also considered moist signs for many purposes.

When the first white explorers reached the shores of the American continent, symbols of the signs of the zodiac were found carved on stone in Mexico, Central and South America. There were three different sets of symbols in these areas, but sea beings were always used to symbolize Pisces and Cancer. While they did not use the crab for Cancer, they all used some species of shell fish. All the symbols resembled the European symbols in some way. Instead of a bull for Taurus, the stag was used in one American zodiac. Gemini was always illustrated by two people. There were always arrows in the Sagittarius symbol. For Leo, the puma replaced the lion, but in no case did a sea being appear for any sign other than Pisces and Cancer, although occasionally, the Capricorn goat was shown with a tail like a fish or a mermaid.

Many Moon-signers believe that the best time of day for fishing is when the Moon is directly overhead, as well as the two hours on either side of this time. At the New Moon, the beginning of the first quarter (Sun and Moon conjunct), both the Sun and the Moon are directly overhead at noon (halfway between dawn and dusk). At the beginning of the second quarter (the Sun and Moon square), the Moon is overhead at midnight (halfway between dusk and dawn). At the beginning of the fourth quarter (Sun and Moon again square), the Moon is overhead at dawn, when the Sun is rising.

This theory holds that the next best time for fishing is when the Moon is straight "down" on the other side of the Earth. This is midnight at the New Moon; dawn at the beginning of the second quarter; noon at the Full Moon; and dusk at the beginning of the

---

Fish may be frozen in a variety of forms or cuts, as shown here.

Whole — as it comes from the water.

Fillets — sides of the fish cut lengthwise away from the backbone.

Drawn — whole fish with entrails removed.

Dressed or pan dressed — whole fish with scales and entrails removed, and usually with head, tail, and fins removed.

Steaks — cross-section slices from large dressed fish.

fourth quarter. Generally, during the summer, the best fishing times are one or two hours before and after sunrise and sunset.

An Eerie Experience

I have a friend named Lucy Hagen, a great fisherlady who has won many prizes in fishing tournaments. She once told me of an unusual fishing experience she and her fishing companion had one August night.

"We were fishing rather late that night on the lake," she said, "when we started noticing that the fishing, which had been excellent, was starting to taper off. Stranger still, all the usual night noises quieted. Gradually the crickets, cicadas, whipoorwills, doves, and the big, awkward water turkeys, all became silent. We had forgotten that this night was the date of the partial eclipse of the Moon, but now we became aware and sat in the boat watching as the Earth's shadow continued to cover the Moon. Everything was almost unbelievably silent — there was no sound, no movement, and the fish, too, had completely disappeared.

"We continued to fish but had no luck for the rest of the evening, even though we kept on for about an hour after the eclipse had passed. It was an eerie, mystifying experience.

"Finally, we gave up and went home. Curious to see what would happen, we returned the next morning at about 5 A.M. and things had returned to normal and we caught our quota of fish in a short time."

)))

The Moon's Influence on Fish

Some outdoorsmen think that the appetites of fish are greater when the Moon is in the two signs of Cancer and Pisces. Perhaps they become more careless at such times, because they are driven by hunger, and thus are caught more easily.

It is also a strange fact that more BIG fish are caught when the Moon is in Cancer and Pisces. As a rule big fish are less given to carelessness — having survived for a time, they have learned caution. But even though they have more fish wisdom, they get hooked when the Moon travels into these two signs.

The records would seem to indicate that Pisces is the very best of all signs for fishing, but Cancer is next. Fishing will be good when the Moon moves through Pisces. There is also a very noticeable lull when the Moon passes through the in-between signs — Aries, Taurus, and Gemini — until it reaches Cancer, when fishing is again good.

Many consider Scorpio, because it is a water sign, good for fishing.

Clams and Crabs

Dig clams the first week of Libra (September 23 to 30). Clams are best and most plentiful at the time of the Full Moon. The best time for crabbing is also at the Full Moon, when the meat is full and juicy.

❦ ❦ ❦

STONE FRUITS OF AUGUST

August is the great month for stone fruits: peaches, sun-ripened and delectable, are coming in for canning; plums for jelly, jam, and wine; and apples for applesauce and apple pies. There seems to be no limit to the goodies — sometimes coming on so fast and so abundantly that the homemaker feels frustrated and frazzled, anxious to get everything put away before it becomes overripe or spoils. The weather is often as hot as the hinges of Hades. At this point I am reminded of the advice given in an old cookbook — and old cookbooks are delightful because they often wax conversational and you feel as if you have a friend in the kitchen with you.

"Plan your preserving, ladies, and try to have your fruit ready early in the morning before the heat of the day. Do not undertake to do too much at a time. Have your jars washed and sterilized, your preserving kettle cleaned and ready. Your tested recipe should be at hand so you do not have to waste time hunting for it. With these matters attended to, you may proceed with your mind clear of minor worries. When your canning is completed and the jars cooled and ready for storing, wash your face, brush your hair, brew yourself a nice cup of hot tea and set down and rest a spell."

Even today this advice sounds pretty good.

Applesauce

Applesauce is so easy to make. My first batches go into the freezer in June when my June apples ripen. Liking applesauce a bit tart I take them when they are still somewhat green, and core and quarter them, cooking over very very low heat. When cooked, I add sugar to taste. Some batches also have spices added. A few freezer bags of others I leave unsweetened for my mother's favorite applesauce cake. Cakes made from scratch have personality box cakes will never achieve.

I cook my apples unpeeled, running them hot and mushy through my food mill (obtainable at hardware stores). This removes seeds and peelings and the whole operation can be done with soul-satisfying speed.

By the time my fall apples come on in late August or early September, the spring supply has been used up. I proceed to make my applesauce as before but usually the later, firmer apples have to be cooked a little longer and water added from time to time so they will not scorch.

If you are afflicted with rheumatism, backaches, arthritis or chills, you should carry three horse chestnuts (Aesculus).

TALL COLD DRINKS

Those old southerners really knew how to live — they had mint julep. August is a month for herbal beverages — tall cold drinks and hot, spicy teas. As Rudyard Kipling said:

Excellent herbs had our fathers
of old
   Excellent herbs to ease their
   pain,
Alexanders and marigold,
   Eyebright, orris, and ele-
   campane.

Basil, rocket, valerian, rue
   (Almost signing themselves
   they run),
Vervain, dittery, "Call me to
   you,"
Cowslip, melilot, rose-of-
   the-sun;
Anything green that grew out of
   the mould,
   Was an excellent herb to our
   fathers of old.

Sweet birch (*Betula lenta*) is first on my list of the tall colds. Just about every part is usable. The oil of the young buds, leaves and twigs of sweet birch is a cousin, in taste, to oil of wintergreen and imparts an aromatic flavoring to tea. Boiled for just one minute, chilled and served with sugar or honey and ice, it makes a light summer drink, particularly acceptable to children.

Sumacade is next. Sumac (*Rhus*) makes an equally refreshing, though acid, drink — somewhat similar to lemonade. The Indians loved it. Sumac is a woody shrub with velvety branches and feathery leaflets, growing in dry open fields from Maine to Manitoba and southward. It also grows along roadsides but I don't advise gathering it there as it may have been sprayed. *Rhus glabra*, or smooth sumac, grows well in Oklahoma, and I gather the fully ripe, red, tightly clustered berries, if possible, before a thundershower. I put the whole heads into a large container, cover them with cool well water and beat them with a block of wood. The juice is then strained at least twice to remove the malic acid hairs and any other debris. This drink is delicious on a hot afternoon — sweetened or drunk "neat." You can make it into an alcoholic drink if you like, a sumac collins. Just be careful how much you drink — and let somebody else drive!

A *word of warning* — there is a poison sumac, but little danger of getting the wrong one if you know your sumacs. The poison berries are white and grow in loose, lacy racemes, while the edible *Rhus* are red and grow in tight clumps.

A delicious nonalcoholic tea made from any of the **mint** family (*Labiatae*), known for their square stems, makes a good drink on a sultry August afternoon and may be taken either hot or chilled.

> If you would attract love, draw money, or wish to ensure sexual potency, carry the root of ginseng (Panax quinquefolius).

Practically all Indians of the Southwest have made **cota** tea (*Thelesperma gracile* and *T. megapotamium*) from ancient times to the present, often traveling many miles to gather the plant for drying. As the cota is harvested each plant is wrapped in a circle and tied in the middle with some of the same fiber. The tea is made by placing a bundle of either the fresh or dried plant in a pan of water, bringing to a boil, and then reducing the heat. It is simmered until the desired strength is reached.

≫→   ≫→   ≫→

Possum Grape Drink

Gather grapes of the kind that remain sour after they ripen when frost has fallen on them. Hang up to dry. To prepare, pull grapes from stems and wash. Stew in water. When done, mash in the water and let set until seeds settle. Pour off juice, replace in pot and set on stove. When juice boils add a little cornmeal to thicken. Remove from stove. Sweeten to taste and serve hot or cold.

Pansies, kiss me quick, or johnny jump up — a Scottish fable says the lower petal is the mother with two gaily dressed daughters beside her. The small upper petals are her stepdaughters, twin Cinderellas.

SEEDING PANSIES

For pansies in the Spring, you must sow the seed in the fall. I tend to wax evangelical when I speak about pansies. Pansies say, "it's spring," blooming long before less hardy annuals. They are at their best during the cool of very early spring in beds or low borders. They are easily grown and so hardy, their foliage remains green and attractive for long periods even in winter. They bloom, and bloom, and *BLOOM!*

"Sow the seed in August in flats in a cool, shady place and keep the soil moist at all times. When the plants are large enough, transplant into frames. Cover with coarse material for winter protection and set plants out in permanent beds in the spring." from *Watkins Household Hints*, 1945.

Pansies tend to disappear for me when hot weather strikes but in more northern regions they will continue to delight much longer. Here is an item of December 27, 1877 from the Farmington, Maine Chronicle: "Mrs. O.B. Butler gathered from her garden several perfectly developed pansies Friday, 21st inst. Pretty well for December, in Maine."

As our winters are mild I planted my pansies one year in open ground in the late fall. Soon I noticed the foliage was disappearing. Examination showed no insects present. One night my son returned from a late date and there was a rabbit happily munching on pansies in the moonlight. We put a low wire fence around the area and that was that.

Vital Tropical Rain Forests

Recently there has been great concern about the deforestation of tropical rain forests, so that the secrets of many plants that can heal and feed the world are being lost. For example, in deforested central Panama, average annual rainfall has dropped by 17 inches in the last 50 years. Some scientists believe that the spreading of the Sahara is due in part to the shrinking of equatorial forests.

A rain forest is a vast storehouse of organisms that can be used for human benefit. For instance, rain-forest plants and animals are the source of at least one-fourth of ingredients for prescription drugs on the market today. The snakeroot plant of India's monsoon forests yields the alkaloid reserpine — the base of many tranquilizers. The corkwood tree of eastern Australia provides scopolamine, used to treat schizophrenia. The plant derivative curare, used by Amazon Indians to poison their arrowheads, is an agent for treating Parkinson's disease. Researchers estimate that some 1,400 plants in tropical forests have potential anticancer properties. Countless more plants await discovery.

COMPANION PLANTING

As insects and plant diseases change and adapt, becoming impervious to chemicals used in their control, it becomes necessary to explore alternatives. One of these, of course, is companion planting. So just what is companion planting, and how do we use it?

Briefly, it is placing plants in close proximity so they may help each other grow, or repel their enemies, which may be insects or even other plants. It may be succession planting; for instance, corn, which needs nitrogen, may follow a crop of early peas, which restore nitrogen to the soil by drawing it out of the air. Because of its high saponin content, spinach is useful as a pre-crop and does especially well planted with strawberries. The solanine in tomatoes will protect asparagus against asparagus beetles. In turn a chemical derived from asparagus juice has been found effective when used on tomato plants as a killer of nematodes.

Companion planting may take the form of **"barrier plants:"**

★ Chives or garlic between rows of peas or lettuce should control aphids.
★ Marigolds between hills of cucumbers, marrow, squashes, or melons should keep cucumber beetle down.
★ Nasturtiums between rows of broccoli should keep aphids down and help control harlequin bugs.
★ Rosemary, thyme, sage, catmint, hyssop or, preferably,

mixtures of these between rows of cabbage should keep away the white or imported cabbage butterfly.
★ Tansy (a useful but little used pot herb) between cabbages should help control cabbage worms and cutworms. Plant tansy also around door openings to keep ants out of the house. If you have ants coming in from below, cucumbers repel them.
★ Tomatoes near asparagus should keep down asparagus beetle. Parsley is also good planted with asparagus.
★ Chives between roses should reduce the incidence of aphids.
★ Other plants that have been found repellent against a broad spectrum of insects are marigolds, asters, chrysanthemums, pyrethrum daisy, and such herbs as anise, coriander, and basil.

August Planting

August is an excellent time to start planting your fall garden. For one thing I have found that fall planted vegetables — squash for instance — have fewer insect enemies in the fall. No matter how hot and dry the weather, I always plow up a space and plant turnips the last of August. The seed seems to pick up a little moisture and sprout quickly with the first fall rain. I sow all kinds of greens in the fall — greens (and lettuce) will stand quite a bit of cold. Cauliflower does well as cooler weather approaches. Brussels sprouts even benefit from a light freeze. Onion sets are often available in the fall and I can again have fresh onions for the table. Fall, too, is the time I replant my yellow or white onions which have sprouted.

Diversification is needed in the process of building a farm or a garden, just as in the growth of an organism. This means using a variety of different crops, as I have noted, and also crop rotation, previously mentioned. Fortunately a variety of produce is just what the homeowner wants.

Nature abhors idle ground. If she has her way she will always have roots hanging into the topsoil to prevent erosion. She almost never leaves wide, unplanted, unmulched areas between growing plants. Furthermore, her plants, in most instances, grow very closely together.

Broadcasting Seeds

Nature, unlike we who make gardens, does not plant in long, straight rows. She prefers to broadcast her seeds. Of course, we can't follow her method entirely or we would have a weed patch, but we can still learn a lot.

Instead of planting onions in a single row like a flock of ducks following each other I now plant a staggered row on each side of the first row. When they are large enough I pull every other one for green onions, leaving wider spaces between those intended to be used at maturity for dry onions.

I put lettuce plants between broccoli, cabbage or Brussels sprouts while the plants are small. Quick-growing lettuce is up and out of the way when the slower-growing brassicas need the room.

I get more mileage out of my compost because I know that all vegetable plants do not have the same feeding requirements. First we have the heavy feeders such as broccoli, Brussels sprouts, cabbage, cauliflower, celeriac, celery, chard, cucumber, endive, kohlrabi, leek, lettuce, spinach, squash, sweet corn and tomato. These I plant in soil newly fertilized with well decomposed manure or other organic matter.

If you follow these heavy feeders with beets, carrots, radishes, rutabagas or turnips, which also thrive on finely pulverized rocks and compost, you will still have vigorous plants, as their nutritional needs can be met without additional fertilizing.

Legumes, the third in the food chain of succession plantings, include broad and lima beans, bush and pole beans, peas and soybeans. These are the soil improvers, collecting nitrogen on their roots from the air and restoring it to the Earth.

Companion plants may be "helpers," they can act as supports for other plants. Cucumbers can vine up sunflowers, and at the same time provide the sunflowers with a living mulch to keep their roots cool and the soil from drying out.

Planting squash and pumpkins with corn has been a well known farm practice for a long, long time. If you have raccoons you will know why. Coons like to stand up and look around while they eat, instinctively keeping watch for possible enemies. With squash or pumpkin vines all over the place, and possibly tripping them up, it's not easy to do this. The big leaves also deter them.

Two-Level Gardening

Other types of companion planting include "two-level" gardening. This is accomplished by planting together vegetables that occupy different soil strata — asparagus with tomatoes, kohlrabi with beets, beets with onions, garlic with tomatoes, carrots with tomatoes, carrots with peas, leeks with vine plants, corn with beans (pole) or black-eyed peas.

Be careful, however, never to plant together those plants that will need to compete for the same space and light, or those with root excretions that may react unfavorably on the companion plant — such as dill and carrots, or onions with beans.

Timing Crops

Nature has a way of anticipating when it is time for a particular crop to emerge or mature, and the environment has been readied for the next one. Like nature, we can learn to anticipate the needs of plants in the maturing phase. Plant beets, for instance, about thirty inches apart between rows, in the plot reserved for late potatoes. Beets can be counted on to grow well in the cool of late fall, just as they did in the cool and moisture of early spring. Potatoes grow quickly in warm weather, produc-

ing shade for root crops that need moisture and a cool soil.

Don't be in a hurry to cut down your cornstalks. Starting a fall garden in hot, dry midsummer isn't easy, so take another lesson from Nature who starts hers in the cool shade of tall sunflowers. Let your stalks remain standing and cultivate down the middle of each row, cutting the corn roots to make later removal easy. In the tilled area you can plant turnips, cabbage, late peas, collards, beans, rutabagas, and some types of lettuce (most lettuce will not sprout if the temperature is over 70°. I find that, given a little moisture, the seeds will sprout quickly in the shade. When the little plants become better established, and the sun less warm, it is time to pull the cornstalks and give the new plants more light. But don't throw away those cornstalks — lay them between the rows and use them for mulch — walking on them will soon reduce them to shreds and later they can be plowed under.

These are only a few of literally hundreds of ways that companion planting can be of tremendous value to the gardener. My book, *Carrots Love Tomatoes: Secrets of Companion Planting,* enumerates all these ways in detail for vegetables. *Roses Love Garlic* performs the same service for flowers.

Marigolds (Calendula officinalis), *picked at noon when the Sun is hottest, will strengthen and comfort the heart.*

Natural Dyes

Onion skins (yellow-gold). Bring water in dye pot to a boil. Add 8 ounces onion skins and simmer one hour. Add 3 ounces of alum (which sets the color) and 1½ ounces cream of tartar, stir and simmer together 15 minutes. This procedure produces a somewhat pastel yellow.

For *bright yellow* add ½ ounce of stannous chloride and 1 ounce cream of tartar instead of alum and tartar above. Use same procedure.

For a *deep gold*, mordant ½ pound of wool in 1½ ounces potassium alum and 1½ ounces cream of tartar for one hour. Add 8 ounces onion skins and simmer in another pot 45 minutes. Add wet mordanted wool and simmer one hour. Cool, rinse, and dry.

There are different varieties of onions. Each will produce slightly different colors, and in combination with different mordanting agents, will produce a large variety of fabulous yellows and golds.

It is difficult to get the same shade each time you dye, even when you carefully measure materials. It is suggested that cloth, wool, linen, and so on intended for a garment or rug be all dyed at one time in the same dye bath.

Marigolds (orange yellow). Soak 8 ounces marigold flowers in water for several hours, then simmer together 1 hour. Add one pound of wool, and simmer together ½ hour. Add ¼ ounce stannous chloride and 1½ ounces cream of tartar. Simmer together another ½ hour. Cool, rinse, and dry.

Acacia Flowers (bright yellow). Soak 1 pound of blooming acaci in water overnight. Simmer next day one hour. Add one pound unmordanted wool, wet, to pot and simmer together ½ hour. Add ½ ounce stannous chloride, stir and simmer another ½ hour. Cool, rinse, and dry.

Madder (creamy orange). Soak 8 ounces madder root in dye pot overnight. Next day, bring pot to simmer for one hour. Add one pound of wet wool and simmer together another hour. Remove wool, add ½ ounce cream of tartar, and ½ ounce stannous chloride. Replace wool, simmer together one more hour, cool, rinse, and dry.

Logwood (purple). Allow 6 ounces logwood chips to soak in warm water for 3 days. Bring to simmer for one hour, and add one pound wet wool to dye pot for 45 minutes. Remove wool, add ½ ounce stannous chloride and 1 ounce cream of tartar. Reenter wool and simmer another half hour. Cool, rinse, and dry.

Cedar (light green). Simmer for 2 hours in dyepot containing 5 gallons water, 1 pound cedar twigs and needles. Allow to cool overnight. Next day, bring pot to simmer again. Add wet wool, layering between twigs and needles. Simmer 1 hour. Remove wool from pot, add 1½ ounces cream of tartar and ¼ ounce stannous chloride and stir well. Return wool to pot, simmer 1 hour together. Remove wool, rinse, and dry.

DYEING WITH HERBS

The pioneer woman had to do the washing, spinning, winding, knitting, and weaving of the wool. She often dyed it as well. Sometimes the cloth made was part linen and part wool, and this was called linsey-woolsey. It still itched.

Both wool yarn and linen tow were usually dyed. Wool was usually dyed with a liquid made from bark of walnut or butternut trees, and so most pioneer clothing was brown in color. In dyeing flax, more variety was possible. Warm red colors could be obtained by boiling sumac berries, or by using madder, which was carefully hoarded by the pioneers. Browns came from walnut bark, chestnut, or black oak, and yellows from peach or hickory bark. Oak and maple bark made shades of purple. A delicate gray or dove color, much admired by the pioneers, was made from cedar berries. Indigo for dyeing cloth blue was sometimes used, but it was expensive.

★ ★ ★

Puffballs for Breakfast

Sometimes on an early August morning I like to go out and search for puffballs (*Lycoperdon perlatum*). Newborn overnight, this delicacy just makes my day if I am lucky enough to find a patch. After dashing them under cold water to remove the tiny granular prickles, I slice them thin, sauté them in butter in a covered skillet, and take them out when they are limp and heated through but not fried. They are put aside while I whip up a simple omelet, seasoned with salt and pepper, a sprinkle of garlic chives and a dash of nutmeg. Part of the mushrooms are added to the beaten egg, the rest when I flip the omelet over just before it is served. This is one of the very best ways I know to start a new day.

Dr. W.W. Ray who wrote *Common Edible Mushrooms of Oklahoma* states "all Puffballs are edible but only when the flesh is soft and white, cheesy in texture and free from insects throughout the entire ball. Small Puffballs should be cut in two for examination before they are cooked."

When 5 or 6 inches in diameter, they may be peeled and sliced and then baked like eggplant.

✦ ✦ ✦

Virgo the Virgin   *(August 23 - September 22)*

Harvest Moon
SEPTEMBER

Digging root crops ★ Harvesting "top crops" ★ All-purpose tomato juice ★ Eggplant needs a better press ★ Labor Day ★ Watermelon rind pickle ★ The County Fair ★ Growing giant veggies ★ Preparing vegetables and fruits for Exhibition ★ Preserving herbs ★ Using herbs right ★ Gathering wild grapes ★

HARVESTING PROPERLY

SEPTEMBER IS TRADI-TIONALLY the time for harvesting and storing vegetables, and we moon-sign followers think that the waning moon is the proper time for these operations.

Indian Prayer
Thank the Lord of Harvest
Bless the work of our hands.

Digging Root Crops

Root crops you wish to save for seed should be dug during the third quarter, and other harvesting should be done during either the third or fourth quarter of the moon. At this time nature seems to cooperate, for the dry, barren zodiac signs are considered the best for successful harvesting. Virgo (August 23 to September 23) is ideal for digging root crops, being earthy as well as dry. If the third quarter of the moon coincides with Virgo's reign, so much the better. You can confidently dig beets, carrots, chicory, peanuts, potatoes and turnips. And remember also what I told you in March about digging at the right time of day. Root crops dug in the late afternoon will keep better because the energies gathered during the day are in the plant in the most concentrated form.

Libra (September 23 to October 23) balances moist, semifruitful characteristics with airy, masculine tendencies. Harvesting may also be done at this time, and it is particularly favorable if the Moon is in the third or fourth quarter during the last week of September.

If **early potatoes** have been hilled properly to protect them from light and heat, they may be left in the ground until September. But watch them carefully — if summer temperatures have been high, and rainfall heavy, harvest them earlier, for they may start to sprout. After digging, move them promptly to a shaded area to prevent sun and wind damage. These are the ones to be held for winter storage. They should be cured about ten days at room temperature, because cuts will not heal properly if they are placed at once in cool storage.

Potatoes dug in September should be handled gently while being sorted and cured. Plan to use the imperfect ones first, transferring the best to a dark, moderately moist, airy cellar and spreading them two to four deep in bins.

Sweet potatoes do not keep well or very long in southern Oklahoma so we exercise great care when digging them, being careful to inflict very few bruises as they are very tender. Those we keep are cured for ten days to two weeks in moist heat, 80° to 90° F, and then stored in rather small flat boxes to be placed where the temperature is cool and even. Once sweet potatoes are stored, do not move them about. Changing their position shifts the position of the juice and may cause them to rot. Take as needed without disturbing the rest.

In Oklahoma **peanuts** do exceptionally well as a second crop, following early beets or some fast-growing crop like spinach. Storing them presents no problem, as shelled, bagged, and frozen peanuts will keep indefinitely. We also carefully saved the peanut hay — a sweet treat for our two milk goats. And if we missed a few peanuts they were particularly relished as they munched on the hay. It is best to dig peanuts with a garden fork.

Harvesting and Using "Top" Crops

Gardens tend to look rather frazzled in September with a few notable exceptions. The tomato is one, quite often eggplant is still holding up well, and green peppers are just coming into their fall glory.

As a thrifty-minded gardener I'm dedicated to keeping my foot out of the supermarket door, so *on to the tomatoes*, every one of which can be used.

There are so many different ways of using **tomatoes** and preserving them — whether they be stewed, fried, juiced, pureed, preserved, pasted, cocktailed, catsupped, pickled or sandwiched with bacon and lettuce — that none need ever be wasted. A really good crop makes the gardener feel "tomato rich." Like housewives everywhere I do a lot of tomato canning, usually saving the perfect ones for this. Tomatoes should be harvested between ten in the morning and not later than three in the afternoon to obtain maximum quality. This rule also holds for other "top" crops.

After I have canned the pick of my crop I always have a lot of small, slightly bruised, a bit over-ripe, or otherwise imperfect to-matoes. With thrift deeply in-grained in my mental makeup I've found a good way to use even these. I wash, trim, and sort them and then place them, tightly lid-ded, in my Dutch oven over a very low flame, stirring occasionally so they will not scorch. They soon soften and then I put them through my food mill, which effectively re-moves seeds and skins. When they are cool enough to handle I put the rich juice in pint-size freez-er bags and store them for winter use. The addition of butter, salt and pepper, and a tablespoon or so of sugar makes this into the best soup you ever tasted on a cold winter day. It's good also in stews or meat soups to give added flavor.

Peppers, both hot and sweet, were in early American gardens and are thought to be native plants. Sweet peppers now come in all sorts of shapes and even different colors, including bright yellow. Burgess offers the famous "stuff-ing pepper," Hybrid Gypsy, a sweet, greenish gold hybrid, also excellent for salad. The fruits turn red upon full maturity. Peppers produce exceedingly well in the fall when cooler, hopefully rainy weather gives them a new lease on life. Early day cooks made them up into pickles and relishes and I also do this. But I also put away in my freezer an ample supply for winter stuffed peppers. Choosing

sizes as nearly uniform as possible, I cut off the tops, scoop out the seeds, and "nest" the peppers so they will take up little space. Then I remove the stem, chop up the tops and store these also in small bags along with the peppers to be added later to the stuffing.

The **eggplant,** also at its best in September in my garden, is a native of the Old World tropics, according to Sturtevant. It was not an ancient vegetable in Europe, but was well enough established there in the 16th century to be among the annuals brought to America for household-garden cul-tivation. Fruits of these early egg-plants were probably smaller than the largest kinds grown today, and were white and yellow as well as the familiar purple (which is why they were called *egg*plants). You can still get the white ones (which I have grown successfully), as a number of nursery catalogs still list them. Stokes Seeds, Inc., for example, lists the 152A Casper (70 days) as a "beautiful, ivory-white" vegetable with "snow-white flesh" in its 1987 catalog.

The 19th century New York seedsman Joseph Harris wrote, "There is no difficulty in raising this delicious vegetable in the open air, after you have got the plants. But the plants are tender and must be raised in a hotbed or in boxes in the house. Sow the seed in this latitude the first or second week in April, set out the plants in the garden the first or second week in June, in a loose, warm soil. Select a warm, sheltered location, and keep the ground mellow and free of weeds. Hill up a little as the plants grow, and keep off the potato bugs." He's said it all — the only thing I might add is to dig compost into the planting spots generously before moving seedlings to the garden, and use compost as a hilled-up mulch when plants are half grown. Eggplants like to eat well.

Labor Day Watermelons

Labor Day has become a symbol of the end of summer. Observed on the first Monday in September as a legal holiday throughout the United States, Puerto Rico, and Canada, it has always been one of the favorite holidays of the rural farm family — a day of rest and recreation, a day for a huge picnic. It is a time for rejoicing, a foretaste of the big Thanksgiving feast to be held later in the year.

Like many holidays it has its own traditions, fun, and contests. In our part of the world, which is justly famous for growing fine watermelons, there were always seed-spitting contests when the melons

---

Watermelon Pickles

3 quarts prepared watermelon rind (about 6 pounds unpared or ½ large melon)
¾ cup salt
3 quarts water
2 quarts ice cubes (2 trays)
9 cups sugar (white)

3 cups white vinegar
3 cups water
1 tablespoon whole cloves (about 48)
6 1-inch pieces stick cinnamon
Red or green food coloring (optional)
1 lemon thinly sliced

Pare the rind and all pink edges from the watermelon. Keep the rind in plastic bags in refrigerator until enough for one recipe has been collected. Cut into inch squares or fancy shapes as desired. Cover with brine, made by mixing the salt with 3 quarts cold water. Add the ice cubes. Let the dish stand 5 to 6 hours. Drain.

Rinse in cold water. Cover with cold water and cook until fork tender, about 10 minutes. (Do not overcook.) Drain.

Combine sugar with vinegar, water and spices tied loosely in a cloth bag. Add red or green coloring, if desired. Boil 5 minutes and pour over watermelon with spices. Add lemon slices if desired. Let stand overnight.

Heat to boiling. Cook until fruit is translucent and hot throughout, about 10 minutes. Pack hot watermelon loosely into clean hot jars. Open the spice bag and add one piece of stick cinnamon to each jar. Cover with boiling syrup to the top of jars. Adjust the lids. Process in a boiling water bath for 5 minutes. Yield: 4–5 pints.

(cooling all day in the well) were brought out and served in the evening. My husband, who was a great seed-spitter, always looked forward to this and entered into the contest with great gusto.

Needless to say, we housewives, who wasted nothing, always gathered up the left-over watermelons and put them carefully aside in the back of our old Fords to be taken home. The next day we all got busy and made watermelon pickles. This recipe is about the best I have ever used.

❦ ❦ ❦

THE COUNTY FAIR

Putting aside food for winter was not the only reason for digging root crops carefully, harvesting top-of-the-ground fruits gently, canning, preserving and jelly making. September, in Oklahoma, is the time of the County Fair.

A fair is a special kind of event for the purposes of buying and selling, holding contests, and having a good time. The name comes from the Middle English *feire*, from Middle Latin *feria*, meaning "weekday," "fair," or "holiday," according to Webster's. But fairs were held long before the Romans' time, first having developed as a way to facilitate peaceful trade between tribes. Thousands of years ago, tribesmen would come together at certain spots to exchange goods. They were often at war with men of other tribes, but they declared a truce at the "fair ground." They regarded the fair ground as a holy place and believed that the gods would punish anyone who fought or cheated there.

Marco Polo returned to Europe from China in the late 1200's, telling of the fairs of Kinsai, the great capital city ruled by Kublai Khan, and the center of trade of all China. The fairs took place in ten great squares four miles apart down the main street of the city. Half a million customers came to these fairs. Each square had a great palace where officials settled arguments about trade. The fairs were held every third day. Tremendous amounts of fresh meat, vegetables, fruits, wine, and jewelry were sold. Five and a half tons of pepper, one of the most prized spices of the time, were sold in Kinsai every day. The fairs of Kinsai, as Marco Polo described them, were beyond the imagination of his European listeners, and many people did not believe his stories.

Fairs were also held in North America at a very early date. The Aztecs of Mexico held weekly fairs in honor of their gods, with special courts of law. The greatest fair took place in Mexico City in front of the temple. Cortez' Spanish soldiers, who saw this fair, were astonished at its size, orderliness and cleanliness. Strict rules of honesty were followed. Products such as stone implements, cloth woven of cotton and other fibers, chocolate, tobacco, and garments of feathers were for sale.

Much of the trade was carried on by barter, but tin and gold were also used.

In Colonial America fairs were patterned after the lively market fairs of England. In the early 1800's, farm societies that hoped to improve American farm products began to hold exhibitions at the market fairs. They offered prizes for the best examples of certain farm products — a practice continued today — and for useful inventions. In 1810 the Berkshire Agricultural Society, organized by a country gentleman named Elkanah Watson, put on a fair called the Berkshire Cattle Show, a forerunner of the county fair.

Prizes were given for many oth-

Giant sunflowers are easy to grow. The bright golden heads don't really follow the sun, once they have bloomed — they do so only while still in the bud.

er products besides livestock. For the first time women took an active part in fairs. They sent in their jellies, pickles, mincemeat, and other household goods, and received medals and prizes for the best. This type of fair became popular throughout America, especially in farming areas. Corn huskings, sack races, quilting bees, athletic contests and horse races were added as time passed. Now there is usually a carnival as well, with ferris wheels, concession stands and cotton candy, hamburger and hot dog stands, in addition to the general exhibition building and livestock barns.

Winning at the fair was important. At stake was more than the prizes and the prestige of the individual farmer. A winner in the grain contest would soon find he had customers eager to buy his seed so they might also harvest a superior product. Those who had prize-winning livestock could sell their animals at higher prices and charge higher prices for breeding.

In the matter of vegetables it was usually the largest tomato, pumpkin or squash that won (though not always, as I will tell you later). Quality was important, too, and still is today. Combine the two and you have a real winner.

Grapefruit-size Tomatoes

Derek Fell, whose farm is located near Gardenville, Pennsylvania, relates his experience in growing tomatoes "as big as grapefruits," weighing over 2 pounds each and full of delicious flavor.

He grows them like that consistently, every year, relying mostly on compost to maintain soil fertility. Here is how he does it:

The variety selected is extremely important, and in my experience the hybrid variety called Supersteak VFN is best. It is not only the largest size tomato I've ever seen, but it also grows fruit that is smooth skinned, round in shape, deep red in color and more flavorful than other large-fruited varieties such as Beefsteak and Ponderosa. Also, it has three kinds of disease resistance the other varieties don't have.

Second, a compost-rich soil is vital. Tomatoes require excessive amounts of moisture to produce large, blemish-free fruits, since it is water that swells the fruit, and fluids that transport food from the roots to all parts of the plant. Compost has several benefits over other soil amendments: it has excellent *moisture retention*, yet allows excess water to drain freely; it improves *soil texture* with its fibrous structures and pockets of air, allowing plant roots freedom to grow and absorb moisture; it acts as a fertilizer, adding to the soil beneficial plant nutrients and trace elements."

(I might add here that one of the best things you can add to a compost heap is nettles, free for the taking if you find a patch.)

Derek Fell makes his compost in a compost bin that is scientifically designed to make tons of compost quickly and continuously, simply by dropping garden and kitchen wastes in at the top and shoveling rich, compost out at the bottom within a matter of weeks. You can accomplish the same thing, but more slowly, by making a compost heap and turning it.

Soil Preparation

In the spring he spreads his compost from the bin onto his garden to a depth of 3 inches. He mounds the soil into raised beds 2 feet wide and 6 inches high to accommodate each row of tomatoes. A handful of granular fertilizer high in phosphorus, which helps speed fruit formation and ripening, is worked into the soil at each planting hole. He then covers the bed with a strip of black plastic to smother weeds and prevent moisture loss through evaporation. Also, the plastic warms the soil early so the tomato plants get off to a good start.

Starting Plants

To beat the weather he starts his tomatoes indoors from seed eight weeks before setting them outdoors, using empty quart-capacity milk cartons as plant pots (he's a man after my own heart). These allow his tomato plants to develop extra-large root systems so that when transplanted they overcome transplanting shock quickly and help the tops grow vigorously. On cool nights the plants are covered with bottomless plastic gallon-capacity milk jugs to protect them from danger of frost.

He waters the rows frequently

during the growing season to keep the soil moist (but not water-logged), and gives a booster application of dilute liquid fertilizer (fish emulsion) when the first fruits start to enlarge.

Using this system of growing tomatoes Derek Fell not only harvests giant-size tomatoes, but his first Supersteaks ripened around July 4th in a year when his garden had experienced a heavy snowfall on April 1st and a last frost on May 1st.

Varieties

While Derek Fell's choice of Supersteak VFN is an excellent one for growing giants, it is not the *only* choice. Delicious (Burpee and others) is the seed that produced the world's largest tomato — a whopping 6-pound, 8-ounce beauty grown by Clarence Dailey of Monoma, Wisc. and listed in the Guinness Book of World Records. Most fruits of this variety weigh over a pound, have excellent flavor and smoothness, with very little cracking, and solid interiors with small seed cavities; perfect for slicing. They are widely available and may be ordered from Burpee's.

R.H. Shumway has Abraham Lincoln, which may weigh from 1 to 2-plus pounds. For such a large tomato it is remarkably smooth and free from cracks and seams.

Other Giants

There are other giant vegetables besides tomatoes that are fun to grow as well. One of our oldest seed and nursery houses (and I might also say one of our finest, both in quality and integrity), Henry Field's, has a lot to say about growing biggies. With the becoming modesty always evidenced by our leading seedsmen, they state:

Giant Vegetables Are Not Just For Fairy Tales. First, start with the right selection. According to Donna Carlson, Customer Service Manager for Henry Field Seed and Nursery Company of Shenandoah, Iowa, it is possible to design a garden that is sure to earn you a reputation as a 'giant among gardeners.' 'The secret,' she says, 'is really genetic. If you plant seeds for ordinary-size vegetables, no matter how much fertilizer and water and sunlight and care you provide, you'll still have ordinary-size vegetables. But if you plant seed for giants and provide all those things, you'd better have a lot of storage room!'

Although there is no evidence that Cinderella's pumpkin was grown from Atlantic Giant seed, the variety does produce pumpkins large enough to hold a full-size person. Developed by Howard Dill and marketed by Henry Field's, the variety has reached 493½ pounds — a world record. The vines can grow to 90 feet and the pumpkins gain up to 15 pounds a day during the summer growing season. By autumn Atlantic Giants can grow so large that it takes eight men to lift them and a commercial scale for the weigh-in!

Giant Growing Tips

Once you've chosen your giants, you need to tailor your growing practices to suit their big appetites. Vegetables are mostly water, and they can not attain their optimum size if they are stressed by lack of moisture. If you keep them weed free, and give them plenty of water, sufficient fertilizer, protection from harmful insects and disease, and shelter from the wind, you can easily grow prize winners for the county fair.

❦ ❦ ❦

Record-Breaking Pumpkins

If your ambitions reach beyond the local fair and into the record book, the 500-pound-pumpkin barrier remains to be breached. Howard Dill, the current record holder, uses the following method for growing record pumpkins:

Starting plants indoors (and under the right sign) to give them a head start is especially important in short-growing-season areas. Dill grew his record breaker in Canada, using seed started indoors.

Since pumpkins need plenty of sunlight and well-drained soil, select your site carefully. Then give your pumpkins plenty of room — Dill spaces them 25 feet apart. Giant pumpkins also need plenty of food. To provide it, Dill digs a pit 4 feet wide, 6 feet long, and nearly 2 feet deep. He fills the pit nearly to the top with 2–3-year-old cow manure, and covers this with his best top soil, to which he has added fertilizer. Into this hill he sets his started plants when the soil has warmed up in the spring. He provides plenty of water — several dozen gallons a day — because even one day without sufficient water can slow the giant's growth. Providing these things will result in enormous pumpkins, but if you're shooting for a record, the vines will require special attention as well.

Watch over them carefully in June and July and prune away any fruit that sets too early or too close to the root. In late July, let just one fruit set, about 15 feet away from the root. Through August, topdress with manure tea or fertilizer, paying particular attention to the "knees" of the vine —those knobby junctures where tendrils reach down into the soil to form a kind of secondary root system.

During the time the plants are growing and setting fruit, provide wind protection — Dill uses 4-foot-high windbreaks of plywood and particle board. Then inspect the pumpkins daily and be alert for any problems so they can be handled quickly before they slow your giant's 15-pound-per-day growth rate. Following Dill's methods, you'll have only one pumpkin per vine, but it may be the one that reaches 500 pounds and puts your name in the *Guinness Book of World Records!*

Barring that, and provided you are on good terms with your fairy godmother, you could park the Ford in the garage and take a fine pumpkin coach to the Halloween ball...

Exhibiting at the Fair

So now you've grown your giants — what are you going to do with them? The obvious answer is exhibit at the County Fair. But just how are you going to do that? As with everything else there are rules. The largest vegetable in its class does not always win because other things are taken into consideration. Most county fairs have a rule book printed well in advance, and usually a copy of this may be obtained from your County Agricultural Extension Agent. This will list the various categories of livestock, baked goods, clothing, and so on, the prizes in each class, and the dates for entry and closing.

Rules differ a little from place to place. Generally speaking, however, to be successful with exhibition vegetables it is necessary to take every care to ensure that they are prepared and staged in the most effective manner. Each vegetable must be selected with care and arranged so that it shows to the best advantage.

Choosing Specimens

The specimens chosen should be uniform in size, shapely and free from blemishes. The general rule is to pick vegetables in prime eating condition.

★**Peas** and **lima beans** must be well filled out and fresh. When gathering peas, handle them by the stalks so the waxy "bloom" will not be rubbed off. (Should this happen there is still a trick you can use. If the bloom on the pods is poor you can improve it by laying the pods in a piece of folded flannel and holding them over the steam from a kettle for a few minutes after they are picked.)

★**Potatoes** should be shapely, shallow-eyed, free from disease, and unblemished. It is a good idea to place them in a shallow box as soon as they are lifted and cover them with a damp cloth to prevent the skins from becoming discolored.

★**Root crops** such as beets and carrots should be lifted carefully to prevent their being damaged. They make a better appearance on the show table with foliage attached, provided it is fresh, clean and undamaged by insects. If the rules state "with cut foliage," the leaves of carrot, turnip and parsnip should be cut off to within an inch of the base, but those of beets should be twisted off. Potatoes, beets, carrots, turnips and parsnips must be sponged gently in clear water, and all fibrous roots should be trimmed off. The long varieties of carrots, beets and parsnips must have roots that taper evenly.

★Wash **celery, leeks** and **Chinese cabbage** and cut the roots off neatly. Sometimes it is best to trim off a few of the outer leaves.

★Choose **snap beans** that are straight, firm and crisp; stringy beans should be discarded, even if they are large.

Ideal **leeks** are long in the stem, well blanched, clear-skinned and not "bulbous" at the base.

★The curds of **cauliflowers** should not be discolored and must be of even size and rounded shape.

Cauliflowers are prepared by cutting off the leaves level with the curds. Just like you usually see them cut in the supermarket.

★The amateur exhibitor is apt to choose the largest specimens of **cabbage,** but those of medium size, firm and free from holes caused by slugs and caterpillars, are preferred by judges. Remove cabbage stems and outer imperfect leaves.

★Strip a husk from a section of each ear of corn and cut it off near the base.

★**Tomatoes, eggplants, peppers, squash, apples** and **pears** should be carefully wiped and polished. Tomatoes should be ripe, clear-skinned, of good color, firm and fresh.

★**Turnips** with small tap roots, tender flesh and undamaged skins are required for exhibition.

★Loose skins should be removed from **onions** and the necks tied. If rules call for them to be exhibited with tops on, do what the rule book says; otherwise long tops may have a few inches cut off so they will present a better appearance. Onions should have clear skins and small necks.

Transporting and Displaying

Greens and tops of root vegetables can be kept fresh by harvesting well in advance and hardening overnight in a cool place, in water, or sprinkled with water. If unwilted and of good color at the end of the hardening period, they will probably stand up through the show.

Be extra careful in transporting your fruit and vegetables to the show. For transit, flat boxes or baskets should be used. Each specimen must be wrapped in tissue paper, with moss or cotton placed between the layers. The heaviest specimens should be placed at the bottom and the lightest and most easily damaged, such as tomatoes, on the top.

Lay out pea or bean pods side by side so they can be easily seen and counted by the judges. Turn tomatoes stem end down; fruits, stem end up. To display a vegetable collection, make an arrangement with squash, melons and other large items at back, and corn, root vegetables, and so on radiating from the center. Place smaller vegetables in the foreground.

If you display fruit here is a suggestion. As mentioned before, fruit packed in nettle (stinging nettle) hay ripens faster. Nettle also deters fermentation, keeps fruit free from mold, and aids keeping qualities.

Secrets of a Prize Winner

My mother took winning first prize at the county fair very seriously. She had to! My father died when I was nine years old and, as I have said, I grew up in the lap of poverty. Then, as now, you lost your home if you couldn't pay your property taxes — and there was no "welfare" to step in and pay your bills for you. You made it on your own, or else. All year we would scrimp and save so that we could pay our property taxes in the fall — and winning a little prize money at the fair helped.

That little house we lived in was just about all we had.

In those days there were few ways for women to make money, but my mother was an excellent cook. She sold cakes, cookies, bread and rolls, did fine sewing, and held her head up proudly. And she taught me to do the same.

I remember her strategy as she readied her baked goods for exhibition. In the cookie exhibits, for instance, there were three categories — sugar cookies, fruit cookies, and nut cookies. She made the same dough for all three, merely decorating them differently — and she usually received the blue ribbon. Her bread and cakes were so light they almost floated. Being also a pretty woman, she had more than one proposal of marriage. (In the early days of the West women were scarce, very scarce, and it was not at all unusual for a widow to receive a proposal of marriage even as she rode home from her husband's funeral. In one instance, a fight took place at the cemetery over who would have the privilege of driving the widow home. And girls married young — I had my own first "offer" when I was twelve! Any woman who wanted to "get hitched into double harness" had a wide choice of suitors.)

My mother was a real prize winner in more ways than one, and I watched her with admiring eyes and basked in the reflected glory. But the year I turned ten I wanted some of that glory for myself. I determined to bake a fruit cake and enter it in the county fair. I had never baked one before,

but I just knew I could. My mother tried her best to persuade me to try something easier — fruit cakes can be somewhat difficult even for an experienced cook. But no, my hard little head was made up. I baked the cake and it was duly entered.

As it chanced, mine was the only entry that year in the fruit cake category, and I felt absolutely sure of winning first prize. It was, however, the disappointment of my life. We were a bit late in getting there the day the bakery exhibits were judged — perhaps a merciful Providence so arranged it — and I was appalled when I looked and saw my cake decorated with a *white* ribbon. Here it was, the only entry in its class, and the judges thought it was so bad they had given it *third* prize!

I cried all the way home and I've been mad at fruit cakes ever since.

For Fragrant Linen

Our grandmothers dried flowers of lavender, loving them for the nice fragrance they gave to clothing and linens. The leaves and seeds also went into sachets. You can easily grow lavender, a perennial, from seeds, cuttings, or root divisions. Give it a light side dressing of wood ashes in the spring.

HARVESTING AND PRESERVING HERBS

September is an excellent month to cut and preserve herbs intended for winter use in seasoning various dishes. They are best when dried fresh and lose their quality as they age. Herbs can also provide creative, tasteful alternatives to salt for flavoring foods. This is important for those on a salt-free diet. Others may be trying to reduce and salt often causes water retention. So do yourself a flavor — through the skillful use of herbs and spices, imaginative flavors can be created and simple foods made into gourmet delights.

Herbs and spices differ only in that herbs tend to be plants grown in temperate areas while spices grow in tropical regions. Many people prefer to grow their own herbs, just as their grandmothers did, so they will have a fresh supply throughout the growing season, thereby assuring top quality. Professional cooks prefer fresh herbs, if available. But fresh herbs are less concentrated, and two to three times as much should be used if a recipe calls for dried herbs.

If growing herbs for drying, the harvesting should be done in the morning after the dew has evaporated but before the sun is very bright. The essential oils in herbs will evaporate into the atmosphere during the day, so it is important to collect them when their flavor is at its peak. Cut only the amount to be used in one day.

The herbs should be dried in bunches or laid on screens in a warm, dark, well-ventilated spot.

Rosemary For Remembrance

This neat and lovely plant, with its tiny blue flowers, has been famous for centuries as a healing plant. A general feeling of well-being was thought to be prompted by rosemary tea. The boiled leaves were applied to gouty legs. Extracting the oil from the leaves by pounding them with a little sweet oil in a mortar, an ointment was made. This was incorporated with melted petroleum jelly and the resulting ointment used for scratches and cuts. It is said the ancient Saxons made similar use of a rosemary ointment.

The name "Rosemary" comes from the latin *rosmarinus*, meaning *sea dew*. In masses, blossoming rosemary looks like blue-gray mist blown over the meadows from the sea. Oil of rosemary is used in perfumes and cooks use the plant for seasoning. The plant is also an emblem of fidelity and remembrance. In *Hamlet* occurs the often-quoted remark of Ophelia, "There's rosemary, that's for remembrance."

An attic is ideal, although closets or dry basements will suffice. The temperature should not be over 90 degrees. If it's too hot, the herbs will cook. The length of time required for drying will vary according to the thickness of the plant parts.

Herbs should be stored away from direct sunlight to prevent bleaching. Be sure they're well labeled. Most dried herbs will keep for at least one year in glass or plastic containers, but eventually they lose most of their potency and should be discarded. Certain herbs, such as chives, parsley, French tarragon, mint, basil, lovage and sorrel, keep well in the freezer. Put them into individual plastic bags or small plastic jars and freeze them.

Herbs are wonderful for so many purposes — you can cook with them or landscape with them. Use them to control bugs in the garden or for medicinal purposes — even for home crafts. More about all this a bit later on.

Cooking with Herbs

For cooking, which we are concerned with now, a good general rule is not to mix two very strong herbs together, but rather one strong and one or more milder flavors to complement both the stronger herb and the food.

Here are some cooking tips with herbs and spices:

★In general, the weaker the flavor of the main staple item, the lower the level of added seasoning is needed to achieve a satisfactory balance of flavor in the end product.

★Dried herbs are stronger than fresh, and powdered herbs are stronger than crumbled. A useful formula is: ¼ teaspoon powdered herbs = ¾ to 1 teaspoon crumbled = 2 teaspoons fresh.

★Leaves should be chopped very finely because the more cut surface is exposed the more flavor will be released.

★A mortar and pestle can be kept in the kitchen to powder dry herbs when necessary.

★Scissors are often the best utensil for cutting fresh herbs.

★Be conservative in the amount of an herb until you're familiar with its strength. The aromatic oils can be strong and objectionable if too much is used.

★The flavoring of herbs is lost by extended cooking. Add herbs to soups or stews about 45 minutes before completing the cooking. For cold foods, such as dips, cheese, vegetables and dressings, herbs should be added several hours or overnight before using.

★For casseroles and hot sauces, add finely chopped fresh or dried herbs directly to the mixture.

★To become familiar with the specific flavor of an herb, try mixing it with butter and/or cream cheese, let it set for at least an hour, and spread on a plain cracker.

Beware when purchasing herbal salt blends. Many are merely herbs added to salt. Read the ingredients carefully or just blend your own combinations.

Dried herbs should be stored in plastic bags, boxes or tins rather than in cardboard containers. Keep the containers out of the direct sunlight (because that will bleach their color and reduce their strength) and don't place them too near the stove (to avoid high humidity).

Relative Strength of Herbs

Strong or dominant flavors. These should be used with care since their flavors stand out — approximately one teaspoon for six servings. They include bay, cardamom, curry, ginger, hot peppers, mustard, black pepper, rosemary and sage.

Medium flavors. A moderate amount of these is recommended — one to two teaspoons for six servings. They are basil, celery seed and leaves, cumin, dill, fennel, French tarragon, garlic, marjoram, mint, oregano, savory (winter and summer), thyme, and turmeric.

Delicate flavors. These may be used in large quantities and combine well with most other herbs and spices. This group includes burnet, chervil, chives and parsley.

Herb Blends

Herbs can be combined for specific foods. Having the combinations on hand will speed cooking and enhance your reputation as a gourmet cook. The herbs can be added loose or wrapped in cheesecloth (removed before serving). Here are some suggestions for blending herbs:

Egg herbs. Basil, dill weed (leaves), garlic, parsley

Fish herbs. Basil, bay leaf (crumbled), French tarragon, lemon thyme, parsley (options: fennel, sage, savory)

Poultry herbs. Lovage, marjoram (two parts), sage (three parts)

Salad herbs. Basil, lovage, parsley, French tarragon

Tomato sauce herbs. Basil (two parts), bay leaf, marjoram, oregano, parsley (options: celery leaves, cloves)

Vegetable herbs. Basil, parsley, savory

Italian blend. Basil, marjoram, oregano, rosemary, sage, savory, thyme

Barbecue blend. Cumin, garlic, hot pepper, oregano

French herbal combinations. *Fines herbes:* parsley, chervil, chives, French tarragon (sometimes adding a small amount of basil, fennel, oregano, sage or saffron)

Bouquet garni mixtures. Bay, parsley (two parts), thyme. The herbs may be wrapped in cheesecloth or the parsley wrapped around the thyme and bay leaf.

Basic herb butter. One stick unsalted butter, 1 to 3 tablespoons dried herbs or 2 to 6 tablespoons fresh herbs, ½ teaspoon lemon juice, and white pepper. Combine ingredients and mix until fluffy. Pack in covered container and let set at least one hour. Any of the culinary herbs and spices may be used.

Garlic butter. Divest garlic cloves of hard outer covering and put through food chopper or garlic press. Add 2 tablespoons of puree to 1 pound of butter or 4 sticks of margarine. Optional: Parsley flakes may be added.

Herb vinegars. Heat vinegar in an enamel pan and pour it into a vinegar bottle and add one or several culinary herbs (to taste). Do not let the vinegar boil. Let the mixture set for two weeks before using. Any type of vinegar may be used, depending on personal preference.

Herb Blends to Replace Salt

These can be placed in shakers and used instead of salt.

Saltless surprise. 2 teaspoons garlic powder and 1 teaspoon each of basil, oregano, and powdered lemon rind (or dehydrated lemon juice). Put ingredients into a blender and mix well. Store in glass container, label well, and add rice to prevent caking.

Pungent Salt Substitute. 3 teaspoons basil, 2 teaspoons each of savory (summer savory is best), celery seed, ground cumin seed, sage and marjoram, and 1 teaspoon lemon thyme. Mix well, then powder with a mortar and pestle.

Spicy saltless seasoning. 1 teaspoon each of cloves, pepper, and coriander seed (crushed), 2 teaspoons paprika, and 1 tablespoon rosemary. Mix ingredients in a blender. Store in airtight container.

WHAT GOES WITH WHAT

Soups	Bay, chervil, French tarragon, marjoram, parsley, savory, rosemary
Poultry	Garlic, oregano, rosemary, savory, sage
Beef	Bay, chives, cloves, cumin, garlic, hot pepper, marjoram, rosemary, savory
Lamb	Garlic, marjoram, oregano, rosemary, thyme (make little slits in lamb to be roasted and insert herbs — garlic slivers are particularly good used like this)
Pork	Coriander, cumin, garlic, ginger, hot pepper, pepper, sage, savory, thyme
Cheese	Basil, chervil, chives, curry, dill, fennel, garlic chives, marjoram, oregano, parsley, sage, thyme
Fish	Chervil, dill, fennel, French tarragon, garlic, parsley, thyme
Fruit	Anise, cinnamon, coriander, cloves, ginger, lemon verbena, mint, rose geranium, sweet cicely
Bread	Caraway, marjoram, oregano, poppy seed, rosemary, thyme
Vegetables	Basil, burnet, chervil, chives, dill, French tarragon, marjoram, mint, parsley, pepper, thyme
Salads	Basil, borage, burnet, chives, French tarragon, garlic chives, parsley, rocket-salad, sorrel (these are best used fresh or added to salad dressing. Otherwise, use herb vinegars for extra flavor)

GATHERING WILD GRAPES

There are a number of different species of wild grapes. My own favorites for wine and jelly making are the tiny blue-black grapes we call "possum grapes," which festoon the trees, often by roadsides, and are free for picking in September.

Here is the Indian recipe for Possum Grape Dumplings, which are often served as dessert at Indian dinners and gatherings. Also, according to tribal custom, Grape Dumplings, sometimes called *Walakshi*, were furnished by the bride's relatives at weddings. The bridegroom's relatives furnished the venison.

★ ★ ★

Possum Grape Dumplings
(Walakshi — *Choctaw*)

Gather possum grapes when they ripen in the fall. They grow in the woods and along creek banks throughout Indian country.

Cook the wild grapes until they boil, using just enough water to cover. Strain through a clean sack, keeping the juice alone. Sweeten it with sugar or honey. Bring the juice to a boil and add dumplings (see below). Cook, covered, until dumplings are done, stirring occasionally.

The housewife who doesn't have a supply of wild grapes may use store-bought unsweetened grape juice.

Dumplings

---

1 cup flour	¼ teaspoon salt
1½ teaspoons baking powder	1 tablespoon shortening
2 teaspoons sugar	½ cup grape juice

Mix first five ingredients and add juice until a stiff dough is made. Roll out very thin on a floured board. Cut pieces two inches long and ½ inch wide. Prepare juice by adding ½ cup sugar to 2½ cups grape juice. Mix well bring to a boil and add a dash of lemon juice. Drop dough pieces into boiling juice mixture. Cover and cook about 12 minutes. Serve warm. *Yield: about 5 servings.*

★ ★ ★

Libra the Balance *(September 23 - October 22)*

Hunter's Moon
OCTOBER

*Peach canning time ★ Apple butter ★ The Medicine
Show ★ Cutting wood by the Signs ★ Circus day ★
Drying Apples ★ Green tomato relishes ★ Katydid
love call ★ Mormon hospitality ★ Roasting venison ★
Freezing fish for winter meals ★ Celebrating
Halloween ★*

WHEN I WAS A LIT-
TLE GIRL we used to
have a peach tree we
called our "October peach." I
don't know if that was its real
name or not — I just know those
wonderful peaches with the blush-
ing, bright red cheeks ripened
in early October. When they ripened, my father would pen the
chickens in another area so they
would not peck the fruit, and we
would harvest the peaches at the
peak of their juicy best. Most of
our earlier canned peaches having
been used, my mother would "put
up" these for winter, carefully
saving the stones and peelings for
peach brandy.

October Apples

Many of our apples, too, would
ripen late in the fall and be ready
for harvest at what my mother considered the "right time," that is,
from September 23 to October
23. She believed that any crops
harvested under Libra should be
reaped during the old phase of the
moon, the waning third or fourth
quarter, thus counteracting the
moist influence of the Scales, and
any bruised spots would heal up.
When fruit was picked during the
New Moon, she contended, the
bruises would rot. And we did not
pick apples for cider or winter
keeping until the sign of Libra.

Of course October was also "cider making time," and my father made both sweet and hard cider. And "apple butter making time" just naturally follows cider making time. Here is an apple butter recipe from an old cookbook which follows pretty well the way my mother made it.

Apple Butter

This is generally made by the large quantity. Boil down a kettleful of cider to two-thirds the original quantity. Pare, core and slice juicy apples, and put as many into the cider as it will cover. (These need not be all of one variety, you can use Delicious for sweetness, winesaps and even a few crab apples.) Boil slowly, stirring often with a flat stick, and when the apples are tender to breaking, take them out with a perforated skimmer, draining well against the sides of the kettle. Place in a large crock. Put in a second supply of apples and stew them soft, as many as the cider will hold. Take from the fire, pour into the crock with the first batch; cover and let stand 12 hours. Then return to the kettle and boil down, stirring all the while until it is the consistency of soft soap, and brown in color. You may spice to taste if you please. Keep in stone jars in a dry, cool place, and it should keep all winter.

Autumn, in our climate, is also a good time for planting new fruit trees (or any trees or shrubs), they will grow a little under the ground during our mild winters and be well established by spring. New strawberry plants, too, can be planted during the fall.

It was even better to wait to harvest apples "for keeping" until the waning moon under Scorpio (October 23 to November 22). Old-timers believed that Scorpio's watery and fruitful sign "fixed the sugar and juice" in winter apples. And these were carefully stored in nettle hay.

Late Potatoes

In my garden there are usually a few late potatoes to be dug, both sweet potatoes and "Irish" potatoes. I often think about how the latter got their name, for they are not *Irish* potatoes at all. Potatoes originated in South America. Most botanists agree that the white potato comes from a species found in the high plateaus of Peru and Bolivia. The potato was probably first mentioned in a book by Cieza de Leon in Cornica de Peru, published in Seville, Spain in 1553. He recorded that potatoes were grown in Colombia and Peru in 1538.

Spanish explorers introduced potatoes to Europe, probably as early as 1550. Potatoes appear in the records of two hospitals in Seville in 1573. From Spain potatoes were taken to Italy, then to England and Ireland.

The potato grew so well in Ireland, and had such great food value, that the Irish adopted it as their main food. They became economically dependent upon potatoes. In 1845 and 1846 the Irish potato crop failed because of a late-blight plant disease. As a result, thousands of Irish starved to death or migrated to the United States. Migration was definitely preferable. Not generally known, the Choctaw tribe of Oklahoma raised money to send to the Irish famine sufferers in 1847. Potatoes were probably introduced into North America in 1621. They may have been brought to Virginia from England by way of Bermuda. The white potato became known as the *Irish potato*, because Irish immigrants brought potatoes with them when they settled in Londonderry, N.H., in 1719.

★ ★ ★

All my life I've felt that I was born both happy and lucky. As a child I could walk through a field of white clover and look down and pick up four leaves as I went. I did not know until later in life that I could dowse for water but there were other things. Often I would get quick flashes in my mind about something that was going to happen in the future. I did not know, as a child, that this was the gift of premonition. When something like this occurred, I just told my mother I "had a funny feeling." I did not think of this as unusual; I thought everyone was like that. One day she warned me not to speak of this to others. "This comes to you from me, child," she said, "and my mother and my mother's mother, far back, but

you must not talk about it; people will think you are crazy."

The flashes have not necessarily been of impending evil or disaster, as such things often are, but usually take the form of a warning of something I should, or should not do ... a trip I should or should not take, something I should sell or buy. Could this have come to us from a long-ago Irish grandmother?

★ ★ ★

Herbal Medicines and "Medicine Shows"

My mother had a lot of Indian friends who respected her greatly for her knowledge of herbs and herbal remedies. Sometimes, even today, when I take the time to read the fine print on a medicine bottle, I notice that some of the plants she used for specific ailments are still right there being used today. Recently eyebright and many others have been rediscovered.

In the old days, doctors were few and far between. There was little regulation in the Old West, and sometimes they were not really doctors ... they just claimed to be. There was no way for people to check up on them; often they just drifted into a community and "hung out a shingle." Sometimes they really were pretty good and helped people, having somewhere, somehow, picked up some medical knowledge. They would also grow their own remedies, just as the settlers did, and would make up various concoctions. Sometimes these mixtures worked. And then, quite probably, there would be a "Medicine Show" on the road, traveling from place to place and offering to cure everybody of just about any ailment that troubled mankind. The cure for everything often was contained in the same bottle, and frequently purported to be made of a lot of strange things including snake oil.

One year, in early October, one such show, calling itself "The Quaker Healers," arrived in Ardmore, Indian Territory. They claimed they would "lecture and *heel*" (probably a newspaper typo) on "Main Street, opposite the Banks," and what they promised to do was little short of miraculous. With a lot of people being gullible, the "healers" usually did a brisk business.

The shows were also a form of entertainment in places that didn't see much from one year to the next; they played in little towns where they didn't have a movie theater, a drugstore, a doctor —or a sheriff.

The con artists also had a good sense of the dramatic; they put on a good show and everybody loved it. Often the performance included music, a guitar or some other instrument, singing and dancing, possibly a clown or two. There was always a lot of noise and action, and the audience got worked up to fever pitch. At the most appropriate psychological moment, one of the medicine show troupe would start extolling the virtues and curative qualities of their particular product, and another member would start circulating through the crowd, selling right and left. By the time the purchasers found

that the product didn't cure anything, the medicine show was long gone and difficult to trace. Quite often the "cure" would contain a large percentage of alcohol, which gave — even to the ladies who were teetotalers and would never touch "spirits" — a temporary feeling of euphoria. When that wore off, they were right back where they started. Sometimes the concoctions would contain purgative herbs, and a good cleaning out in fall or springtime usually made people feel better anyway. Which reminds me of something else that was a necessity back in the "old days."

Firewood Lore

Since for most people in frontier days, wood was the only means of keeping warm in the winter and fueling the kitchen range so meals could be cooked, keeping the woodpile stocked was a very serious matter.

Signs of Rain

If summer has been dry, it may still be dry in October, and I have more than once observed a strange thing. Springs that have gone dry, or nearly dry, will start running again just *before* a rain. It's hard to find an explanation for this, but watch and see if this happens where you live. Others I have mentioned this to in different sections of the country have told me they've seen it happen also.

Toadstools, too, often appear just *before* a rain.

Regarding the best time to cut timber there are two schools of thought. Most agree that it should be cut in the time of the waning moon, but there is some disagreement as to the correct month. One of the old books says that August is the best month, probably because it is generally hot and dry. Another book directs that to cut hardwood timber to make it durable, the best months are October, November and December.

December and January, in the old of the moon, is when the sap is down. All kinds of timber that sheds its leaves in the fall should be cut in the third quarter of the moon, if possible in the winter. It is more durable when cut in the best month, December. Evergreen timber must be cut in the second quarter of the moon in the fall and winter.

In recent times there may still be those who remember that in France woodcutters once advertised that "the wood was cut in the waning of the moon."

That these beliefs are very ancient is shown by the words of Plutarch, a Greek moralist, who wrote of this more than two thousand years ago:

> The Moone showeth her power most evidently in those bodies, which have neither sense nor lively breath; for carpenters reject the timber of trees fallen in the ful-moone, as being soft and tender, subject also to the wormes and putrefaction, and that quickly by means of excessive moisture.

The Circus Comes to Town

Besides the Medicine Show there was another entertainment likely to appear in October — the circus. At this time the southern and southwestern states were still warm, so they were usually last on the circuit before the show was retired to winter quarters.

Circus day was different from any other. Weeks before the circus came to town, gaily colored posters showing clowns, lions, tigers, and elephants were pasted up on billboards and buildings and in the windows of stores. The posters promised that the circus would be "the greatest show on earth" and gave glowing descriptions on its star acts. Large newspaper ads were taken well in advance to announce the circus's coming.

In the old days, smaller circuses traveled from place to place in wagons. With the coming of the railroads and more convenient transportation, however, a circus might come to town on its own railroad train.

The circus came to America from Europe around 1792. George Washington attended Rickett's circus in Philadelphia while he was president. Rickett's was a small show, held in a small building, but George Washington liked it, especially the military riding acts, the jugglers, the clowns, and the music.

There were no elephants in American circuses until 1797. Later Phineas T. Barnum, the great circus pioneer, would buy Jumbo, a huge elephant, from the London Zoological Society for $10,000.

Jumbo's admirers in England protested the sale, and tried to prevent it. The publicity created by this disturbance helped to make Jumbo one of the most famous of circus elephants.

American circuses grew with the country, moving westward as the frontiers moved westward, and the wagons transporting the animals had to be strong, sturdy and large. Roads were rough and often muddy. A hippopotamus wagon required fourteen horses to pull it. No circus in the early days could be certain it would arrive in time for its scheduled performance.

The first railroad circus cars were built in 1872 and were used to move the Barnum Circus, which developed into the Barnum and Bailey Circus, the largest in the United States. James A. Bailey took it on tour of Europe in the 1880's. The show was a sensation.

When the Barnum and Bailey Circus returned to the United States it found a strong rival had sprung up. This was the Ringling Brothers Circus, started by five brothers at Baraboo, Wisconsin, in 1884. Though the two great shows were combined into one in 1919, the Ringling Brothers Circus was still a separate entity when it performed in Ardmore, on October 14, 1902.

As I mentioned in February, if a circus comes to town it is a good opportunity for an enterprising gardener to ask for the cage and stable cleanings for his compost heap. Manure is manure wherever you can get it!

Sundials in Colonial Gardens

Sundials are very ancient. No one knows who invented them — they just evolved. For centuries gardeners have found them particularly appealing, perhaps because sundials serve as sculptural ornaments, as well as attractive timepieces. Sundials were a part of many colonial gardens and some still exist, bearing the date when they were placed. If you would have an old-time garden, think "sundial."

Today, there are over a dozen different types, but all have a common element. Generally, the dial plate is the surface of the sundial where hour lines are inscribed, marking the hours of the day. The dial plate may be placed horizontally, vertically, or at a particular angle in between, depending on the type you choose.

Most sundials use a rod or plate called a "gnomon" to cast a shadow. The edge of the gnomon, known as the style, actually focuses the shadow on a specific spot on the dial plate, indicating the time.

The horizontal sundial is the most common type and is usually mounted on a post or pedestal and often used as the focal point of a formal garden, or as a pleasant accent amid flower borders.

HARVEST HOME

October is the time to harvest the small beets, carrots, turnips, and celeriac you may have missed on an earlier harvesting. Pull off the last tender okra pods from the bare, stiff stalks, now practically denuded of all their leaves except at the very top.

It is time now, too, to bring in all the squashes, for frost will fall alike on the ripe and the unripe. Bring in the few remaining dark green or bright-gold acorn squash, the long green- and white-striped crooknecks, and the dark, rough Hubbards. I always have good luck growing a second planting of summer squash such as Butterbar in the fall of the year. Seemingly, the squash bugs that may have devastated the planting (or tried to) early in the spring rarely attack it in the fall. I like to outwit the bugs — it makes me feel like a "mad scientist"!

Dried Apples

In early times drying fruit was often the only way people had of preserving it for winter, and dried apples for pies were looked upon with favor. We can still use this method. Apples can either be sliced up into thin slivers or cored and sliced into rings. Women who worked with old-fashioned apple peelers and corers often became very adept at the job, and sometimes made a game out of it, contesting with several friends to see who could prepare the most apples in a given period of time — again, turning work into fun.

Sometimes the apple rings were strung on a broomstick or a pole; while slices were spread out on boards. Depending on the weather, they were set out in the sun or in front of the fireplace. Generally speaking, if the weather was dry, two or three days of "sunning" would produce a rubbery, brownish product that might not look very appetizing, but when reconstituted on a cold winter day and baked into a pie wasn't half bad at all. If you dry fruit in this way, protect it at night, either by taking it in or covering it well so it won't pick up moisture and retard the drying process.

Since we have modern ovens, it is also a good idea to heat the dried slices for a few minutes at 225° F to kill any germs. Store the apples in sacks in a dry place. Peaches and apricots may also be dried, as well as many berries.

Late Tomatoes

In a warm autumn, you may find you still have tomatoes late into the season. Often, when a really cold spell threatens, you can continue to have fresh tomatoes for the table for several weeks simply by pulling up the vines and placing them to hang in a warm dry place. The tomatoes will continue to ripen, though they will not grow any larger.

Some thrifty colonial housewife of long ago must have developed the idea of using the smaller green tomatoes in such things as Chow Chow, India Relish, Green Pickle Relish, and my mother's favorite relish, Piccalilli.

Piccalilli

1 quart green tomatoes, chopped
1 cup (2–3 medium) sweet red peppers, chopped
5 cups (about 2 pounds) cabbage, chopped
1 cup (2–3 medium) green peppers, chopped

1½ cups (2–3 large) onions, chopped
⅓ cup salt
3 cups vinegar
2 cups brown sugar, firmly packed
2 tablespoons whole mixed pickling spices

Combine vegetables, mix with salt. Let stand overnight. Drain. Press in clean, thin white cloth to remove all liquid possible. Combine vinegar and sugar. Tie spices loosely in cloth bag, and add to vinegar mixture. Bring to a boil. Add vegetables, bring to boil, simmer about 30 minutes or until just enough liquid to moisten vegetables. Remove spice bag. Pack boiling hot into clean hot jars. Fill to ½ inch from top. Adjust lids. Process in boiling water bath 5 minutes. Yield 5–6 pints.

Aloe (Aloe vera) *guards against evil influence and prevents household accidents.*

An infusion of orange peels (Citrus sinesis) *when drunk will guard against future drunkeness.*

SIGNS OF THE SEASON

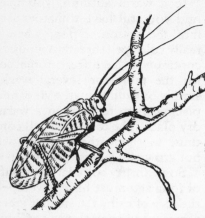

The name "katydid" comes from the love call of the male of certain eastern species, made by rubbing the bases of the forewings together.

Katydids

Katydids are an insect whose song I love to hear. They usually begin "singing" at twilight and keep it up throughout the night. They are heard most frequently in late summer and autumn — even in October there are a few of them left. And I think this relative of the meadow grasshopper is very attractive to look at. Its name comes from the love call of the male insects of certain eastern species. Other species make different sounds. Katydids rub the bases of their front wings together to make these notes. Little cross ridges on the wings form a sort of scraper. Most katydids live in trees and shrubs. They feed on leaves and young twigs, but they do little damage compared to that done by many other insects. Katydids lay their flat, oval, slate-gray eggs from early in the fall until frost appears. The warmth of early spring causes the eggs to split along the edges, and the small katydids appear. The little ones look just like their parents but do not have wings. Katydids are an attractive green color.

The Mormon cricket is not really a cricket, but belongs to the family of katydids and green grasshoppers. It can be very harmful to crops. Don't confuse this little beastie with katydids. Mormon crickets are brown or black and grow about 2 inches long. They have wings but cannot fly. In 1848 a plague of Mormon crickets threatened to ruin the crops of the Mormon settlers in Utah, when flocks of sea gulls suddenly appeared and ate the insects. In Utah there is a monument to the sea gulls.

Wild Geese on the Move

I always think of October as the time when the wild geese fly south. Sometimes, even now, I will wake up in the middle of the night, throw on my robe, and go outside and watch them in their flight against the moon, honking as they go. I don't cry easily but somehow it is a sight that always brings tears to my eyes — I am so happy that there is something left that is wild and free. The geese fly in a V-formation and I have been told that the leader is nearly always a wise old female. She does not necessarily lead the formation all the way; when she gets tired she drops back and another female takes her place.

A VISIT TO THE MORMONS

When the wild geese started coming over, I always knew that before long my husband and I would hitch up our trailer to the pickup and head for Colorado for the deer-hunting season. One year, however, he decided to go to Utah instead and I was delighted. Now I would have a chance to meet and talk with the Mormon people. I have always admired the Mormons. To me they have always seemed such a wholesome, *happy* people. Their religion permits dancing and other fun and entertainment, while at the same time preserving a strict moral code. Anyone who has ever been their guest soon learns that the Mormon women are great cooks, gracious hostesses, and lovely to look at with their fresh, clear complexions.

The Mormon people eat well. They are thrifty and industrious and highly skilled in both agriculture and animal husbandry.

Mormon Specialties

People of many nationalities have been welcomed into the Mormon church and Mormon cooking reflects this. Some of those I enjoyed most seem to reflect the German influence. Their gravy, for instance, is made exactly the way my mother made it. This was common fare among the early settlers and is still hearty and nourishing for many of their descendants, who like to make it with ground beef or frizzled ham or bacon, and serve it over baked potatoes. The pioneers often spooned it generously over meat pies, made from small pieces of leftover meat or poultry cooked together with such vegetables as carrots, potatoes, turnips, onions, and seasoned with salt and pepper.

Foraging in the Mountains

I did not spend all my time visiting with our Mormon friends. I also spent several happy days roaming over the mountains, living in the travel trailer, and renewing my friendships with women I had met before — from Texas, Arkansas, and other states. The beauty of the mountains in Colorado and Utah is just unbelievable. Some years it snowed heavily and it was more difficult for us flatlanders to get about; other years it was warm and sunny. When the weather was fine I would gather wild rose hips, sack them up carefully, and bring them home with me to be processed later.

Pinto beans grow exceptionally well in Colorado, and we always made a point of bringing home a lot of these for our own use, and extra for family and friends.

Something else we brought back without fail was a bushel of Colorado or Utah apples — they grow the finest Rome Beauty apples that I have ever tasted. My only regret was that we did not have room enough in the trailer to bring back *two* bushels.

Swiss Apple-Cherry Pie

This recipe delightfully and unusually combines two of Utah's most popular fruits.

It's hard to improve on a good thing but I like to add just a tiny dash of salt.

pastry for a 2-crust pie
4 large cooking apples
6 tablespoons butter
2½ cups pitted sour red pie
  cherries (fresh or canned)
1 cup sugar

2 tablespoons flour
2 teaspoons ground cinna-
  mon
½ teaspoon grated nutmeg
cream or evaporated milk

Make pastry for two-crust pie. Pare apples, core, and slice. Melt 2 tablespoons butter and brush on bottom of pastry shell. Arrange a layer of apples on bottom of shell. Mix dry ingredients and sprinkle portion over layer of apples. Arrange a layer of red cherries, then sprinkle with some of dry ingredients; then a layer of apples and dry ingredients; a layer of cherries and dry ingredients; and end with a layer of apples. Top with dots of remaining butter. After top crust is added to pie, rub crust with cream or evaporated milk and sprinkle with mixture of ½ teaspoon sugar and ¼ teaspoon ground cinnamon. (Here again I like to add ¼ teaspoon of nutmeg.) Bake in 425° F oven for 30 to 40 minutes.

When my hostess served this, we were also free to cover our slice with a dollop from a big bowl of real whipped cream.

★ ★ ★

GONE FISHING

When we returned home the weather was usually still quite warm. If we had a few days of vacation left, we would unload the trailer, get a supply of fresh clothing and take off for Lake Texhoma for a few days of fishing. Fish caught in late fall, as in early spring, have much firmer flesh because the water is cooler. We always liked to put down a good supply of fish in our freezer; fish, along with venison, gave us a change of pace. Note the diagram I have drawn (p. 138); you can cut fish the way professionals do and serve it in a lot of different ways.

Fish is best when it is truly fresh, just caught, cleaned and put in the pan over a campfire. I always carried a large skillet in the trailer for this purpose so the fish would not be crowded. And I turned the fish just once — when the first side was crisp and golden.

I prepared the fish by dipping it in one beaten egg with 1 tablespoon of milk (or water) and then rolling it in bread crumbs, seasoned all-purpose flour (often I put a teaspoon of dried parsley or thyme in the flour), or cornmeal. I poured enough cooking oil into the skillet to bring it about ¼ inch up the sides.

Small fish may be fried whole. Larger fish should be boned and cut in steaks or fillets before they are fried.

Try olive oil sometime for cooking your fish. This mono-unsaturated oil is good for you and smells and tastes delicious. The nutrition expert, Jane Brody, says there is good news for those who are health conscious but not quite ready to give up the tasty fats. Studies made by Dr. Scott M. Grundy at the University of Texas at Dallas and Fred H. Mattson of the University of California at San Diego have shown that mono-unsaturated fats such as olive oil may be preferable to the polyunsaturated vegetable oils and margarines in helping to lower the risk of heart disease by lowering damaging blood cholesterol. Olive oil also has the advantage of a longer shelf life and is less likely to become rancid.

More Foraging

To go with the fish I always hunted around for whatever the land might provide. I knew that if I could find them, oyster mushrooms would be a tasty treat. They grow on logs or dying trees from October through January. Along streams and ditches are the most favorable places to look. It is an easy form to recognize, and its flavor and texture are good. Insects do not usually infest the mushroom, and even when it freezes its texture and flavor are not altered. Astrological lore tells us to pick mushrooms at Full Moon when they are most plentiful.

When the moon is at the full,
   Mushrooms you may freely pull;
But when the moon is on the wane,
   Wait till you think to pluck again.

In preparation for cooking, one should use the strip of flesh extending inwards from the outer edge about 1 to 2 inches. This is the most tender part.

The October earth is a veritable treasure house of starchy wild roots. Cattails (*Typha latifolia*), arrowheads (*Sagittaria*), day lily (*Hemerocallis fulva*), wild potato (*Psoralea esculenta*), evening primrose (*Oenothera biennis*), and Jerusalem artichoke (*Helianthus tuberosus*) — all supply nutritious food and are there for the digging. Use them like potatoes or cook as you would a turnip-like vegetable.

And if, in my ramblings, I found some wild grapes still clinging to the vines, I gathered them eagerly to make dumplings, Indian style (see "September") or to take home for late fall jelly-making. Muscadines ripen in the fall and are delicious.

Spearmint (Mentha spicata) *is useful in all healing applications, especially in aiding lung diseases.*

HALLOWEEN TRADITIONS

October seems to hold a lot of opportunity for fun, not the least of which is the festival of Halloween, celebrated on October 31. Its name means *hallowed* or *holy evening* because it takes place before All Saints' Day. It is a time for parties for both young and old, with delicious food and drink to be served, following tradition for the most part, but with some new twists added from time to time.

There are special games played at Halloween, such as bobbing for apples and telling fortunes and ghost stories, these latter before the flickering flames of a fireplace in a darkened room.

Since apples were plentiful in the fall, apple-bobbing seems to have just naturally developed. Apples are floated in a large tub of water, usually an old-fashioned wash tub. You are not allowed to use your hands, which are usually placed behind your back or at your sides. The idea is to grasp an apple with your teeth, and, incredibly, some people do manage to do this. If done in the right spirit, it's lots of fun and lots of splashes.

Ghosts and Goblins

Many superstitions and symbols are connected with Halloween. The Irish have a tale about the origin of jack-o-lanterns. They say that a man named Jack was unable to enter heaven because of his miserliness. He would not enter hell because he had played practical jokes on the devil. So he had to walk the earth with his lantern, a

coal stuffed into a hollowed-out turnip, until Judgment Day.

The Druids, an order of priests in ancient Gaul and Britain, believed that on Halloweem ghosts, spirits, fairies, witches and elves came out to harm people. They thought the cat was sacred and believed that cats had one been human beings but were changed as a punishment for evil deeds. From these Druidic beliefs comes the present-day use of witches, ghosts, and cats in Halloween festivities.

Though witches, especially those of Halloween, are usually portrayed as crones — wrinkled old women — some believed witches to be young and beautiful. From this we have the phrases "bewitched," "enchanting" or "charming," indicating influence a lovely woman exerts.

The black cat was considered to be the most prevalent form a witch might take. This is evident today when we fear the consequences of a black cat crossing our path. Or, sometimes, a black cat was said to be the "familiar" of a witch, helping her cast evil spells.

The Druids had an autumn festival called *Samhain* (pronounced SAH win), or *summer's end*. It was an occasion for feasting on all kinds of food that had been grown during the summer. The custom of using leaves, pumpkins and cornstalks as Halloween decorations comes from the Druids. The early peoples of continental Europe also had a festival similar to the Druid holiday.

American Halloween

Halloween was not a particularly significant holiday in the early days of the United States. Most Protestant denominations do not celebrate All Saints Day, and the early settlers chose to hold their harvest celebrations on Thanksgiving Day. But it was impossible to completely ignore the traditions of thousands of years, and in colonial times "Mischief Night," which occurred around October 31, was a time of harmless pranks and ghostly storytelling, apple-bobbing, taffy pulls and hayrides.

With the arrival in the 1800s of the Irish and Scottish immigrants, the celebration of Halloween in this country took on its modern form. American pumpkins replaced Irish turnips for jack-o'-lanterns, and trick or treating combined "souling" (visiting homes and offering prayers for the dead in return for gifts of food) with parading to scare away evil spirits. Many people took up the practice of partying with appropriate harvest foods and games.

The custom of a Halloween parade comes from the ancient days when Celtic priestesses moved through the moors, singing and chanting to frighten away the harmful spirits who were thought to have freedom to roam about on this one night of the year.

Personalized Pumpkins

If you grow your own pumpkins, especially if you have children or grandchildren, they can be personalized. Using an ice-pick or other sharp instrument, scratch the child's name on the pumpkin when it is partially grown. This scratch will heal over, becoming slightly raised, and the result is very attractive.

Halloween Folklore

Egg shells should always be burned or crushed into small bits, to prevent chickens from becoming bewitched.

If you are bewitched, lay a broom before the door. The "rules" decree that the first person to come in and pick up the broom, is the witch.

If you think you are bewitched, beware of the first person coming to borrow from you — it is the witch!

Scorpio the Scorpion   *(October 23 - November 21)*

Beaver Moon
NOVEMBER

Time to mulch strawberries ★ Foiling moles ★ Setting fence posts ★ Folklore of trees ★ Signs of rain ★ Fall-planted sweet peas ★ For bigger and better bulbs ★ Field dressing deer ★ Curing chickens of the sniffles ★ Advantages of goat keeping ★ Superior Achievement in Agriculture ★ Keeping colds away ★ A jolly fall happening: "Welcome to the Wurstfest" ★ Beauty secrets ★

OLD-TIMERS had a lot of little verses like the following, often quoted as weather predictions.

Mackerel sky,
  Five miles high
Lets the earth
  Go three days dry.

But someone else was just as likely to quote one that was the exact opposite:

Mackerel sky,
  Rain is nigh.

What on earth did they mean by a "mackerel sky"? Webster says a mackerel sky is one covered with rows of clouds, resembling the patterns on a mackerel's back.

Which verse should you put your faith in? While rain can be wonderful for newly planted winter wheat, it is just the opposite if you are trying to get the hay baled. Well, "you pays your money and takes your choice." You can believe in either one, so just enjoy yourself.

Scorpio (October 23 to November 22) seems to hold a grudge because its weather is neither autumn nor winter. Though the Moon is passing through its fruitful sign, the Sun refuses to cooperate, and Scorpio — slow to storm, slow to warm, watery, fruitful, feminine — becomes frustrated and misanthropic.

LAST GARDEN TASKS

For the most part, gardening comes to a screeching halt. The weather is cool, and with the possible exception of lettuce and spinach, nothing much will sprout anymore. I'm usually still planting spinach in November. With a bit of luck it will live through the winter and, if it comes up thickly, I will dig it up before the spring plowing, and then transplant it for an early crop.

Mulch & Fertilize Strawberries

November is the time to heap straw around the strawberries. To prevent winter injury apply the mulch before temperatures drop below 20° F, but after two or three hard frosts have occurred. The plants should be covered to a depth of 2 to 3 inches with the mulch. You may also successfully plant strawberries in the fall, even in late October or early November, though spring planting is more usual. Be sure plants are well mulched before severe weather arrives.

An old seed catalog describes hardwood ashes as an excellent fertilizer for strawberries, as well as for cabbages, potatoes, onions, fruit trees, corn, and beans. A typical application of one pound of ashes for each 10 to 20 square feet was applied in the spring when the winter mulch was removed.

Caring for Trees

Though Scorpio is puzzled about November weather, you need not be. Moon-signers believe that the propagation of hardwoods is best done on the growing moon under Scorpio. Hardwoods include all kinds of deciduous trees and shrubs, as well as evergreens, yews, boxwood, and hollies. Make up the slips under this fruitful, watery sign by cutting shoots off the plant, tying them in bundles, and keeping them in damp sand in a cool, dark place. Then in February or March, while the first quarter of the Moon passes through the moist sign of Pisces, plant them outdoors in rooting sand.

If you have noticed sick or ailing trees, usually discernible by the color of their foliage, give them special care in November. Cut off dead limbs, if any, paint the cuts with wound dressing, and make a note in your garden book to give them a good dressing of compost in the early spring to encourage new growth.

Indian Summer Fishing

Sometime in autumn, you are just bound to experience that wonderful time of year called Indian summer. The fall equivalent of spring's "Blackberry Winter," Indian summer is that warm spell of a week to ten days that you usually get in October or November. Preceded by cold, it is sure to be followed by another blast from the

North, so make the most of it.

If you have a yen for fresh fish, pick a bright warm day and sally forth. Bluegills, perch, and catfish are usually hungry during the last few weeks before freeze-up. To collect their favorite food, earthworms, pick a moist, humus-laden spot and drive a wooden stake four or five inches into the ground. Rub the wood with the back of a hammer so that it gives off dry, grunting sounds, which call up fishing worms. The curious, or frightened, creatures will obligingly come out of the ground.

🍃   🍃   🍃

Mole Foiling

Sounds that penetrate into the ground also affect another creature you may have to deal with at some time or other: moles. Early-day gardeners had a number of ways of foiling the moles, one of the best known being the "castor oil bean" treatment.

"Last spring," reported a nineteenth-century gardener, "I went over our grounds and with a trowel opened the mole tracks, put in a few beans, and covered them. This operation I repeated several times in the course of a few weeks.... We were scarcely troubled with the little torments after that." This gardener added that a cat was worth its weight in gold for catching moles.

Moles are said to find the odor of elder offensive, and an 1860's gardener asserted, "After I placed elder leaves in the runs the moles abandoned them."

Cats are also great snake catchers, even of rattlesnakes, the mother cat teaching her kittens how. Dogs, too, catch and kill snakes. This ability seems to vary, however, from one individual to another.

A Maryland gardener of the 1880's favored a different treatment. "I place the heads of salted herring in the ridges where the moles run. I find this an effectual remedy." A gardener in Kentucky in 1886 reported a mole-foiling method that would, at least, seem to smell better: "Plant tulip bulbs in old tin pans, then sink them in the [flower] beds." Both pans and bulbs were taken up after the bulbs had bloomed and the foliage had matured, and stored for replanting in the fall.

Other tricks include placing pinwheels or empty bottles in the runways to make a noise that frightens the moles into leaving.

Though moles make unsightly ridges, there is something to be said in their defense. Unlike their vegetarian cousins, gophers, moles are insect eaters, and when the insects the mole eats are destructive ones, he does the gardener a favor. A gardening magazine of the 1880's reported: "It is said that in a certain locality in France the chafer grubs became so numerous and destructive that gardening had to be given up. To rid the gardens of the pest a number of moles were introduced and in the course of a season or two the culturists were enabled to raise good crops." The report does not, however, state what they did with the moles afterward.

Setting Fence Posts

Set fence posts or telegraph poles when the Moon is in the third or fourth quarters. The fixed signs, Taurus, Leo, or Aquarius, are best for this.

Old mountaineers say, "Dig a hole on the new of the Moon and you will have dirt to throw away, but if you dig it on the old of the Moon, you'll not have enough to fill it back again. Dig a post hole on the growin' of the Moon. Dig it ever so deep and so big around as you want, and put the post in it.

It'll be loose all the time and never settle. Dig the same kind of hole on the old of the moon, just the same size, and sink your post. It'll settle as tight as you could want — like it took roots and growed there."

In the old days, a lot of fresh-cut, uncured fence posts did take root and "grow there," especially if they were planted under Cancer or Pisces. There are stands of Osage orange and green ash all over Oklahoma that originally started life as fence posts.

Folklore of Trees

★ If a tree will not bear fruit, drive nails in it.

★ Trees for building purposes should be felled in late November or in December.

★ When transplanting a tree, be careful to have the same side facing the south before and after it is moved.

★ Wood from a tree struck by lightning should never be used in the construction of a house or barn, or they in turn may also be struck by lightning.

★ If a pregnant woman helps plant a tree and takes hold of it with both hands, the tree will bear doubly well.

★ You will become blind, so they say, if you look up into a tree while a woman is in the tree.

★ ★ ★

WEATHER SIGNS

Folklore Signs of a Hard Winter

It is a sign of a tough winter:

★ When there is an unusually large crop of nuts or acorns, and when heavy moss appears on the north side of trees.

★ When maple and sassafras sap goes down early in the fall.

★ When grape leaves turn yellow early in the season.

★ When there are thick husks on ears of corn.

★ When hornets have triple insulated nests.

★ When wasps are sealing twice as many live spiders in the mud incubator tubes to feed their babies when they hatch.

★ When cattle get rough coats, and when rabbits and squirrels have unusually heavy fur.

★ When wooly bear caterpillars are dark from "stem to stern": if dark only in the middle, only the middle part of winter will be hard; if the ends are black, the beginning and the end of winter will be hard.

Signs of Rain

★ When, standing on high ground, you have a clear view and the horizon is unobstructed from all quarters, you may expect rain within forty-eight hours.

★ If it begins to rain after seven o'clock in the morning, it will continue to do so all day, and may also be an indication that it will rain for three days.

★ When it is raining and the sky brightens and darkens alternately, it will rain all day, with a good chance of clearing at sundown.

★ It is a sign of continued rain if smoke from the chimney hovers low over the housetops. When it is ascending straight into the air, there will be clearing weather.

★ A foggy morning is usually the forerunner of a clear afternoon.

★ Mushrooms and toadstools are numerous just *before* a rain.

★ "If the down flyeth off Dandelion when there is no winde, it is a sign of rain."

★ When the flowers of the pimpernel close during the day, it is a sure sign of rain; thus this plant is known as the poor man's weather glass.

★ Bees are sensitive to the increased humidity that usually precedes a shower, and always return to the hive to escape a wetting.

FALL BOUQUETS

Planting Peonies

Peonies belong to the buttercup family. Many of the cultivated varieties common in America are the offspring of two species of the eastern hemisphere, the common peony of Southern Europe and a large group of hybrids known as the Chinese peony. The large flowers of the common peony are lovely to look at, but they do not have much fragrance. Many of the Chinese peonies bear double, sweet-scented blossoms. Although the tender buds may be winter- or frost-injured, peony plants are very hardy and require no special winter protection. However, after frost has killed the foliage, it should be cut off slightly above the ground level, not deep enough to injure the buds at the crown (top) of the cluster of roots.

It is a mistake to plant peonies in a border facing east, for in that position the flower buds are liable to be damaged by the early morning sun if it happens to shine on them after a frosty night. Peonies in a border facing south, southwest, or west, are unlikely to suffer harm in such circumstances, and if well cared for and located, they will bloom for a long time, 20 years or much longer. Don't transplant them once they are established.

Once established, peonies are vigorous, leafy plants that take up a good deal of room. For this reason they are best planted in open spaces or among shrubs, rather than used too prominently in a mixed flower border — although they make a nice backdrop to other summer flowers.

Sweet Peas

The 1987 Burpee catalogue devoted its front cover and an entire ten-page section to sweet peas. Who doesn't love their fragrant and delicately beautiful blossoms? Two secrets will make it possible to grow superior sweet peas just about anywhere: compost and fall planting.

Until the hot weather hits, sweet peas really are a delight, especially when provided with the best of conditions. You can't fight the climate, but you can outwit it by fall planting, particularly if you live in the South or Southwest. An older gardening friend of mine always had the most beautiful spring sweet peas I have ever seen. She planted them in November, and I have learned to do so also.

In the North, if you don't plant sweet peas in the fall you can do so in spring as soon as the soil has started to warm up.

The other secret ingredient is compost. Although Northern gardeners with light loam or sandy

In the fall remove the tops of peonies, iris, and dahlia, where borers might hide for the winter.

soil need make little preparation for sowing, there's a lot of mystique to soil preparation for sweet peas. One method involves digging a special, narrow, 2-foot trench and replacing the soil with one part soil, one part peat, and one part sharp sand. To each bushel of this mixture add 2 ounces of bone meal and about one quarter bushel of well-decomposed manure. For areas not so alkaline as mine, add in addition 4 ounces of ground dolomite (magnesium) limestone and 3 ounces of ground chalk limestone.

With this preparation you'll get earlier and superior results. Sweet peas have an undeserved reputation for being difficult: give them good soil and late fall or early spring planting, and they'll give as good a show as any annual planted under ordinary conditions.

How To Have Bigger Bulbs and Better Bloom

You may have noticed that bulbous plants such as tulips, daffodils, hyacinths, all kinds of lilies, and crocuses, seem to do their best the first year after planting. They then gradually diminish in number and size of bloom each year until they finally disappear.

This happens even in the best-cared-for gardens where plenty of fertilizer is applied. My first-year bulbs, produced commercially in Holland or Florida, are packed with plant nutrients that are directly responsible for their growth and bloom and their brilliant color, but in order to enjoy this a second year, I have to buy new bulbs. Regardless of the care I give them, my bulbs never regain their original size, even those I plant in very fertile soil.

Why? Simply because my soil, like most soils, is not high enough in the one specific element so vital in the production of sound, healthy bulbs: potash. Potash makes all the difference in the world in the size and blooming ability of a bulb. Why potash? To better understand this, let's see just what potash actually does for bulbous plants.

When potash is readily available to bulbous plants, their manufacture of necessary carbohydrates, both sugars and starches, proceeds at a very rapid rate. Since carbohydrates are chiefly responsible for building plant cells, the more carbohydrates produced, the bigger the plants will grow. As the plants grow bigger, they develop greater root systems capable of extracting still more potash and plant food from the soil. The more food taken up by each plant, of course, the more nutrients the bulbs will have for storing. And the bigger the bulbs, the more magnificent display you will have in spring.

Potash is also beneficial in counteracting excess nitrogen in the soil, which results from overuse of manures. Too great an amount of nitrogen in the soil causes bulbous plants to lose their resistance to disease.

So I heartily recommend that you use a fertilizer high in potash in conjunction with well-decomposed compost to keep your bulbs flowering beautifully year after year.   ❦   ❦   ❦

FOR BETTER-TASTING GAME

Hunting seasons differ from state to state. After we returned in the fall from Colorado or Utah, where the season is earlier, if Carl had failed to get a deer, he still had a chance to hunt in Oklahoma. This happened only in rare years when the autumn was still hot and dry and the deer had not yet come down from the higher elevations to spend the winter on lower, warmer ground.

Deer multiply very rapidly, particularly now that their natural enemies, pumas (sometimes called mountain lions) and bobcats, have mostly been killed off. Deer, eating and destroying crops, can be very detrimental to farmers if their numbers are not thinned out from time to time. And venison, if correctly prepared, is a very delicious meat. It is unfortunate that many hunters kill their deer and then do not use it. Some of them do this because they have had a bad experience with wild meat. Their misconception that all wildlife has a strong or "gamey" flavor probably was brought on by one or two poorly prepared meals. If game is not properly handled, the end result quite often is not very good; so how does one go about properly preparing game?

You won't find the answer in an ordinary cookbook. The key to better tasting wild meat is in the care you give it within the first few hours after the animal has been taken. A few major points of game care are vitally important.

Field Dressing Deer

The most important thing in field dressing any animal is to keep it as clean as possible. The time to think clean is even before the game is in hand: A basic tenet of cleanliness is to make a clean kill. This is not just another bid for sportsmanship, although that is reason enough to take care when using a rifle on big game; a clean kill definitely has an effect on the flavor of the meat. An animal hit in the paunch (the abdomen) has had its muscles bathed in adrenalin and various digestive juices, and the deer meat may thus become dark and tough.

Even if you've made a good shot, take care with the knife when cleaning any game. Avoid cutting an internal organ during the opening of the carcass. Some animals have scent glands. If these are to be removed, remember to clean your knife and hands before dressing the rest of the animal.

After the body cavity has been opened and cleaned, care should be taken to keep hair, feathers, dirt, and insects out. Lots of washing with cool water helps remove foreign matter and blood, whether a small rabbit or a whopper whitetail or muledeer.

In today's diet-conscious society, most are familiar with the terms saturated and unsaturated fats. Domestic meat has saturated fats, and these give it the juicy qualities we all love. The unsaturated fats of wild animals have strong flavors, so they should be removed as thoroughly as possible. Game species tend to have their fat deposits located under the skin in particular regions in the body, rather than marbled throughout the meat. This make fat trimming simple.

Cooling the Carcass

Another important step is cooling the carcass. If an animal is not cooled properly after it has been cleaned, the meat may spoil or sour. Simply because there is more meat, the larger the animal, the more you need to worry about getting it cooled down. A deer's chest cavity should be propped open after it has been cleaned. The body may be covered with an open-weave cloth to keep insects out but let air in.

Smaller animals and birds present less of a cooling problem. If you are going to be in the field for just a few hours, you can carry your small game in a hunting jacket game bag with no heat problems. But in warm weather small game need ventilation also.

Small game cools more rapidly. It wouldn't be wise to bundle a bunch of birds or rabbits into a tightly closed plastic bag. Be sure to keep small game out of the reach of dogs, or you may reach home with an empty sack.

Transporting

An area often overlooked is transporting your day's bag home or back to a camp. Don't put it in a plastic bag, trunk of your car, or a closed camper for a long trip home.

The right way to transport big game is to place the carcass, with the skin still on it, in the back of a pickup or open trailer. The body cavity should be left open, but covered with an open-weave cloth. Under dusty conditions, it may be necessary to cover the game loosely with a tarp. If you are going only a few miles, the car trunk will do.

Aging and Freezing Game

Some hunters like to *age* their game. Aging is the natural breakdown of proteins and muscle tissues that makes meat more tender. Some folks feel the sooner you freeze the game the more tender it will be. If the meat is frozen before rigor mortis sets in, however, tissue breakdown will not take place

and the meat will be tough.

Aging times vary as widely as hunting methods do. Large mammals, such as deer or elk, should be aged from five to ten days.

Aging calls for hanging the carcass, in a cool, dry place, and the best place might just be a meat locker or walk-in. In Colorado or Utah, when the weather was cold and possibly snowing, my husband would hang his deer from a tree limb, after "bleeding it out," and "field dressing." It was then covered and allowed to age for several days before taking it in to the packing plant. In warm Oklahoma we took it to our butcher to be placed in his meat locker before cutting.

While your deer or elk carcass is aging, the outer layer of tissue will become dry and stiff. This is called "casing out," and is added protection for the meat. This tough outer layer will be cut away at butchering time, revealing tender, well-aged meat.

Smaller mammals and birds, such as squirrels and rabbits, do not need to be aged and can be cleaned as soon as you like — in fact, the sooner the better.

Any wild meat not cooked immediately should be frozen for future use. Large pieces of meat must be protected by thoroughly wrapping in freezer-proof packaging, such as freezer paper. Small game like fish can be frozen in serving portions in milk cartons filled with water. Whenever you are ready for a meal, just thaw, soak briefly in salt water, and cook.

Fatless venison steaks, marinated for two hours in olive oil and lemon juice, broiled and turned frequently over hot coals until ruddy brown, sprinkled over with paprika and pepper and salt, daubed with butter, and eaten "hot off the griddle" are greatly to be recommended!

Providing nutritious and good tasting meals from the wild won't be as easy as shopping from the supermarket, but I firmly believe in using what you kill, not just killing for sport or because the law allows a certain number of a given species to be taken legally. It might take some practice with a skillet or your roaster to find the best way to prepare each game species, but give your game its due respect in the field, and those folks gathered at your dinner table will be *treated* to wild meat, not just *subjected* to it.

My father was a hunter, my four older brothers hunted, my husband hunted, and now my son goes forth each year to bag his deer — in bow season and muzzle-loader season, as well as the regular hunting season. Whatever he is lucky enough to get is always carefully prepared for use and never *wasted*. We're descendants of those old pioneers who used everything. Remember?

A Near Barn Burner

Domestic animals and poultry are occasionally subject to illness, and chickens sometimes seem to have a sickness similar to the common cold that plagues us human beings. A disease, once it appears, can go through a flock of chickens like wildfire.

When we were first married, my husband worked in the Swift and Company hatchery, and we kept a large flock of White Rock hens so that we would have fertile eggs for the hatchery. One wet, cold November they got sick, sputtering and sneezing much as people do when they have a bad cold. We had heard that smoke from hot tar would cure this condition, and we determined to try it. The method advised was to pour tar into a shallow pan, heat a flatiron, and put the iron into the tar. The resultant smoke — and this generated a lot of smoke — was supposed to be used in the poultry house with all doors and windows shut. The windows of our poultry house could be opened and closed, but there was also chicken wire screening on them on the outside. We stuffed papers and rags all around the cracks and the place was almost hermetically sealed. My husband went in with the tar and the hot iron....

I stood outside nervously fiddling with the latch. Eventually deciding all was well, I returned to the house and started preparing the evening meal. I waited and waited. The meal was cooling, and Carl still hadn't showed up. I decided to go back out and see what was going on, but just then he came in the door, blurry-eyed and fit-to-be-tied. Inadvertently (and I honestly didn't do it on purpose), I had tripped the latch and locked him in. He had finally managed to free himself by opening one of the windows and tearing off the screening.

And *that time* we really did have a barn burner! But neither the chickens nor Carl had a cold for all the rest of the fall and winter.

The Kid Who Thought She Was a Chicken

One of the funniest things that happened with that flock of White Rocks was the incident of the goat kid who thought she was a chicken. For a number of years we kept white Saanen milk goats: very affectionate little animals and great pets, as well as fine milkers. As a matter of fact, we raised our own "kids" on goat milk, not because they were ill but just because we all liked its taste. From time to time, however, there were many sick children who really needed the goat milk because their little bodies could not assimilate other types of milk. Goat milk, you see, is so healthful and easily digested because it is naturally homogenized, having very small fat globules. Goats are healthy little animals anyway, rarely if ever having brucellosis and other problems of cows.

One day a man from the county health department showed up, accompanied by a man he introduced as one of the local doctors. Darn near scared me to death! I wasn't aware that we had broken any laws and when they asked to see our animals, our dairy barn, and our milking stand, I almost had a nervous breakdown. And they took special note of my two rosy-cheeked children.

They looked at everything, still saying very little and left. A few days later I had a call from the doctor asking if we would be willing to sell some of the milk to a patient of his, a small baby having

a digestive problem. This wasn't a convenient time — the goat kid was still nursing — but the doctor explained the child's need was great; her life might even depend on receiving the goat milk.

We decided to wean the kid, a little too soon, but we would manage. The goat pen and run were adjacent to the chicken yard, so we put Bitsie in with the chickens, and I patiently stayed with her until she began to get the idea that the milk in the pan was for her. Goat kids can be taught this at an early age if necessary.

I am happy to say that the baby lived and thrived. In time she was joined by three brothers, none of whom had her problem, but the parents decided to raise them on goat's milk, too.

Where she would sleep at night was a problem Bitsie solved for herself. Where else but up on the roost with the chickens? Goats are great climbers, and getting up there was easy. She would settle down, and the chickens, who did not mind at all, would roost all around her, perfectly content.

We enjoyed this situation and would often go out at night to look at the scene, but it was just too hilarious to keep to ourselves. Whenever we had visitors in the evening, we would insist that they go out with us to admire our chickens. Thinking us a bit zany (nothing unusual for the Riottes) they would politely follow us out. We would open the door, turn on the light, and they would look. All of a sudden somebody would catch sight of that little white goat head sticking out with practically nothing else showing but the chickens all around her. When one of our lady friends almost fainted at the sight we stopped the practice, but we kept going out to look ourselves.

Our Victory Farm

Making a garden, keeping milk goats, chickens, ducks, geese, white rabbits, and a few other projects brought us some unexpected publicity. Back during the Second World War, everybody was getting excited about raising food. William G. ("Bill") Skelly, president of the Skelly Oil Company, was one of the great pioneers in the oil industry, and he started a program to encourage agriculture. The award — $100.00, a dinner to which winners could invite their friends, gold lapel pins, and so on — was usually given to large farms and ranches, but we were billed as having the "smallest farm in America." In time we were visited by the Skelly representatives, who inspected everything, and a bit later we were notified that we would be given the award and would be interviewed on radio. I still have the plaque, entitled "SUPERIOR ACHIEVEMENT IN AGRICULTURE."

Chervil for Bruises
A popular treatment for bruises, dried chervil was moistened with water and bandaged on.

KEEPING COLDS AWAY

Folklore Remedies to Cure a Cold

★ Put seven beans in your pocket. Each day throw one bean away, and at the end of the seven days your cold will be gone.
★ Sore throat: Wear one of your long stockings around your neck, with the foot under the chin. This is said to be good for head colds, too.
★ Eating horseradish is said to cure a cold, as is rubbing goosegrease on the chest, and eating chicken soup.

Garlic and Cleanliness

Garlic, a remedy for colds as well as many other things, is also believed to prevent them. I have literally tons of garlic in my vegetable garden, in my flower beds, and around my fruit trees. And I like garlic in everything. Of course the odor is a problem, but chewing parsley and brushing your teeth well, both before and after, will usually get rid of that. I spend a lot of time exercising outdoors, both walking and working, so I seldom have a cold, but, especially in winter, wherever you go you are almost constantly meeting people who have the sniffles. When I was a volunteer worker with the hospital auxiliary, we often had so many flu patients when the flu season arrived that we had to put beds out in the halls. I made it a special point to remember to swallow a few cloves of garlic every morning before I went on duty. I cut them into slivers, but did not chew them. Swallowing them whole like a vitamin pill, I thus avoided "garlic breath." I don't know, maybe I was just lucky, but I never did pick up a cold or flu during all the years I worked. Something else the head nurse told us to do: "Wash your hands frequently." Whenever I return home from visiting, church, or the grocery store, wherever I might have touched a door handle, the first thing I still do is wash my hands, before I start to prepare a meal or whatever I have planned to do. I have great faith in both garlic and cleanliness.

Recipes for a Cold Day

Herb Teas

Infuse the dried or green herb leaves and stalks in boiling water, and let them stand until cold. Sweeten to taste. Add ice if you like, but chilling in the refrigerator is better.

★ Sage tea, with a small bit of alum dissolved in it and sweetened with honey, is good as a gargle for a sore throat.
★ Chamomile and gentian teas are excellent tonics taken either hot or cold.
★ The tea made from blackberry root is said to be good for

summer disorders, while that from green strawberry leaves is an admirable and soothing wash for a cankered mouth.

★ Catnip tea is the best panacea known to nurses for infant colds and colic.

★ Tansy and rue teas are also useful in cases of colic, as are fennel seeds steeped in brandy.

★ Sweetened mint tea, made from green leaves crushed in cold or hot water, is palatable and healing to the stomach and bowels.

Apple Toddy

Boil a large juicy pippin apple in a quart of water. When it has broken to pieces, strain off the water. While the juice is still boiling-hot, add a tumbler glass of fine old whiskey and a little lemon juice, and sweeten to taste. Take hot at bedtime for influenza.

Always remember this:

Just because a plant is labeled an "herb" doesn't mean that it is necessarily good for you, or even harmless. Many herbs are more toxic that magical. Some herbs, such as foxglove, are poisonous but have excellent medicinal qualities and are seemingly magical when used in the right way at the right time and place.

Headache Remedy

If grandfather had a headache grandmother prepared a tea of catnip, which was also considered to be a stimulant and tonic. Bruised catnip leaves were also once considered to relieve both toothache pain and hemorrhoids. Catnip was also considered to be an aphrodisiac, but apparently only among cats.

Arrowroot Wine Jelly

In the early days you couldn't run down to the corner drugstore to fill a prescription — there just wasn't one there to run to — but granny or the herb-woman usually had something that would cure the condition or at least alleviate the pain. Some were very tasty. This was one of the most pleasant "for building up an invalid," as well as a noble inspiration to make for Christmas gifts.

Wine jelly also adds zest to sauces and gravies, and is especially good served with lamb or baked ham. Combine it with yellow prepared mustard for a superb sauce or basting agent.

1 cup boiling water

2 heaping teaspoonfuls arrowroot

2 heaping teaspoonfuls white sugar

1 tablespoon brandy or 3 tablepoons of wine

Boil together until thickened, stirring all the while. Eat with cream, flavored with rose water and sweeten to taste.

The Wurstfest

November is traditionally hog-killing time. Did you know that sausage has its very own festival? And that all sausage is not made from pork?

Deep in the heart of Texas lies the Hill Country, a land so beautiful, so peaceful, so quiet that every day seems like a Sunday morning. The area is teeming with white-tail deer. Here, too, you will find big hungry bass, gray shadowy catfish, and frisky perch waiting under cypress roots for your lure or fly. Hills and trees teem with countless species of wild birds, their bright colors untouched by the dismal soot of pollution. Bluebonnets and devil's paintbrush, each in its season, provide eye-catching color everywhere.

Would you believe that this landscape, so thoroughly American, provides the setting for that most delightful German happening, the *Wurstfest*? Though Old World in concept, this glorious ten-day romp honoring the sausage at the beginning of November each year is carried out with truly American zest and energy.

Here is New Braunfels, a city of some 20,000 people, many of whom are of German descent. It was founded over 130 years ago in the midst of Mexico and Western cultures, by a German prince and his followers.

These German aristocrats, like so many others who came to our shores, sought freedom; many, possibly most, of their descendants today speak "High German" as well as English. At first, unused to working with their hands, they had a difficult time of it like so many early settlers. In time, however, they made it, and their beautiful little city, located not too far from the Gulf Coast, is known for its *Gemuetlichkeit* — good fellowship in the German manner — for New Braunfels still retains the Old Country atmosphere along with the charm and color of the new.

Wurstfest, where sausage is king, is a storybook holiday. To experience a social gathering anything like its frolicsome fun you'd have to be in Munich at Oktoberfest. While sausage is its reason for being and its featured attraction, each year sees added entertainments for the enjoyment of everyone.

Many visitors come back year after year, for it is a time for *ist das Leben schoen* — being happy and living the good life. You can feast on all kinds of sausage, and you "can have it your way," either smoked and crisp or hot and

A call to the New Braunfels Chamber of Commerce, or a letter to Wurstfest, New Braunfels, Texas 78130, will get you a descriptive folder. If you are an out-of-stater you can get an excellent state highway map by writing to the State Department of Highways and Public Transportation, Travel & Information Division, P.O. Box 5064, Austin, Texas 78763.

juicy, wrapped if you like in homemade bread. You can sample strudels and *Kartoffel* (potato) pancakes made from old German recipes, drink a delicious cup of potato soup made with dill and cream, or taste *Bratwurst mit Sauerkraut*, the "national" dish of Texas-Germany. You will find all this at the Marktplatz, along with typical Texas foods as well — tamales, tacos, and corn on the cob.

Naturally I did what I always do when I am exposed to unusual and very delicious food: I kept right on going until I got the recipes for the dishes I most enjoyed. This time I bought a cookbook of German recipes.

Sweet-Sour Potato Salad

8 potatoes
1 stalk celery, diced
2 hard-cooked eggs, sliced
1 onion, minced
3 sweet-sour pickles, diced
1 tablespoon minced parsley
4 slices bacon

2 eggs, well beaten
1 cup sugar
¼ teaspoon dry mustard
½ teaspoon salt
¼ teaspoon pepper
½ cup vinegar, diluted with
½ cup cold water

Boil potatoes in their jackets. When tender, peel and dice. Add celery, hard-cooked eggs, onion, pickle, and parsley. Beat eggs, and add to them the sugar, spices, and diluted vinegar; mix well. Fry bacon until crisp and brown; drain on toweling and dice. Pour egg mixture into the hot bacon fat, and cook, stirring constantly, until thickened, about 10 minutes. Pour over potato mixture, add diced bacon, and mix lightly.

Spicy Apple Coffee Cake

2 cups sifted flour
1 tablespoon granulated sugar
3 teaspoons baking powder
¾ teaspoon salt
4 tablespoons shortening
½ cup grated nippy cheese
⅔ to ¾ cup milk

2 or 3 apples, cored, pared
  and sliced thin
⅓ cup brown sugar
½ teaspoon cinnamon
¼ teaspoon nutmeg
1 tablespoon butter

Sift flour, sugar, baking powder and salt together. Cut in shortening and cheese. Add milk to make a soft dough. Turn out on lightly floured board and knead ½ minute. Pat dough out in ungreased 9-inch layer cake pan. Arrange pared, sliced apples in petal design over top. Sprinkle with brown sugar, cinnamon, and nutmeg, and dot with butter. Bake in hot oven 425° F, 25 minutes. *Makes 1 9-inch coffee cake.*

❦ ❦ ❦

AN OLD-FASHIONED BEAUTY SECRET

Does the cold of November seem to shrivel the skin of your face and hands? My mother's sister, Aunt Henrietta, who was famous well into old age for her lovely complexion, had a remedy for this. Several times a week she would treat her skin to an old-fashioned version of the modern sauna — but the water she used was much hotter than the electric facial sauna generally achieves.

She would fill a large pot with water and bring it to a boil and then carry it to a steady table. Sitting in front of the steaming pot, she would drape a towel over her head and shoulders, so as to envelop both herself and the pot in a towel tent. Since this was very hot, she lifted the towel occasionally to get a couple of gulps of fresh, cool air during the sauna period. *And she was always careful to keep her face at least a foot away from the steaming pot.*

The Herbal Steam

Adding a few fragrant herbs to the hot water makes this so pleasant it is almost a religious experience. The skin of the face will always improve with the help of the humidity and the temperature of a facial steam, and the effect is intensified with the addition of either a mixture of herbs or some specific herbs for specific purposes. It is recommended particularly for any skin with large pores or impurities.

A general mixture of dried herbs for improving the skin of face and neck includes:

Sage (whole leaves if available)*
Peppermint (whole or
    shredded)*
Chamomile flowers*
Basil (small quantity)
Lime flowers
Elder flowers
Marigold petals

Nasturtium flowers
Cornflowers
Lavender flowers
Verbascum flowers
Nettle leaves (if available)
Fennel
Yarrow (if available)
Salad burnet (if available)

*Essential herbs for a facial steam. The others are helpful as an addition and provide also good specific effects from each herb.

Facial steams are not intended for, and in fact should not be used at all on, very dry skin, because it is usually too thin and too sensitive to heat, particularly if there are any dilated red veins visible on the face. Also the steam is not good for people with heart trouble, difficulties in breathing, or asthma.

Try this sometime and examine your skin after five to ten minutes under the facial sauna. Take note of how plump and smooth your skin is: lines seem to disappear and your skin feels very soft, a vivid demonstration of the effect simple water has on the beauty of the skin. Some of those old beauty treatments still work pretty well today!

For Rosy Cheeks

In the 1890's it was practically social suicide if a woman was reputed to "paint" her face. But the smart gals got around that by using a freshly cut beet to provide cheek rouge. The red juice is a temporary skin dye —harmless.

Luffa Gourds for Lovely Skin

The highly versatile luffa gourd was early recognized by our grandmothers and great grandmothers as a cosmetic aid and, interestingly, it is still sold commercially, in spite of heavy competition from synthetic sponges. I saw them advertised recently at fancy prices in a book of beauty supplies and preparations. Grow your own. Here is how an 1894 Vaughan catalog describes the method of preparation: "Let the gourd ripen on the vine (it turns from green to yellow when ripe), then cut it open, remove the seeds and strip off the skin. The inside fiber is then washed and is ready for use." Luffas, used as bath sponges, help to remove old, dried surface skin, thus promoting both health and beauty.

Gifts from the Garden

★ Canned peaches, marmalades, chutney, pickles, pepper relish, jelly, jams.

★ A collection of homegrown, hand-collected vegetable and flower seeds.

★ Sachets of lavender, rose petals, or other fragrant homegrown flowers: use orris root, from an iris species, to hold the scent.

★ Plan ahead and grow ornamental hot pepper plants from seed started last spring and raised on the patio or apartment porch during the summer; Park's Tequila Sunrise is both delicious and pretty.

★ Grow Park's popcorn "Pretty Pops," with its brightly colored kernels of red, blue, orange, black, yellow and purple that turn white when popped; these are not only ornamental but of superb flavor, nutty and crunchy. Five ears are generously borne on 6-foot plants. The ears can be used as a table decoration as well as for popping.

THANKSGIVING

Thanksgiving is also a November "happening" that we enjoy celebrating each year. Undoubtedly wild turkey was served at that first Thanksgiving feast for the simple reason that there was no other kind. As I have mentioned before I love the old-fashioned cookbooks because of the personal opinions and conversational tone the author often takes. One author waxed somewhat lyrical on the wild turkey:

Wild Turkey and Giblets

"Draw and wash the inside very carefully, as with all game. Domestic fowls are, or should be, kept up without eating for at least twelve hours before they are killed; but we must shoot wild when we can get the chance, and of course it often happens that their crops are distended by a recent hearty meal of rank or green food. Wipe the cavity with a dry soft cloth before you stuff.

"Have a rich force-meat (meat chopped fine for use in a stuffing), breadcrumbs, some bits of fat pork, chopped fine, pepper, and salt. Beat in an egg and a couple of tablespoonfuls of melted butter. Baste with butter and water for the first hour, then three or four times with the gravy; lastly, five or six times with melted butter. Dredge with flour at the last, froth with butter, and when he is a tempting brown, serve. Skim the gravy, add a little hot water, pepper, thicken with the giblets chopped fine and browned flour, boil up, and pour into a tureen. In the South the giblets are not put in the gravy, but laid whole, one under each wing, when the turkey is dished. Garnish with small fried sausages, not larger than a dollar, crisped parsley between them.

"Send around currant jelly and cranberry sauce with it."

Cranberry Jelly

Wash and pick over: 4 cups cranberries (1 pound). Place them in a saucepan. Cover with 2 cups boiling water. As soon as the water begins to boil again, cover the saucepan with a lid. Boil the berries 3 or 4 minutes, or until the skins burst. Put them through a strainer or ricer. Stir into the puree 2 cups sugar. Place over heat and bring to a rolling boil. If you want cranberry sauce, remove from heat at once. If you want to mold cranberry jelly, boil about 5 minutes, skim, then pour into a wet mold. The cooking periods indicated are right for firm berries. Very ripe berries require a few minutes longer.

More Thanksgiving Recipes

Plan ahead and make this stuffing up a week or so in advance and store it in the freezer. Here is how.

Herbal Turkey Stuffing

1 pound bulk pork sausage	8 cups cubed corn bread
1½ cups chopped onion	16 slices white bread, cut in
1½ to 2 teaspoons salt	½-inch cubes
2 teaspoons dried whole sage, crushed	2½ cups turkey or chicken broth
1 teaspoon dried whole rosemary, crushed	2 eggs, beaten
¼ teaspoon pepper	About ⅓ cup butter or margarine, melted

Cook sausage and onion in a medium skillet over low heat till sausage is brown and onion is tender. Drain. Place in a large bowl, and add next six ingredients, mixing well. Do not add eggs or broth. Place mixture in plastic freezer bag and store in freezer until wanted.

On Thanksgiving morning, thaw dressing and add eggs and broth when you are ready to stuff your turkey. Preheat oven to 325° F. Remove giblets and neck from turkey; reserve for gravy. Rinse turkey thoroughly with cold water; pat dry, inside and out. Stuff dressing into both neck and body cavity of turkey. Tie ends of legs to tail with cord; lift wingtips up and over back so they are tucked under bird. Brush entire bird with butter or margarine; place on rack in roasting pan, breast side up. Bake, basting frequently. *Stuffing is sufficient for a 16–18 pound turkey.*

Giblet Gravy

Chicken or turkey liver, heart, and gizzard	4 tablespoons flour
¾ teaspoon salt	4 tablespoons fat or drippings from chicken or turkey
⅛ teaspoon pepper	3 cups giblet stock

Wash liver, heart, and cleaned gizzard. Cover gizzard and heart with cold water, add salt and pepper, and simmer until tender. Add liver and cook 10 to 20 minutes longer. Drain, saving stock, and chop giblets fine. Brown flour in fat, stirring constantly, cooking about 5 minutes. Add giblets and stock. Cream or milk may be used for part of the stock. *Makes 3 cups gravy.*

Sagittarius the Archer   *(November 22 - December 22)*

Cold Moon
DECEMBER

Starting gift plants ★ Shrubs for winter beauty ★
Maple goodies ★ Heirloom quilts to treasure ★
Making rugs ★ Christmas cookie tree decorations ★
Old-fashioned corn husk dolls ★ Cooking your goose
★ Kentucky Bourbon Cake ★

At Christmas play and make good cheer,
For Christmas comes but once a year.
— FROM A HUNDRED POINTS OF GOOD HUSBANDRY (1557),
BY THOMAS TUSSER

THE ZODIAC PERIOD OF CAPRICORN (December 22 to January 20) is said to hold earthy, moist, productive, and feminine tendencies. Radical pruning of grapes, according to Moon-signers, is effective if done during Capricorn's rule when the Moon is in the second quarter. Pruning under the sign of the goat supposedly influences new grape vines to reach upward toward the "knees," and if they are pruned on the increasing Moon, grapes will grow round and juicy.

Graft fruit trees and vines during fruitful signs of the Moon, cutting your grafts from good bearing stock while trees and vines are dormant, December to March. Keep the graft branches in a cool, somewhat moist, dark place. Graft onto host plants just before the sap starts to flow.

Grafting is best done while the Moon is passing through the watery signs of Cancer, Scorpio, or Pisces, or the earthy, productive sign of Capricorn, or when specific days are ruled by those signs. Do not graft on Sunday, however, because that day is ruled by the Sun and believed to be dry and barren.

Pruning fruit trees, on the other hand, is thought to be most satisfactory when accomplished under a "hostile" sign such as Aquarius and may be delayed until the last two weeks of January. Top-pruning trees under a sign hostile to vegetation encourages trees to spread horizontally, according to Moon-sign believers, and grow low to the ground.

However, should a hostile day-sign (daily moon's place) coincide with a zodiac period of dry, barren, masculine, and fiery characteristics, the result could be extremely rough on growing things. This double negative should be used for killing noxious or unwanted growths, grubbing and trimming to destroy.

Moon-signers believe that the barren sign of Aquarius (January 20 to February 19) is most favorable for pruning fruit trees if the day is not doubly hostile to vegetation. The moon should be in the last quarter.

END-OF-YEAR CHORES

Starting Gift Plants

If you have not already started to propagate some of your house plants to give for holiday gifts, early December is not too late.

Long ago, ladies considered houseplants very precious. When they secured a new variety they would guard it jealously. My mother, who was sometimes a bit naughty, would carry a folded bread wrapper in her purse (plastic bags being unknown at the time) just in case she could talk someone into giving her a "slip" (as cuttings were called in those days). Once, she could not resist, when her hostess was out of the room preparing refreshments, snipping off a tiny bit of a cherished plant and slipping it into her purse. She carefully tended the cutting and it grew. Every time her friend came over I had to run out and hide it. One day she came over unexpectedly and I remember what a dreadful time my mother had trying to explain.

Propagating House Plants

The most rapid way to propagate house plants is by division or offsets, as stem cuttings may take over a month to produce well-rooted plants.

Use **division** to propagate plants that increase by forming crowns (new plant groups) by the old plants. Falling into this category are African violets, *Sansevieria* (Mother-in-law's-tongue), *Spathiphylum*, Chinese evergreens, and many ferns. To divide the plant, remove it from the pot, and then cut or pull the crowns apart, making sure that each portion of crown has some roots attached.

Pot the divided crowns in well-drained potting medium composed of equal parts of loam and leaf mold with some sand. Vermiculite added to the soil will help to keep it from packing.

Plants that form **offsets** or plantlets are: Aechmea, hen and chickens, spider plant, bromeliads, Boston fern, strawberry geranium, kalanchoes, good-luck plant, devils-backbone, life plant, and bryophylum.

You will also find that offsets, on a short or long stem, can be cut from the mother plant and potted. Plantlets on kalanchoes, good luck plant, devils-backbone, life plant, and bryophylum, may be removed individually or the entire leaf may be placed on perlite and peat. After the plantlets have formed roots they may be repotted. Remember, kalanchoes belong to the succulents and they will not tolerate poorly drained soil or overwatering.

While **stem cuttings** take a little longer to produce an established plant, many plants are easily propagated by this method — just start a little earlier to have plants pretty enough for gifts by Christmastime. Coleus, impatiens, and Swedish ivy will root in one to two weeks in just plain water. Put three- to six-inch cuttings in water, removing any leaves that fall below the water level. Put the container in bright light but not in direct sunlight.

Begonia, fiddle-Leaf fig, syngonium, and monstera may also be rooted like this but will take a lit-

tle longer. In time a mass of roots will develop and when this happens, pot in good potting soil as previously directed.

Using Rooting Medium

These plants are not by any means the only ones that can be easily propagated for gifts. Grape ivy, croton, aucuba, zebra plant, schefflera, ti, dracena, sanderiana, hoya, maranta, peperomia, hastatum, Christmas cactus, and numerous other houseplants can be propagated by stem cuttings in a rooting medium. Before making your cuttings you should have a pot or pots of rooting medium ready. Here is a good mixture: ½ coarse sand, ½ peat; or ½ perlite and ½ peat. Stem cuttings three to six inches long should be taken, removing the lowest set of leaves. Sometimes it helps to get rooting started if you dip the lower inch of the cutting in a rooting hormone.

Be sure your pot has good drainage. The medium should remain moist but not soggy during the propagation period. Insert the cutting one to one and one-half inches

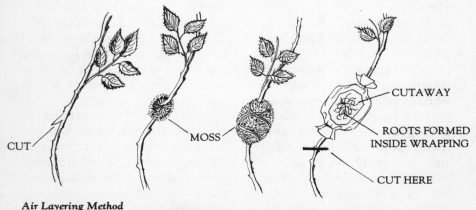

CUT

MOSS

CUTAWAY

ROOTS FORMED
INSIDE WRAPPING

CUT HERE

Air Layering Method
In the air layering method, make a notch in the stem and then wrap it in sphagnum moss.

into the rooting medium. Any leaves that would be below the medium should be removed.

A cover of plastic such as a clear plastic bag (or shower cap) tied over the pot but not in contact with the cuttings, will greatly aid moisture retention. Such bags as are found at grocery stores, or for larger cuttings, the dry cleaner's, may be used. Snip a few holes in the plastic to allow for air exchange. Put the covered pot in bright light but not in direct sunlight.

Caring for Your House Plants

Once your plants root and start into growth there are still a number of factors to be considered if you would have a good looking plant for gifting.

Light is very important. If the spot you picked out for your cuttings after they start into growth does not have enough light, consider using either regular fluorescent lights, or the wide-spectrum fluorescent lights that are also acceptable for flowering plants.

Water your plants when they need it. Do not base watering on some routine practice. Check the soil to determine when it is still moist. Some plants like to be evenly moist, others like to dry out slightly between waterings. Some plants, like aloe vera, should not be watered at all during the winter.

Leaching refers to a process of thorough watering where a large quantity of water is washed through the soil. An example of this is, fill the pot up ten times in a row and let the water drain out.

Leaching will help to eliminate excess fertilizer salts. When a plant is brought into the house environment it needs only about one-tenth of the fertilizer required by a plant grown in a commercial greenhouse. Plants you've had in your home for some time may also benefit from leaching as they eventually accumulate salts. Try leaching your container plants once a month with a solution of Epsom salts ($MgSO_4$). Use at the rate of one tablespoon in a gallon of water as an aid to removing sodium from the soil.

You can minimize the need for leaching if you make sure that each plant, when watered, has sufficient water applied so that some drains through the drainage hole. If you are to be successful with houseplants drainage is very important. After you water a container and the water drains through, either dump it out or provide a layer of pebbles in the saucer so the container can rest above the drainage water.

Other Houseplant Tips

★ Fertilizer should be given sparingly — too much may even kill your plant. Timing is also important. A half-strength fertilizer applied four to six times a year, preferably in the summer or when plants are making their best growth, is generally sufficient.

★ Give your plants a vacation outside in summer. Also, if you have a plant that is looking peaked and the weather is mild, put it aside in partial shade, and water it well and usually it

The lovely gloxinia thrives in compost, peat moss, and sand, and receives maximum benefit from the use of earthworm castings. Use one cup of castings per 6–8-inch pot.

will start a rapid recovery.

★ A curious plant, easily propagated, is the "pregnant onion" (*Urginea maritima*, Scilla.) This amusing oddity, sometimes called sea onion because it originated on the seashore, forms little bulblets on its sides, which eventually burst through the paper-thin covering. Simply plant the little bulblets in good potting soil.

★ Aloe vera plants are also easily propagated. Simply pull off the little plantlets that form around the mother plant and place them in potting soil and they will take root. The aloe vera plant has been called "the drug store in a flower pot" because of its healing qualities. Keep a small plant handy on your kitchen windowsill. Should you burn yourself, clip a small portion and rub it on the burn. It will take the sting out almost immediately and aid in the healing process.

★ If you would keep the beautiful gloxinia growing it will thrive best in compost, peat moss and sand and benefit greatly from the use of earthworm castings.

★ The best time to propagate gift plants, by whatever means is chosen, is under the favorable signs of Cancer, Scorpio, and Pisces.

Shrubs for Winter Beauty

Wintersweet (*Chimonanthus praecox*) is one of the finest of all winter-flowering shrubs, especially prized for its sweet fragrance. The flowers, almost one inch across, translucent yellow on the outside and purple in the center, appear over a long period from December on, depending on the latitude and the severity of the winter. Cut flowering branches make an excellent indoor display. Wintersweet grows to 12 feet in height and 8 feet in width and is clad in rich dark green leaves that turn a pleasing yellow-green in autumn. In very cold areas it will do best if grown against a wall for winter protection and reflected heat.

Westonbirt dogwood (*Cornus alba "Sibirica"*) is grown for winter beauty, its rich, deep red stems presenting a striking contrast to winter snow or evergreens. This clone has better twig color than other similar dogwoods, is of upright growth, and has handsome foliage all summer, even under hot conditions. In autumn its pale blue berries are beloved of birds. It grows to about 6 to 7 feet and prefers moist soil, sun, or shade. It should be pruned hard in early spring to encourage growth of the young, brightly colored stems.

Hazel (*Corylus avellana "Contorta"*) is a plant Nature must surely have designed as a copy of the famous Medusa of legend — only it is not poisonous. This one, discovered in England, is a real conversation piece, with fantastically twisted, almost corkscrew-like branches. For a real landscape highlight, plant it where you can enjoy its bizarre silhouette against the winter snow. It is also a favorite of flower arrangers and easy to grow, reaching 8 to 10 feet in either sun or shade. (Cannot be shipped to Oregon or Washington).

Few shrubs are so well known as **Carolina allspice** (*Calycanthus floridus*), sometimes called "sweet-scented shrub," "sweet shrub," or "strawberry shrub" because of the heady fragrance of its dark burgundy flowers. It blooms from mid-May to June, but the glossy corrugated foliage will persist well into late November or early December, and the wood, and roots, too, produce a camphor-like fragrance when crushed. Reaching 6 to 9 feet tall with a spread of 8 to 12 feet, this is a neat, very decorative native shrub, excellent used on a patio or outdoor living area. Trouble free, it will grow in almost any soil and has enjoyed widespread popularity since early colonial times.

Cornus stolonifera "Flaverimea," like *Coalba* "Sibirica," is an outstanding source of winter landscape interest for its vivid yellow twigs. White flowers are followed by white berries in late summer and fall — another bird attractant. It does best in moist soil and should be given a severe spring pruning to encourage new growth.

The lovely **weigela** "Bristol Ruby" flowers in both spring and autumn. Immense quantities of almost black buds open to create a dazzling display of sparkling ruby flowers. After the spectacular spring flowering, there is a fine show of these hummingbird-attracting flowers throughout the summer and late autumn. Free-blooming Bristol Ruby grows 6 to 9 feet and should be planted in full sun in moist soil.

Sea Buckthorn (*Hippophae rhamnoides*) is an attractive deciduous shrub with bright silvery leaves resembling those of the willow. It is highly valued for the multitude of showy orange-yellow berries that cling closely to its thorny twigs, forming a colorful display from September well into the late winter. One of the best shrubs for winter color, it also forms a formidable hedge plant. It thrives in dry, sandy soils where little else will grow. The vigorous, bushy *Callicarpa bodinieri* grows 6 to 10 feet tall, with slender, erect branches covered in August with thousands of small lavender flowers in dense cymes. The blooms are followed by masses of violet-purple berries, which often persist until Christmas. Noted for its exceptional flowering, it is also a great favorite in flower arrangements and is easily grown in sun or shade.

The fragrant **witch hazel** (*Hamamelis*) blooms at a time when there is hardly anything else flowering outdoors. The bright flowers endure even zero temperatures.

They thrive best in somewhat moist, peaty and sandy soil, in sun or shade. The well-known medicinal lotion is derived from an extract of the plant dissolved in alcohol.

Witch hazels are noisy plants! Go into a witch hazel thicket on some fine morning in winter and sit down on the drift of dead leaves that carpet the woods floor. The silence is broken now and then by a sharp report like a bullet striking against the bark of a nearby trunk, or skipping among the leaves. Perhaps a twinge on the ear shows that you have been a target for some tiny projectile, sent to its mark with force enough to hurt.

The fusillade comes from the ripened pods, which have a remarkable ability to throw their seeds, and thus do for the parent tree what the winged seeds of other trees accomplish. The lining of the two-celled pod is believed to contract, producing a spring that drives the seeds forth with surprising force when they are loosened from their attachment. Frost and sun seem to decide just when to spring the trap and let fly the little black seeds. It has been recorded that one seed fell as far as 18 feet from the base of the parent trees.

The Indians of America were the first people to use the bark of the witch hazel for curing inflammations, making an infusion of the twigs and roots by boiling them.

Maple Goodies

Those of you who live "up North" might consider what a treat it would be for your friends "down South" to sample some of those maple goodies. Maple sugar is made chiefly from the sap of the sugar maple tree. Late in the winter and early spring the farmers of New England, New York, Pennsylvania and Canada begin their yearly job of tapping these trees — something else the early settlers learned from the Indians. They bore a hole about 3 inches deep into the tree trunk, at a height 3½ to 4 feet from the ground. Then they drive a small metal spout or wooden trough into the hole. A bucket hangs from the spout to collect the sap that flows out of the hole, the bucket usually being covered to keep the sap clean.

Each day, the farmers collect the sap in large tanks and take it by sled or cart to the sap house. Here it is boiled until most of the water in the sap has boiled away as steam. This was done outdoors in large iron kettles.

When some of the water has boiled off, maple syrup remains. If the sap is boiled longer it forms maple cream, soft sugar, and then hard sugar. More syrup than sugar is usually made because of the greater demand for it. The syrup is passed through a wooden strainer after it is boiled. It is then so pure that no further refining is needed.

Vermont is the leading maple-sugar-producing state in the United States. Black, silver, and red maples are all sources of maple sugar. Sugar maples also make beautiful shade trees, turning a lively gold in the autumn.

Maple Fondant

4 cups brown sugar	2 cups hot water
2 cups maple syrup	1 tablespoon glucose

Place sugar and water in a large saucepan and heat, stirring until sugar is completely dissolved. Add the syrup. When the syrup begins to boil add the glucose.

Continue boiling, without stirring, until the thermometer registers 240° F or until a few drops form a soft ball when tested in cold water. Remove from heat at once and allow to stand 4 minutes or until air bubbles disappear. Pour into a large wet platter. Syrup should not be deeper than 1½ inches.

Turn the sugar backward and forward, leaving no part untouched, until the whole mass becomes white and opaque. Knead until smooth and free from lumps. Wet and wring a small towel, place over fondant and allow to remain for at least an hour. (This is called the curing process.) Remove the cloth and knead as you would bread dough, until creamy and smooth. This makes delicious centers, which must be allowed to dry before they are crystallized and dipped in chocolate.

HEIRLOOM QUILTS TO TREASURE

Colonial winters were cold, and the log houses of the colonists drafty. But the busy English and Dutch housewife kept her scraps and pieced them together, and the members of her household did not suffer. Large, warm quilts covered the beds, heavy quilted curtains were drawn over the windows, and quilted petticoats were part of every woman's wardrobe. The English petticoat was worn in modest concealment, but the Dutch one was worn highly colored and very much in view.

The patchwork quilts were the ones of which the quiltmaker was proudest, while the piecework bed coverings were most common. This is not so difficult to understand when you remember that the materials had to be either laboriously woven in the home or imported. The appliqué (or patched) quilt, calling for a large, unpieced background and large pieces, was a luxury and a showpiece. But the pieced quilts, using every available scrap of new and old material, were constantly being made and were on every bed. The Crazy Quilt is the oldest and one of the most common of colonial pioneer days because it made use of even the tiniest and most irregularly shaped scraps.

When the quilt was "ready for the frame" it was the custom to ask the women of the neighborhood to come and help with the quilting. Thus the quiltmaking was not only a household art born of family needs, but an interest drawing the busy women into social groups.

The patterns used, many of which have come down to us, were often inspirations of the home: Cake Stand, Windmill, Dresden Plate, and the Tea Leaf. The Bible, so large a factor in daily life, was responsible for such names as Rob Peter To Pay Paul and Jacob's Ladder. The New World worked itself into the quilts in Bear's Paw, Crossed Canoes, Turkey Track, Log Cabin, and Arrowhead. These and thousands of others have spread with the population and now may be found in every part of the country.

While only a very few of the many truly beautiful old quilts have been preserved, quiltmaking itself has passed from mother to daughter, and today many southern homes and community groups are producing worthy descendants of this splendid art.

The padding for quilts comes in sheets of cotton manufactured especially for quilts. Quilting was invented to hold the padding in place. Elaborate patterns came as an afterthought.

For most designs, it is best to follow the outlines of the design. When the quilt is used on the lining side it will duplicate the pattern.

Special needles, short and slender (but with large eyes), are manufactured for quilting, the most popular sizes running from 5 to 9. A variety of quilting transfers are sold by firms that handle needlework patterns and designs.

The quilting, done with No. 40 or 50 thread, should be started at one end and finished at the other, with the fullness kept ahead of the work. Some of the best quiltmakers suggest the use of waxed thread for quilting.

A true bias binding, not more than one-half inch wide when finished, should be used for the edge of the quilt. If the corners of the quilt are slightly rounded a more perfect binding is possible.

Recently I was told a lovely story of how an elderly woman enjoyed fingering over the various patches in a "crazy quilt" she had inherited. In one corner was a patch from her great-grandmother's very best "Sunday-go-to-meetin" silk dress. Over toward the middle was another in deep rose velvet from a cape her sister had worn on the evening she had been "presented to society."

One day when she was not feeling well, she discovered best of all a verse which had been sketched into a patch with letters so tiny that she had to use a magnifying glass to read them:

"Sleep sweet within this quiet room,
　　O thou, whoe'er thou art,
And let no mournful yesterdays
　　Disturb thy peaceful heart.

Nor let tomorrow mar thy rest
　　With dreams of coming ill:
Thy Maker is thy changeless friend,
　　His love surrounds thee still.

Forget thyself and all the world,
　　Put out each garish light:

The stars are shining overhead —
　　Sleep sweet! Good night!
　　Good night!

Though she had used the quilt on her bed for many years, she had never noticed this verse before and she thought how strange it was that the words had been called to her attention at a time when she was depressed and needed them most. The thought came to her that every generation, with all its changes, has a "changeless friend." Then she remembered something else — that "The Comforter" (which a quilt is often called) is another name for the "Holy Spirit."

With this story in mind I would suggest that when your quilt is finished you embroider your signature and the date in one corner, identifying for all time the thing of beauty on which you have spent so many pleasurable hours. Your children and your children's children may be "comforted" by it.

Soapwort

This old-time favorite for cleaning delicate fabrics and shampooing hair was also used by early Americans against the rash caused by poison ivy, presumably to wash the skin. Quite probably it worked if used soon after exposure to poison ivy. Yellow laundry soap was also used. A more reliable remedy is jewelweed, the juice of which may be frozen like ice cubes, bagged and kept on hand during the poison ivy season.

OLD-FASHIONED CORNHUSK DOLLS

Cornhusk dolls were the only dolls that little girls had to play with in pioneer days. As they were not very durable, none of them have survived, but it is a very easy doll to make. All that is needed are cornhusks, string for tying, corn silk for hair, and glue.

The cornhusks can be picked in the corn fields in the fall during the corn harvest or bought in craft stores. They can also be dyed, if you like, with bright colors.

They should be dampened with water before going into the hot dye bath. Leave them in the hot dye until they are the shade you want — the longer they are left in, the darker they will be. When they are the color you desire, take them out and rinse them in cold water. Lay them on newspapers to dry until needed. These colored husks can be used with the natural tan husks as caps, bags, or for clothing.

Lady dolls are the easiest to make, as they stand on their skirts. Cornhusks are easier to work with if they are damp. Dip the husks in cold water, shake off the excess water, and place them on a towel. If they dry out, just dip again.

Begin by taking a narrow strip of husk. Starting at one end, roll up to form a small ball. Place a smooth, slightly wider strip of cornhusk over the ball with it centered in the middle. Use one smooth side with no wrinkles as a face. Tie with string at the neck.

Take a thin strip of cornhusk and roll lengthwise. Tie ends after cutting long enough for both arms. Place arm rolls through husks extending from the head at the shoulder level. Tie beneath the arms.

Place a layer of cornhusks at the waist with the tapered ends to the top where the waist will be. Tie down tightly at the waist. Trim the bottom of the skirt with shears evenly so that the doll can stand on the skirt edge.

Place a strip of cornhusk over each shoulder extending down to cross in the front and back. Tie with a strip of cornhusk at the waist. Trim edges a little below the waist.

Glue dry corn silk on the head for hair. Draw features with a pen. Fashion a bonnet out of cornhusk, plain or colored. Tie the back ends of the bonnet around the neck. Fold a plain or colored wide strip of cornhusk and gather top. Tie with a strip of cornhusk and tie to one arm for a bag. The little cornhusk lady is finished.

She can be fitted out with a variety of accessories, such as a broom, a feather duster, a churn, or even a baby wrapped in a cornhusk blanket.

A cornhusk man can be made the same, except that the skirt is divided before being cut. The husks are tied into pants legs. He will not stand alone but will need support.

DECEMBER RECIPES

Cooking Your Goose

If you had a turkey for Thanksgiving dinner, why not have a goose for Christmas? This is a recipe for wild goose, but could be used for a tame one just as well.

1 loaf stale bread	2 cups celery, finely chopped
1 box corn muffin mix, baked	1 wild goose
1 tablespoon salt	2 to 3 eggs (or more if they
2 teaspoons pepper	are small)
2 tablespoons powdered sage	2 teaspoons salt
½ pound salt pork (or ½	*Note:* This makes a lot of
pound pork sausage, crum-	dressing. Any not used may
bled and fried)	be bagged and frozen — or
2 cups onion, finely chopped	baked separately.

Preheat oven to 350° F. Slice bread and butter each slice lightly. Cut in cubes and toast in oven until slightly crisp. Put in large container and add baked, crumbled corn bread. Add salt, pepper, and sage. Cut salt pork into ½-inch cubes and slowly fry until cubes are crisp and brown. Add salt pork cubes to seasoned bread, retaining drippings in skillet. Add onion and celery to drippings, toss lightly, and fry till just tender crisp. **Do not overcook.** Add celery, onion, and drippings to bread mixture. Add eggs and toss lightly.

Fill the goose with stuffing and sew opening closed, or use skewers and string. Rub the goose outside with olive or salad oil, and sprinkle with salt. If desired, place one or two strips of salt pork or bacon over top of goose. Bake in a shallow, uncovered pan, allowing 20 to 25 minutes per pound. Baste every 15 minutes.

★ ★ ★

The Germans were probably the first to use Christmas tree decorations, using stars, angels, toys, gilded nuts, and candies wrapped in bright papers. Later they added tinsel and lighted candles, cookies and apples. In the United States, early decorations included homemade paper ornaments and peppermint candy canes, along with strings of cranberries and popcorn.

The Christmas tree at our house always included a profusion of cookies in various sizes and shapes. I was the youngest by ten years so I didn't remember much about my family's earliest Christmas trees. One of my brothers, however, once remarked, "Mother always left the tree up for a long time, and she saw to it that there were plenty of cookies on the tree. We boys could go into the living room and eat off the tree practically up until the 4th of July!" Of course, he was exaggerating, but with four perpetually hungry boys my mother knew exactly what she was doing.

It is hard now to find the old, heavy, tinned cookie cutters but I was fortunate about a year ago in getting a set when I went to an auction sale of an old farmhouse. I love my cookie cutters: angels, stars, rounds (big and little), a half moon, a ruffled round, a Christmas tree, and a heart, diamond, club and spade, as well as a peculiarly shaped one I cannot identify, but that looks like an old-fashioned "lady finger" cutter.

Here are two recipes for Christmas cookies that are very good and also easy to make:

Christmas Cut-Outs

½ cup shortening
1 cup sugar
1 egg
2 teaspoons baking powder

2½ cups cake flour
½ teaspoon salt
½ cup milk
1 teaspoon vanilla

Cream shortening well. Add sugar and egg and blend together. Sift baking powder, flour, and salt together and add to creamed mixture alternately with the milk. Stir in vanilla. Chill. Roll out ¹/₁₆ inch thick on pastry cloth, cut in Christmas designs, brush with egg white, decorate if desired. Bake at 350° F 10–12 minutes. *Makes 100 2-inch cookies.*

Molasses Cookies

This one was my brothers' favorite.

¾ cup melted shortening
1 cup molasses
1 cup brown sugar
1 cup thick sour milk or
  buttermilk

6 cups sifted flour
½ teaspoon salt
2 teaspoons ginger
4 teaspoons baking soda
1 tablespoon lemon extract

Mix melted shortening, molasses, and sugar until smooth. Add sour milk, then flour sifted with salt, ginger, and baking soda. Add lemon extract. Mix to a smooth stiff dough and chill until firm. Roll out on a lightly floured surface to a thickness of ⅓-inch. Roll thin for crisp cookies. Cut with cookie cutters into various shapes. Place on greased baking sheet and bake in a moderate oven (350° F) 8 to 10 minutes. Roll thin for crisp cookies. *Makes 150 cookies.*

Kentucky Bourbon Cake

1½ cups raisins
1¼ cups bourbon
4 cups all-purpose flour
2 teaspoons baking powder
1 teaspoon ground nutmeg
1 teaspoon ground mace
1½ cups butter or margarine
2¼ cups packed brown sugar
6 eggs

4½ cups chopped pecans
    (1 lb.)
1 cup chopped candied
    cherries
1 cup chopped candied pine-
    apple
¼ cup chopped candied gin-
    ger
1½ cups orange marmalade

Combine raisins and bourbon; let stand 1 hour. Drain raisins, reserving bourbon. Grease (or spray with Pam) a 10-inch tube pan. Line with heavy brown paper; grease.

Combine flour, baking powder, nutmeg, and mace. In a mixer bowl, beat butter with electric mixer for 30 seconds. Add brown sugar; beat till fluffy. Add eggs, one at a time, beating well. Add dry ingredients and reserved bourbon alternately to beaten mixture, beating after each addition. Turn batter into a large mixing bowl. Combine raisins, pecans, cherries, pineapple, and ginger; fold into batter. Stir in marmalade.

Spoon batter into prepared pan. Bake in a 300° oven for 3 to 3½ hours or till done. Cool 10 minutes. Remove from pan; cool. Wrap in a bourbon-moistened cheesecloth; overwrap with foil. Store in the refrigerator 3 to 4 weeks. Occasionally, remoisten cheesecloth with bourbon and rewrap.

To serve, unwrap and trim with additional candied cherries, if desired. *Makes about 40 servings.*

Capricorn the Goat   *(December 23 - January 20)*

★ ★ ★

This book has been a pleasant journey through the months of the year but it is time now for me to leave you. I do so with an Indian blessing:

> *"May your moccasins make*
> *Happy tracks in many snows,*
> *And the rainbow always touch your shoulder."*

★ ★ ★

Garden Way Publishing Books

Art, Henry, A Garden of Wildflowers: 101 Native Species and How to Grow Them. ($12.95. Order No. 405-0.)

Hill, Lewis, Secrets of Plant Propagation. ($12.95. Order No. 370-4.)

Jacobs, Betty M., Growing and Using Herbs Successfully. ($8.95. Order No. 249-X.)

Philbrick, Helen and John, The Bug Book. ($5.95. Order No. 027-6.)

Ralston, Nancy, and Marynor Jordan, Zucchini Cookbook. ($6.95. Order No. 107-8.)

Riotte, Louise, Carrots Love Tomatoes: Secrets of Companion Planting. ($6.95. Order No. 064-0.) and Roses Love Garlic: Secrets of Companion Planting with Flowers. ($6.95. Order No. 331-3).

Rupp, Rebecca, Blue Corn and Square Tomatoes: Unusual Facts About Common Garden Vegetables. ($9.95. Order No. 505-7.)

Shaudys, Phyllis V., The Pleasure of Herbs: A Month-by-Month Guide to Growing, Using, and Enjoying Herbs. ($12.95. Order No. 423-9.)

Solit, Karen, with Jim Solit, Keep Your Gift Plants Thriving. ($6.95. Order No. 379-8.)

Tilgner, Linda, Tips for the Lazy Gardener. ($4.95. Order No. 390-9.)

These books are available at your bookstore, farm store, garden center, or directly from Garden Way Publishing, Dept. 8600, Schoolhouse Road, Pownal, Vermont 05261. Please enclose $2.00 for Fourth Class or $3.00 for U.P.S. per order to cover postage and handling.

Other Books

Chase, Deborah, The Medically Based No-Nonsense Beauty Book, Knopf, New York, NY (1974)

Davis, Adele, Let's Eat Right to Keep Fit, New American Library, New York, NY (1970)

Fast, Julius, Weather Language: How Climate Affects Your Body And Mind And What To Do About It, Wyden Books

The Foxfire Book, Doubleday & Co., New York, NY (1972)

Harland, Marion, Common Sense in the Household: A Manual of Practical Housewifery, Charles Scribner's Sons, New York, NY (1884)

Harris, Ben Charles, Eat the Weeds, Crown Publishers, New York, NY (1968)

Hayes, Elizabeth S., Spices and Herbs, Lore and Cookery, Dover Publications, New York, NY (1961)

Horwitz, Elinor Lander, Mountain People, Mountain Crafts, J.B. Lippincott & Co., New York, NY (1974)

Jarvis, D.C., M.D., Folk Medicine, Fawcett Crest Publications, New York, NY (1985)

Levy, Juliette, de Bairacli, Herbal Handbook of Farm and Stable, Faber and Faber, Winchester, MA

Miller, Richard Allen, The Magical and Ritual Use of Herbs, Destiny Books, Rochester, VT (1983)

Muir, Ada, The Healing Herbs of the Zodiac, Llewellyn Publications, St. Paul, MN (1983)

The Old Farmer's Almanac, Yankee Publishers, Dublin, NH (yearly)

Riotte, Louise, Planetary Planting, Astro Computing Services, San Diego, CA (1982)

Seddon, George, Your Kitchen Garden, Simon & Schuster, New York, NY (1975)

Stout, Ruth, How to Have a Green Thumb Without an Aching Back, Exposition Press, New York, NY (1961)

Weschcke, Carl, Llewellyn's Moon Sign Book, Llewellyn Publications, St. Paul, MN

Wilder, Louise Beebe, The Fragrant Garden, Dover Publications, New York, NY (1974)

SUPPLIERS

American Astrology, Inc.
475 Park Ave. South
New York, NY 10016
Books

Aphrodisia
282 Bleecher St.
New York, NY 10014
Dried flowers, potpourri

Applewood Seed Co.
5380 Vivian St.
Arvada, CO 80002
Wildflower seed products

Armstrong Roses
P.O. Box 1020
Somis, CA 93066
Roses, fruit & shade trees

ASC Publications, Inc.
P.O. Box 16430
San Diego, CA 92116-0430
Gardening & astrology books

Bluestone Perennials
7211 Middle Ridge Road
Madison, OH 44057
More than 300 varieties

Breck's
Dept. MN, 6523 N. Galena Rd.
Peoria, IL 61632
Bulb importer from Holland

Bunting's Nurseries, Inc.
Dept. MN, Duke St.
Selbyville, DE 19975
Strawberry & asparagus

Burgess Seed & Plant Co.
905 Four Seasons Road
Bloomington, IL 61701

W. Atlee Burpee Co.
Warminster, PA 18974
Seeds, plants

Peter DeJager Bulb Co.
P.O. Box 2010
188 Asbury St.
South Hamilton, MA 01982
Imported flower bulbs

Dutch Gardens
P.O. Box 200
Adelphia, NJ 07710
Imported Dutch bulbs

Dutch Mountain Nursery
7984 N. 48th St.
Augusta, MI 49012
"Berries for the Birds"

Emlong Nurseries, Inc.
Dept. GW, 2671 W. Marquette Woods
Stevensville, MI 49012

Farmer Seed & Nursery Co.
818 N.W. 4th St.
P.O. Box 129
Faribault, MN 55021

Farmers Seed & Nursery
2207 E. Oakland Ave.
Bloomington, IL 61701

Henry Field Seed & Nursery Co.
Shenandoah, IA 51602

Dean Foster Nurseries, Inc.
511 S. Center St.
P.O. Box 127
Hartford, MI 49057
Fruit-bearing plants

Greenlife Gardens Greenhouses
101 County Line Road
Griffin, GA 30223
Epis, succulents, dwarf crape myrtle

Gurney Seed & Nursery
2nd & Capitol Sts.
Yankton, SD 57078
Vegetables & ornamentals

Hastings
434 Marietta St., N.W.
Atlanta, GA 30302

Hemlock Hill Herb Farm
Hemlock Hill Road
Litchfield, CT 06759
Perennial, biennial herb plants

House of Wesley
Bloomington, IL 61701
Seeds & nursery products

Indiana Botanic Gardens
P.O. Box 5
Hammond, IN 46325
Herbs, teas, spices, seeds

Jackson & Perkins
02 Rose Lane
Medford, OR 97501
Nursery stock & roses

Johnny's Selected Seeds
Foss Hill Road
Albion, ME 04910
Garden seeds

J.W. Jung Seed Co.
335 S. High St.
Randolph, WI 53957
Seed & nursery

Kelly Nurseries
726 Maple St.
Dansville, NY 14437
Ornamentals & fruit

Kitazawa Seed Co.
1748 Laine Ave.
Santa Clara, CA 95051-3012
Oriental vegetable seeds

Krider Nurseries, Inc.
P.O. Box 29
Middlebury, IN 46540
Roses & general nursery stock

Lakeland Nurseries
Unique Merchandise Mart (Bldg. 4)
Hanover, PA 17333

Lewis Strawberry Nursery
P.O. Box 24
Rocky Point, NC 28457

Lilypons Water Gardens
6885 Lilypons Road
P.O. Box 10
Lilypons, MD 21717-0010
Water plants

Logee's Greenhouses
55 North St.
Danielson, CT 06239
Exotics, begonias, rare herbs

Llewellyn Publications
P.O. Box 64383
St. Paul, MN 55164-0383
Moon signs planting guide, herb lore books, video

Earl May Seed & Nursery Co.
208 North Elm St.
Shenandoah, IA 51603
General nursery stock, seeds

McFayden Seeds
Box 1800
Brandon, Manitoba R7A 6N4
Seeds, gardening & kitchen supplies, books

Mellingers Nursery, Inc.
2310 West South Range Road
North Lima, OH 44452-9731
Over 4000 garden-related items

Michigan Bulb Co.
1950 Waldorf NW
Grand Rapids, MI 49550
Bulbs, general nursery stock

J.E. Miller Nurseries, Inc.
5060 West Lake Road
Canandaigua, NY 14424
*Fruit & nut trees, berries,
ornamental trees*

Musser Forests, Inc.
Dept. GW, P.O. Box 340
Indiana, PA 15701-0340
*Evergreens & hardwood seed-
lings, ground covers*

Nichols Garden Nursery
Dept. GW, 1190 N. Pacific
Hwy.
Albany, OR 97321
Seed, herb nursery

Northrup King Co.
Consumer Products Division
P.O. Box 959
Minneapolis, MN 55440
Flower and vegetable seeds

George W. Park Seed Co.
P.O. Box 31
Greenwood, SC 29647
Flower & vegetable seed

Plants of the Southwest
1812 Second St.
Santa Fe, NM 87501
Native plants

Putney Nursery, Inc.
Route 5
Putney, VT 05346
*Wildflower & perennial
gardens, landscaping*

Rayner Bros., Inc.
P.O. Box 1617, Dept. GW
Salisbury, MD 21801
*Virus-free strawberries, blue-
berries, asparagus*

**Roses of Yesterday and
Today**
802 Brown's Valley Road
Watsonville, CA 95076

R.H. Shumway, Seedsman
P.O. Box 1
Graniteville, SC 29829
803-663-6276
also: P.O. Box 777
Rockford, IL 61105
*Specializes in open-pollinated
flower & vegetable seeds*

Spring Hill Nurseries
6523 N. Galena Rd.
Peoria, IL 61632
Nursery products

Stark Bros. Nurseries
Box B3641H
Louisiana, MO 63353
America's first tree specialists

Stern's Nursery Farm
607 W. Washington St.
Geneva, NY 14456

Stewart Orchids
P.O. Box 550
Carpenteria, CA 93013
Retail orchids

Stokes Seeds, Inc.
P.O. Box 548
Buffalo, NY 14240

Twilley Seed Co.
P.O. Box F65
Trevose, PA 19047
Specializing in hybrid seeds

Van Bourgondien Bros.
245 Farmingdale Road
P.O. Box A
Babylon, NY 11702
*Over 1,000 varieties tulips,
daffodils, exotics*

Van Ness Water Gardens
2460 N. Euclid Ave.
Upland, CA 91786-1199
Water lilies and related items

Vermont Bean Seed Co.
Garden Lane
Fair Haven, VT 05743
*Specializing in heirloom vari-
ties, theme & trial gardens*

Wayside Gardens Inc.
P.O. Box 1
Hodges, SC 29695
Bulbs, plants, accessories

White Flower Farm
Route 63
Litchfield, CT 06759
Perennial plant farm

INDEX

A number appearing in **boldface** indicates that a chart or illustration appears on that page.